CASTAWAY BOATS

By the same author

Captain Joshua Slocum

Castaway Boats

BY CAPTAIN VICTOR SLOCUM

With Maps by the Author

SHERIDAN HOUSE

This edition first published 2001 by
Sheridan House Inc.
145 Palisade Street
Dobbs Ferry, New York 10522
www.sheridanhouse.com

Library of Congress Cataloging-in-Publication Data

Slocum, Victor, 1872-1949
Castaway Boats / by Victor Slocum
p.cm.
Originally published: New York: L. Furman, c1938
ISBN 1-57409-126-3 (alk. paper)
1. Shipwrecks. 2. Survival after airplane accidents,
shipwrecks, etc. 3. Castaways. I Title.

G525. S567 2001
910.4'52—dc21   2001020079

Printed in the United States of America

ISBN 1-57409-126-3

PREFACE

Sailor, Save Thyself

IN the summer of 1997, after two years of transatlantic cruising aboard a 35-foot yawl, I returned to this coast and found a man named Sebastian Junger on the bill at the Camden Yacht Club to flog a book called *The Perfect Storm*. All aglow with renewed access to perfectly contemporary literature, I devoured the text and was immediately struck by one blatantly unmentioned fact. I dutifully attended the spiel at the club, and on finally reaching the head of the receiving line that formed afterwards, I confronted Junger with my conclusion.

"You missed the whole point of the story," I told him. "No one had to go to those yachts."

I was referring, of course, to the two sailing vessels whose stories are set forth in the second part of the book. One Air National Guard parajumper, we will recall from Junger's account, died after an attempt to remove Japanese sailor Mikado Tomizawa from his boat was aborted as being futile. Meanwhile the skipper of the other boat,

Satori, was forced by the Coast Guard to abandon ship against his will.

Junger looked genuinely startled by my statement. "What do you mean?" he demanded. "Those boats were in danger."

A simple enough mistake to make, for in ocean sailing the distinction between being in danger and actually needing to be rescued can seem to be a fine one, even when it is not. Nor was I surprised later when I found out that Junger, when researching the book, had never even interviewed Ray Leonard, the veteran bluewater cruiser who had owned and sailed *Satori,* a rugged Westsail 32, for more than 20 years. It was a gross omission, for in his book Junger portrayed the man as a sullen introvert who sneaks sips from a bottle while refusing to confront the reality of the storm.

It turned out that Leonard, who once worked at Rockland's Island Institute across the street from where I now sit, is well known in these parts. His reputation is that of a seasoned, deliberate skipper who has weathered a fair share of gales both safely and competently. Had Junger thought to follow the man a bit further on in his story, he might eventually have suspected the truth. For when Ray Leonard came ashore after being "rescued" by the Coast Guard (who had responded to a mayday issued by Leonard's terrified crew without his permission), he did not drop to his knees and kiss the soil in gratitude. Instead, with a deliberate calmness worthy of his vessel's name, he pulled out a chart, listened to a current weather report, and calculated her drift. Eventually he found her, absolutely unharmed, washed up on a beach in Maryland.

Not that I ever thought Junger intentionally distorted things to sharpen his tale. Rather, it seemed clear his unfamiliarity with his subject had blinded him to the story's most ironic twist—that while the crew of the fishing vessel *Andrea Gail*, men who would never think to light off an EPIRB until they were practically underwater, all drowned without a trace in the great Halloween storm of 1991, the search-and-rescue assets of half the East Coast were being squandered, and lives were being lost, assisting yachts that were not in distress.

Even among members of the bluewater community, there is, unfortunately, little discussion these days of the fact that there are many unnecessary rescues at sea. Australian search-and-rescue (SAR) authorities complained loudly when they had to go to Isabelle Autissier during the 1994 BOC round-the-world race, then were embarrassed by the 1998 Sydney-Hobart storm and had to downplay the massive effort required to retrieve 56 sailors from broken boats in that ill-fated race. And these, obviously, were instances in which people genuinely needed to be saved. Very few have thought to complain about the countless inexperienced Walter Mittys we have created in the last several years, who wander the oceans untested in very expensive well-equipped yachts, then quickly call for an evacuation the moment something goes seriously wrong.

I can cite no statistics in raising this point, for none have been compiled, but I can point to some examples in my own experience. In 1992, for example, during Jimmy Cornell's America 500 rally, I recall an Argentinian yacht abandoned by its crew when its spade rudder snapped off en route from Spain to Madeira. The boat was found soon afterwards by a Portuguese fisherman, who salvaged it singlehanded by simply fashioning a jury rudder and motoring into port.

More dramatically, during the 1998 Caribbean 500 rally, in which a portion of the fleet tangled with the remnants of Hurricane Mitch, one crew lit off their EPIRB and abandoned their boat before the storm arrived solely because they were tired and the weather forecast looked bleak. It goes without saying, of course, that the boat survived in fine form and was later recovered. In fact, it turned out the center of storm had missed it by more than 120 miles.

I could go on, but to ice the cake, as it were, I shall merely point to a story making the rounds in the British press this summer. This concerns a sailor, dubbed "Captain Calamity" by British SAR authorities, who is sailing about Ireland and Great Britain in a homemade boat using roadmaps to navigate. Evidently, he has called for rescues more than a dozen times this season, including one memorable day in which he radioed twice for help. I myself have met a couple of fellows like this, and though one cannot help but laugh at their antics, the consequences of their actions can be quite serious. If nothing else, it is expensive to go to these people (an estimated 55,000 pounds has been spent assisting "Captain Calamity" this summer), and in a worst case scenario, as the death of parajumper Rick Smith in Junger's *Perfect Storm* so vividly illustrates, lives may be forfeit.

Still, this is an understandable phenomenon, for the

technology that encourages a passive response to the bluewater emergency has proliferated madly. With satellite navigation and emergency beacon systems, reliable high-frequency radios, satellite telephones, even offshore e-mail, it is all too easy these days to summon help from the outside. It has become the accepted response to offshore predicaments, so much so we have greatly devalued the coin of self-reliance. We forget there ever was a time when summoning help simply was not possible. A time when those who wandered the sea took it for granted that if anything should go wrong there could be no one else to rely on. A time when a shipwrecked man on a beach thought nothing of building a new boat from the bones of his ship and sailing away in it.

The book you now hold in your hands tells stories from that time. Victor Slocum, its author, eldest child of famed solo-circumnavigator Joshua Slocum, was, chronologically speaking, only barely born into it. In all other respects, however, he was born into it with a vengeance. Though he died as late as 1949 after long years of service in steam vessels, his roots were firmly planted in the age of sail that preceded him.

He was born aboard a sailing ship, on the vessel *Constitution*, June 10, 1872, in San Francisco harbor. Subsequently he grew up and came of age aboard a series of sailing vessels commanded by his father on trading and fishing voyages throughout the Pacific. These included the *B. Aymar*, a full-rigged ship, the *Pato*, a 90-ton schooner, the *Amethyst*, and most magnificently of all, *Northern Light*, a sleek clipper. Ironically, Joshua

Slocum's last proper commercial command, *Aquidneck*, a 365-ton barque, in a sense marked the initiation of Victor's own professional career, as he served under his father on this vessel as a full mate. Sadly, *Aquidneck* was lost on the coast of Brazil in 1886, a blow which haunted Joshua, financially and otherwise, for quite some time.

Victor himself went on to a career distinguished in its own right. The details of his biography, oddly, remain a bit hazy. Mel Brown, a descendant who now serves as unofficial family genealogist and is an active member of the Joshua Slocum Society, has yet, for example, to determine exactly where and when Victor was married (though the actual fact of his marriage, to one Estelle Woodruff, is well established). Still, we do know that Victor earned the title "captain" and deserved it as well as his father.

According to one obituary published in the *Vineyard Gazette* on Martha's Vineyard less than a week after his death, Victor spent the bulk of his career skippering cargo vessels for several shipping lines, including the United States Lines. During the First World War, he served as a navigation officer on board the U.S. Navy transport *Monongehela*. Subsequently he retired from the sea, but when the Second World War started he was eager to serve again and succeeded in finding work with the Navy as an inspector of wooden vessels. After the war ended, he spent the twilight years of his life working as a night captain for the U.S. Fruit Company in New York City, where he ultimately died at the age of 77.

In spite of his having pursued a professional life of his own at sea, there can be little doubt that Victor's defining

moment as a mariner came when he was still quite young
and under the wing of his father. He played a very active
role in the famous voyage of *Liberdade*, which he
reprises for us here as an introduction to the several tales
that follow. A young teenager at the time, Victor not only
helped his father build an ocean-going junk-rigged canoe
from scratch after *Aquidneck* was wrecked, he also
helped sail this unlikely vessel more than 5,000 miles
home to North America. It is hard to believe the experience was not a formative one.

The scope of Slocum's great feat of self-reliance, both
Victor's and Joshua's, is only magnified by the fact that it
was born of pride rather than necessity. For we must remember, the loss of *Aquidneck* took place not on some
remote bar or strand, but in the vicinity of a community
of respectable size. Joshua Slocum could easily have ap-
pealed to the charity of fellow mariners for the means to
extract his family from South America. Indeed, the U.S.
consul to Brazil offered to repatriate the Slocums at government expense. But instead some noble perversity, and
perhaps a genuine academic interest in the sea-keeping
ability of small boats, drove Joshua to solve the problem
himself in his own way.

Small wonder then that Victor should have thought to
compile this eclectic medley of survival tales. Certainly
he must have found various aspects of each of them to be
dramatic and compelling, and quite clearly, like his father,
he was actively interested in the phenomenon of the
small-boat voyage. One thing, however, that would not
have struck him as so very remarkable is that the actors

in each of these stories assume from the moment they are thrust into danger that they must be self-sufficient to survive.

Make no mistake, the heroes of these tales are not supermen. In several instances, we find them badly frightened, engaging in base behavior, comic stupidity, even wanton self-destructiveness. Then, as now, it was easy enough to shrink from the reality of the sea. To the extent these men are heroic, it is when they grasp and come to terms with this one simple truth: that the only true salvation a mariner can hope to achieve is that which he engineers for himself.

On a more technical level, we should note that each of these stories also offers a vivid illustration of the advantages of what Steve Callahan has come to call the "proactive emergency craft." The men who survive in these stories do so because they are able to exercise a great deal of control over the direction in which their survival craft travels. It is the key, obviously, to their being able to exercise self-reliance and seize control of their fates.

Clearly, this calls into question the utility of the modern liferaft, considered by most contemporary bluewater sailors to be their safety device of last resort. Like all the fancy communications equipment mentioned above, the liferaft fits neatly into the whole passive rescue scenario. Indeed, what possibly could be more passive? You simply blow the thing up, then sit in it and wait until help comes.

Callahan, who once spent 76 days in a raft in an uncontrolled drift across the Atlantic from the Canaries to the West Indies, is very familiar with the drawbacks of this approach. In the 17 years that have passed since his ordeal, Steve has carefully studied and promulgated the concept of the proactive survival experience. This summer he sends word from up the coast of the launching of the Clam, a prototype of a folding RIB dinghy (or FRIB, as he is pleased to call it) that, like most of the survival craft in the stories in this book, can serve both as a tender to a mothership and as a proactive escape pod in the event of an emergency. With a canopy, drogue, and sailing rig, the Clam can both protect and preserve its occupants while transporting them in any direction they choose.

Had he been armed with something like this when he lost his yacht *Napoleon Solo* in 1982, Steve notes, his own 76-day survival drift could have been reduced to a mere 10 to 14 days. Other famous survival drifts could likewise have been significantly minimized. Maurice and Maralyn Bailey, for example, who were forced to abandon their yacht in 1973 in the Eastern Pacific and drifted 119 days before being picked up, could have reached land in just a week. Bill and Simone Butler, who drifted 66 days in 1989, could have cut their trip down to two or three weeks. And the Robertson family, who were castaways for 38 days, might easily have saved themselves in only six.

I urge you to carefully consider these facts, and this book, when assembling safety equipment and plotting worst-case strategems for your own offshore voyages. Not that you should ignore all the wonderful technology that is available these days. By all means, obtain some of it—if you can afford it. Just remember that all the technology in the world will never change the fact that when your life is at stake, and the sea is your nemesis, the most useful equipment is that which helps you to help yourself.

Charles J. Doane
Rockland, Maine
September 2000

CASTAWAY BOATS

CONTENTS

PAGE

1. INTRODUCTORY 11

2. THE HERCULES CASTAWAYS 41

3. LADY HOBART'S BOATS 68

4. THE ESSEX CASTAWAYS 79

5. THE LORD ELDON'S BOATS 103

6. BEER AND COLD RAW SHARK 110

7. THE OROOLONG SCHOONER 123

8. THE SAGINAW'S GIG 156

9. THE FENUA-URA CASTAWAYS 179

10. SHACKLETON'S BOAT VOYAGE 190

11. THE VOYAGE OF THE WAGER'S LONGBOAT 204

12. THE VOYAGE OF THE JEANNETTE'S BOATS 245

13. THE TOFUA CASTAWAYS 260

14. THE TAWITI CASTAWAY 291

1

Introductory

THE endurance of man and his small boat on the great
ocean is best shown in the annals of marine disaster,
for there only may be found the most notable examples of their sea-going qualities. There also may be
found the records of the crew's power to resist hardship occasioned by hasty preparation and overcrowd-
ing, as well as the obvious necessity of accepting the
conditions of wind and weather without choice. Sailors
have a firm confidence in the seaworthiness of their
boats at the time when they are the only resource, and
tumble in trustfully when lowered away from the ship.

The study of the small boat at sea may have other
than romantic value; it may be the means of inculcating
in the amateur sailor the spirit of self-reliance. To the
single-hander of more mature experience it may become
an inspiration to still more daring exploits. To the tech-
nician it may offer proof that the smaller boat can be
superior to the one of larger bulk and capable of

withstanding incredible punishment from the elements, often to the point of outdoing its human occupants.

Our primitive instinct for space and solitude makes us susceptible to the appeal of stories of the castaway, and anyone who has ever ventured on a boat voyage, no matter how close to the land, will naturally take an interest in them. In this volume are tales of the collision with an iceberg in the gloom of night; a fearful fire at sea—perhaps the most terrifying of calamities; the sullen growl of the mutineer, intent upon the destruction of half the ship's crew; the ship charged upon and destroyed by a whale in defense of his harem of cows; the spectacle of men being dashed against slippery rocks and clinging to them under the crashing seas with surprising tenacity of life; the ship wrecked without warning upon the coral reef in tropical seas; the escapes of boats from the very jaws of the grinding ice-floe. These are only a few of the disasters to be found in the lore of the castaway. For many of their fates are to this day unknown and may forever be in the realm of conjecture.

The claim to the privilege of authorship in this field of maritime experience is based on a life spent very largely on the sea. A life which has given the writer not only much practical experience with sailing vessels and ships' boats, but a close contact with their crews. His interest in castaways was awakened when he became party to the rescue of a boatload of human beings in the South Seas, when, as a mere boy of twelve, he was on a sailing ship, the *Northern Light,* making a passage from New York to Japan. The sailing track from New York to Japan was around the Cape of Good Hope and to the southward of Australia. Sweeping around Tasmania they started to make their northing to the eastward of Australia and thence up through the Pacific Islands, passing between the Solomons and the Santa Cruz Islands.

In an open space of sea to the northward of these two groups at break of day, on the weather bow, we sighted a speck on the sea. It was a boat with a dark rag of sail. The ship, steering full and by on the starboard tack, was ordered hove to. There was great excitement on deck. There came the rumbling of hoarse and unusual orders; royals came in, the mainsail was hauled up, the weather main braces manned and the yards laid aback, and before the *Northern Light* knew it she was brought stock still in her track. The small speck bobbed like a nautilus on the gray-blue ocean as it drifted in to the great black side of the ship. It was not even a small trading vessel as we at first had supposed, but an open boat with five persons in it.

As soon as they came within heaving distance the ship gave them a line to haul them alongside. As two of the people in the boat grabbed the line we could see that they were scarcely strong enough to secure it to haul in; the rest were stretched out, helpless. A gantline was rove off to the cro'jack yard and a bowline on a bight was lowered into the boat; then, one by one, starved and more dead than alive, they were hoisted on deck; all native islanders, an old man, an old woman, and three young men. Their boat as well was taken aboard and landed across the main hatch of the ship. The boat was of a good model, twenty-five feet long, and bore the brand of a Rotterdam builder.

As the natives were dropped on deck the brandy was broken out at once, which no one refused except the old man, who, with a shake of his head, said, "Me missionary," (Christian), and then pointing to himself and then to the sky, said, "Tabu." But when he was moved into the pilothouse and out of sight of the others, which he ascertained by carefully looking about, the brandy was again proffered with better results. He proved to be equal to a regular bosun's nip. After that there was no "tabu" for him, or any of them, for that matter.

The old man's next word was, "Apamama." Apamama was one of the Gilbert Islands, 800 miles to the north and east, which we were to pass to windward. He gradually became more communicative, and, looking at the moon which was then visible during the day, pointed to it once and then clapped and clasped his hands. He then pointed to the sun and held up all ten fingers. By a single word and these signs he made it known that they were from Apamama, and had been out one moon and ten suns, or in other words they had been adrift upwards of forty days. By another sign he indicated that seven had died; there had been twelve when they left the island. The first to perish was the young wife of one of the survivors. Briefly and vividly he told their pitiful tale. The next thing to do was to restore them to health by careful feeding and nursing.

Another chapter of their story was told by the boat

itself when it was unloaded and cleaned. It reeked of
sea slime and of decayed dried fruits. There was a
box of missionary literature including some small geographies, all in a Polynesian language. The maps in
the geographies became useful as a means of communication, for pictures are a universal language. When
clean and dry, their boat was painted inside and out
and a comet was carved on each bow in commemora-
tion of the great comet we had seen from the *Northern
Light* in the Indian Ocean. It was then fitted with a
platform over the thwarts, and a tent was made for
the natives by stretching a tarpaulin over a ridge-pole.
Here they were comfortably and privately housed as
long as the weather remained warm.

When a better understanding had been established,
it was learned that they were native missionaries, that
the old man was a deacon and the old woman his wife.
A party of twelve had been sent by the king on a mis-
sion from Apamama to Nanuti, an island seventy miles
to the southward. On Nanuti they remained for twelve
days, and on the return towards Apamama they had
been blown out of their track and were lost on the sea.

Soon after they were settled in their boat tent, we
were surprised to have the youngest of the men come
aft and ask in broken English, "Captain, where ship
bound?"

"Japan."

"Ship no stop Apamama?"

The young man was told that if it was a possible
thing and the winds permitted, they would be put off

at their own island, whereupon he said: "Captain, I thank you, King very glad, give plenty copra."

The Captain wondered what his chances would be of being made governor of an island, on personally restoring these subjects of His Majesty, but luck was against him. We made Apamama on a dark and squally night, and a sea filled with coral reefs was no place at that time for a big ship. There was, however, another island in a better position, 300 miles to the northwest. This was Ebon, of the Marshall group. This island the Apamamians knew to be hostile to them, and they begged not to be landed there at all. When Ebon came in sight they showed unmistakable signs of terror, as their boat was cleared away for lowering. Two of them even hid under the forecastle head. The Captain felt that he had no more right to cast them adrift than he would any of his own crew, and so all was belayed for the night.

On the next day, Japan was pointed out in the little geography to the deacon, and he looked pleased, as did his wife, and both nodded intelligently. That the deacon knew about Japan, though it was over 2000 miles away, was very plain. He certainly preferred it to Ebon, and it was decided to continue the voyage without further stopping at islands of the wrong kind.

When the ship reached Japan, the natives had been thirty-five days on board, and had journeyed from a region of coral islands and warm seas to one of keen winter winds. As they sailed into colder latitudes, they were clothed according to the falling temperature, the writer's own mother providing for the deacon's wife.

It was a frosty morning when they sailed into Yokohama, and they were seen standing at the rail and
wondering at the "smoke" of their breath when it
struck the cold air. It was the first time since they had
been picked up that they showed wonder at anything.
The deacon, though, gazed in amazement at Fuji, man-
tled in snow and glistening in the morning sun. "Big
island, big island!" he kept exclaiming.

Since the United States Consul had no authority to
take action for the relief of these foreign castaways,
they were turned over to the missionaries, who placed
them in a paper Japanese house. In a few days, the
natives sent for the Captain, who found these people
of the tropics miserably huddled around a charcoal
brazier. Since in this cold Japanese winter such treatment meant almost certain death, the Captain realized
that his duty to the waifs was not yet ended, for they
had to be sent home. Accordingly, he stirred up newspaper publicity in their behalf, circulated a subscrip-
tion list among the European merchants of Yokohama,
and secured, on the first day, funds to the amount of
seven hundred and fifty dollars. Both the United States
and the British Ambassadors put their hands deep into
their pockets, and the responses were so generous that
a notice had to be put in the paper to stop the money
from coming in. The agent of the Pacific Mail Steamship Company offered to transport them all, including
the boat, to San Francisco, so they sailed from Yokohama as passengers on the *City of Tokyo,* while the
Northern Light was still in port.

All five of the castaways reached home. From San

Francisco they were transported to Honolulu and thence to their own island by a trading schooner. They had made a circuit of 11,000 miles, and, having sailed over many seas, and looked upon many a strange sight, including the "big island" blanketed with snow, the survivors of the boat expedition to Nanuti, long given up for lost, were delivered in good health to His Majesty, the King of Apamama. Upon hearing of this safe return, the Captain exclaimed, with Sinbad the Sailor, "Allah is great!"

A few years after the experience with the Gilbert Islanders, it was the fortune of the author to take part in a boat adventure which had the decided aspect of a castaway voyage. It was in 1888 when the bark *Aquidneck,* owned and sailed by his father, Captain Joshua Slocum, was lost in Paranagua Bay, Brazil. The writer was mate. After the hulk had been floated off the bar and towed to a sheltered cove among the arms of the extensive bay, the building of a boat was started on board of the vessel for the purpose of sailing back home. The boat was laid down on the main deck of the *Aquidneck,* and, on account of the available building space, the length was limited to thirty-five feet; beam seven and a half feet; depth three feet. The model was somewhat on the lines of a clipper dory with a flat bottom section of thirty inches. The stern was on the Japanese order, while the high bow was a tribute to the Makah Indians of Puget Sound. The rudder was Chinese and was held in place by wooden gudgeons, which allowed it to be hoisted up or lowered deep in the water as the case required; it was Chinese even to the small diamond shaped holes useful for holding on to the water and making a friction. Points like these the builders had learned in China.

The new craft was novel in many respects and the entire construction was by hand, even the manufacture of the planking, which was whip-sawed out of long logs by native sawyers who worked by the foot. The sawing was roughly done and left many bumps to be removed by jack planes, the hardest sort of labor. It was all very primitive. A sail was rigged over the job to keep it out of the weather, and everything was done in the most thorough manner possible. Ballasting of the boat was largely accomplished by a selection of the timber according to weight. The wide bottom planks were of iron-wood, which would sink like a stone, and all of the planking below the water line was of the same weight, while the top was of light Spanish cedar. The planks were copper-riveted together, lapstrake, which is by all odds the strongest way to build a boat. The fastenings of the boat were the greatest problem. There was a quantity of used muntz metal sheathing on the ship left over from a previous "coppering" of her bottom and this was taken ashore to a forge in a small shipyard, where it was melted and cast into bolts. Tru'nels were made on the foot lathe in the ship's carpenter shop; these were button headed and were used at the top for through fastenings at the clamps. There was an abundance of copper nails on hand, but no rivets for the clinching, and this want was supplied in a curious way by hammering out "dumps" on the anvil and then punching and cutting them up into washers. A "dump" was a large copper coin of half of its intrinsic value in the very ductile metal. The last contribution that the *Aquidneck* made to the new boat was a number of small eyebolts from her spanker boom, which were turned to account for lashing bolts in the deck of the new craft.

Bamboo was used wherever lightness and strength were necessary. It could be obtained in any required length or size, and it entered into the topside fittings and rigging wherever it could be used. The cabin frame was bamboo, lashed together at the joints. The sails, which were of the balanced lug type, were ribbed like bat's wings with bamboo. A large bamboo guard by way of a sponson was lashed to the outside of each gunwale, the individual members being about four inches in diameter and in single lengths which extended the whole length of the boat. These bamboo sponsons produced a balsa effect when completed, and supplied a reserve flotation of four thousand pounds when submerged. This would be invaluable in case of swamping or a capsize.

Both of these possibilities were also kept in mind when the stores were put on board. All perishable goods such as sea biscuit, sugar, tea, coffee, etc., were soldered up in tin units of convenient size. All heavy stores, such as water in casks, were put in the center of the boat and the lighter things in the ends. That made the boat lively in a sea. While preparing for sea, every precaution against disaster was taken, nothing was left to chance. As it turned out on the voyage, it was well that this was so.

As soon as the hull was planked and ready for the water, it was hoisted overboard from the deck of the doomed *Aquidneck* and the two ships, the new born of the old, parted company forever. It was a sad parting, for the *Aquidneck* was a beautiful and noble vessel of whom her people were both proud and fond. Fortunately, she was not long to survive her melancholy fate for she soon burned in Santos where she had been towed to be a coffee hulk. A builder of small coasting vessels in Paranagua who had done some repair work on the *Aquidneck* proffered the use of his dock to the captain as a place to complete the boat, and there she was towed by a small steam launch which was used for lighter transportation in the harbor. This gentleman also offered the use of his house for the shelter of the boat party of four, which included the captain's young wife, Henrietta, and the writer's very young brother, Garfield. The house near the work was gladly accepted, and it was there that Henrietta stitched the sails on the Okhotsk Sea sewing machine—so called from having been acquired by the family, with proceeds of their fishing voyage there. This connected the new boat with a remote part of the Pacific. When the sails were finished, the sewing machine was traded for a grapnel which had been used as a pot hook by Negro slaves on a plantation where the *Aquidneck* was loading timber before she was lost. "Now that the slaves are gone I have no use for the crooked thing," explained the farmer.

When the citizens of Paranagua outside of the friendly shipyard heard of the project of the Americanos to sail the slim little boat to North America, they were often noticed pointing to their foreheads and muttering the Portuguese equivalent of "suicide." The Portuguese heritage of the sea had been long forgotten, and only pollywog sailors were left. To the Americanos, remaining in Paranagua under any circumstances meant exile, which was not to be considered, as long as a ship, however small, could be prepared for a return home. In the course of three months the boat was ready for sea, but the "suicide" theory had reached official ears and this led to difficulties regarding permission to leave port.

It happened that at this time Negro slavery was abolished officially in Brazil by Imperial Proclamation. There was great excitement. Even in Paranagua there were torch processions and speeches at night, with plenty of loudly detonating rockets by day, after the manner of hot headed, vociferous Latins. The boat party mingled with the civilians, shouting "Viva Liberdade" with the loudest of them, until it became a slogan and was declared to be the only fitting name for the little American ship bound on such a great adventure. Secretly she meant "liberty" to her crew also, so they let it stand and painted "Liberdade" on her main beam, after carving her stem-head into the form of the screaming American eagle which had terminated the cutwater of the dear old *Aquidneck*.

The friends of human liberty were pleased, but when a passport was requested at the Alfandega it was discovered that there was an obstacle to the liberty of the seas. The ship was too small to voyage with safety to America do Nord. If a passport to America do Nord was impossible, how about a fishing license? All hands turned to making a fish net which was rigged on a beam and hoisted in the rigging, making the *Liberdade* look like a regular trawler. This did not put the crew back much, for a fishing net was a good thing to have anyway. Upon another application to the Alfandega, a fishing license was granted, "inside and OUTSIDE of the bar."

"How far outside of the bar may this carry us?" the captain asked.

"Quiem sabe," responded the official. "Adios señor, we will meet in heaven."

This meant: "You may go since you insist upon it, but I must not officially know it and you will go to the bottom."

The *Liberdade* was then put on some trial sails about the bay to shake things into place and to make all shipshape. The bar was breaking but the crew sensed freedom ahead. A fresh southerly breeze was blowing outside. The captain decided on a try, and under full sail the boat started for the entrance of the bay. The pilot on a bar-bound coaster which was anchored shouted that the bar was "crudo," at the same time crossing himself and commending the venturesome Americanos to the saints, as they took the line of thundering breakers. One after another, the *Liberdade* mounted the oncoming waves like a sea bird, scarcely wetting her plumage. Straight out and into deep water she went, as though eager to make a safe offing from the rocky coastline before squaring away for Santos, a hundred and fifty-mile run. All hands were delighted at their escape from Paranagua. The broad Chinese sails pulled on every rope yarn as the boat raced down the long backs of good natured seas, homeward bound. The crew was now in the spirit of the voyage, with confidence in the boat mounting every minute.

Twenty-four hours from Paranagua bar to the entrance of Santos, a steamer was met coming out, bound for Rio. It was the steamship *Finance,* an old friend, and by three o'clock the *Liberdade* was on her way out to sea again at the end of a ninety-fathom towline. Captain Baker thoughtfully invited Henrietta and young Garfield on board of the *Finance* for the run to Rio, leaving the captain and mate on the boat to steer and tend line; a situation which was enjoyable at first; "an eleven knot fair wind" they called it, as the boat started to skip along. The towline was taken to the mainmast under the hood where a man stood by it with an axe to cut in case of a bad sheer. Between the alternate tautening and slacking of the line, the boat raced like a porpoise all night, keeping the tiller man busy with his eye on the taffrail light of the steamer. The next morning, the *Liberdade* passed in by the Sugarloaf, still on the towline astern of the *Finance.* It was a wild ride but she made good time, for in forty-eight hours' time she had covered three hundred and fifty miles from her point of departure. It was worth being drenched with a flying spray of brine!

In Rio it was declared by the Alfandega that the

simple fishing license was invalid and that it required a *passe especial* from the Brazilian government, which was courteously granted "out of respect for American seamen." It took about a month to get the new document, which carried with it the Brazilian flag, which, with due ceremony, was hoisted to the mizzen peak of the *Liberdade*. The *Liberdade* took leave of Rio de Janeiro July 23rd, 1888.

Meeting with light head winds, the *Liberdade* made very little progress on the first day from Rio, and finally when night came on she anchored twenty miles east of Rio Heads, near the shore. There was some sea on and when the boat rolled about on her cable a trouble unthought of before came up in Garfield's mind before going to his bunk; "Mamma," cried he, as the little vessel jumped about in the rough sea, tumbling the young sailor from side to side in the small quarters while he knelt seriously at his evening devotion, "mamma, this boat isn't big enough to pray in." This trouble was adjusted in time, and Garfield learned to watch as well as to pray on the voyage with faith that all would be well.

By daylight on the second day, the *Liberdade* was again under way, beating to windward against the old wind and sea. The following night she kept at it, and the next day made Cape Frio. While yet in Paranagua, and preparing for the voyage, the great bugbear in the minds of the crew had been Cape Frio, the stormiest promontory on the whole coast of Brazil. It was always known as a seat of bad weather, covered with clouds and darkness and frequented by heavy squalls at all times. Nearly midday, the *Liberdade*, close hauled and doing well, drew towards the pitch of the cape. The captain was steering, and the mate after swaying up the main halyards and trimming the fore sheet, sat on the fore end of the house to enjoy an orange and the approaching scenery at the same time. Henrietta, from the cockpit, viewed the dark clouds and the rough sea with misgivings and suddenly burst into a fit of hysterical weeping. That was too much for the captain who at once put up the tiller and snapped at the mate for his apparent heedlessness as though the whole thing was his fault. The boat eased up, scooted with a will to an anchorage back of the cape. On examining the large scale coasting chart, it was found that there was a narrow channel separating Cape Frio Island from the mainland, which was available for small coasting craft of light draft. The entrance to the channel was a quarter of a mile wide and formed a tunnel for swift tides in each direction. When the party arrived, they found the tide against them and so anchored and went down to dine on a dumpling stew made by Henrietta as a reward for taking the inside passage. They were aroused a few moments afterwards by a whale coming up underneath the boat, knocking off the false keel and carrying away the anchor warp, together with the slave owner's pothook grapnel. To make the contact more interesting, the whale stretched out and lay close to the boat for a few minutes, quietly blowing as if preparing again to dive. He was considerably longer than the boat and covered with parasites and barnacles. He appar-

The *Liberdade*

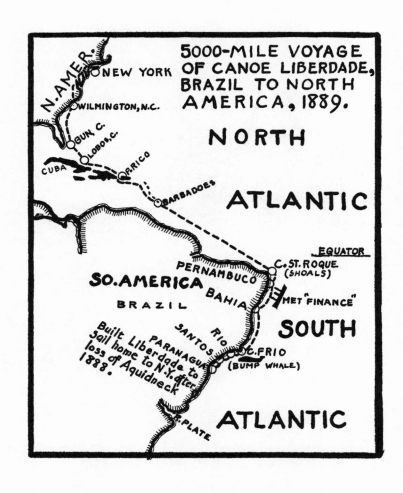

5000-MILE VOYAGE OF CANOE LIBERDADE, BRAZIL TO NORTH AMERICA, 1889.

ently took the boat for some sort of a floating back scratcher, finally concluding however that the rocks were more suited to the purposes of his toilet. This conclusion on the part of His Whaleship was very satisfactory to the crew of the *Liberdade,* who had begun to think of the fate of the ship *Essex.* The channel was used by large schools of porpoise as well as bonito, which made it a most interesting place for fishermen.

While waiting for the tide to turn, the *Liberdade* made sail and ran into Thetis Cove, on the south side of Cape Frio Island, where the British frigate *Thetis* had sunk, with millions of treasure on board. The cove was so snug that the boat tied up to the shore while the crew landed to climb over the cliffs. On making the port behind the island, a settlement of fishermen was found and the headquarters of a diving crew salvaging bullion and silver coin from the sunken *Thetis.* On the beach was all sorts of debris from the *Thetis:* figurehead, small guns, steering wheel and what not. That very day the same whale got into the cove with them and nearly demolished their whole equipment. There was barely enough room for a porpoise, but the whale did not seem to know that.

The natives, as well as the divers, took much interest in the *Liberdade* and her voyage to North America.

"Is North America near New York?" asked the Patron, who owned all the boats and nets in the place.

"Why, North America is IN New York," explained the chief diver, who was a Canadian.

"I thought so," responded the Patron, with a self-satisfied look at the rest of the villagers.

After a brief friendly chat over some coffee, the problems of the *Liberdade's* voyage were discussed and the crew was cautioned by the fishermen against the danger of the balena, which at this mating season were ferocious as they fed along the edges of the coral reefs to the northward. Leaving this haven, a strong southerly wind hurried the boat on, and on reaching out to windward of the shoals off Cape St. Thome the loss of the false keel was first realized.

Sometimes the *Liberdade* came upon coral reefs of a dark night, and her crew, listening to the dismal tune of the sea breaking over them, realized how intensely alone they were; no sign of any living thing in sight, except perhaps the phosphorescent streaks of a hungry shark which told of bad company in her wake and made the gloom of the place still more dismal. One night the crew made shelter under the lee of the extensive reefs called the Paredes, without seeing the breakers in the dark, although they were not far in the distance. At another time, on a dark and stormy night, dragging on sail to clear a lee shore, the boat suddenly came into smooth water. The crew cast anchor and furled sails, lying in a magic harbor till daylight, when it was discovered that they were among a maze of ugly reefs with high seas breaking over them, as far as the eye could reach, on all sides, except at the small place where the boat had entered during the night.

There was fine cruising after passing Cape St.

Thome. Before reaching the Abrolhos the *Liberdade* tied up to the barrier reef and the crew landed to collect specimens of coral. A visit was made to the village of Caravellas, back of the reef, where much whaling gear lay strewn about the place, and on the beach was found the carcass of a whale about nine days slain judging from its stench. Leaning against a smart-looking boat was a gray haired whaleman. Both boat and man were relics of New Bedford, employed at this station in their familiar industry. The old man, thinly clad to suit the climate, was still the sailor recognizable by the set and rig of his gear and by the ample straw hat that he wore and doffed in a seaman-like manner upon receiving a salute.

"Filio do mar do Nord Americano," explained an affable native close by, by way of introduction as soon as it was known that the crew of the *Liberdade*, too, were of the same country. It could not be learned how the ancient mariner came to be stranded in this strange land. He may have been cast there by the whale for ought that could be discovered to the contrary.

With a good growth of barnacles impeding her headway, the *Liberdade* sailed into Bahia for a much needed cleaning and overhauling. With rare courtesy, she was placed in the dock at the Arsenal da Marinha and given every facility at the command of the Port. During the nine days there, the false keel knocked off by the Cape Frio whale was replaced with the addition of an iron shoe which added much to the boat's stability. After the barnacles were removed, two coats of copper paint were put on to keep out the sea worms.

While the crew was up to its eyes in paint, some strong Abolitionists invited them to a formal dinner ashore, given in their honor, but they graciously forgave the crew's inability to accept. There was no doubt of their admiration for the *Liberdade* and what her name stood for.

Five days from Bahia the *Liberdade* rounded the reef at Pernambuco to meet friends again, for all along the coast of Brazil she was preceded by her fame in the papers. The crew was entertained by red hot Abolitionists, and, at their request, the boat was placed for one day on public view at the Arsenal dock.

Leaving Pernambuco, the *Liberdade* headed out by the reef and into the open sea again. It was over two thousand miles around Cape St. Roque to Barbados, the real turning point of the voyage. Cape St. Roque is not as notorious for bad weather as Frio, but it has dangerous shoals extending many miles at sea, and by cutting this corner too closely, *Liberdade* and her crew barely avoided coming to grief. It was after nightfall and she was running before a fresh breeze and a good-natured, quartering sea. It was a fine starlight night and all looked well. Suddenly the boat rose to the heave of a ground swell, and then another heave, followed by the crash of a breaker over the deck. Without waiting for a call, the crew tumbled out. By this time the captain had put the helm down, bringing her head to the sea. With the wind abeam she was under good control. As the boat took the second breaker, the latter roared on toward her like a devouring monster, its form gleaming with agitated phosphorous against a black sky, and the curling crest nearly as high as her mast. The head fell as it curled over the boat and smothered her under tons of water that smelled and tasted of bottom slime. Then the value of the bamboo sponsons became apparent, for without them the boat would have been swamped. As she shook herself from under this breaker, she forged ahead into deeper water where the breakers became less violent, and so into safety again. She had been on the edge of Cape St. Roque Shoals, and the bottom was breaking from a depth of six fathoms. No doubt there had been a strong insetting current that carried her inside of the reckoning. On the rest of the long run nothing out of the ordinary happened, excepting that the mainmast parted company with itself just above the deck, but this was fished.

Nineteen days from Pernambuco, the *Liberdade* made Barbados, where she fitted a new mast. On entering port she was pestered by a native pilot, who got a jolt when he came to collect his bill and found that the boat drew only thirty inches! If alive, he is blinking yet. On the 7th of October she sailed again with the hope that the season of hurricanes was over, although they are known to occur as late as November. Passing through the Antilles around the south end of Sta. Lucia and into the Caribbean Sea, a new period of the voyage was begun. Beautiful islands were passed, one after another—Martinique, Dominica, Guadaloupe and Santa Cruz. Swinging off along the south coast of Porto Rico, the party sailed through the Mona Passage, after a three-day stop at Mayaguez.

They then bore along the north coast of Haiti to the western extremity of the island, from which a departure was made for the headlands of Cuba. Following the Cuban coast as far as Cardenas, they took a final departure from the islands, regretting that they could not sail around them all.

The region on the north side of Cuba is often visited by gales of great violence, making this the lee shore; a weather eye was therefore kept lifting, especially in the direction of their source, which is from north to northwest. However, storms prevailed from other quarters, mostly from the east, bringing heavy squalls of wind, rain and thunder every afternoon. Such storms, once heard, will never be forgotten.

In the night while standing across the Bahama Channel, a glow was made out in the sky ahead which the captain thought was a "norther," until he checked on the glass and found it too high for one of those disturbances. This phenomenon disturbed them somewhat, till the discovery was made, upon nearer approach, that it was but the reflection of the white banks on the sky, and no cause for alarm. Soon after this, up popped the Lobos Cay light, two points on the weather bow. Having a mind to stop at the Cay for water, they fetched in under its lee and came to, in one and a half fathoms of water, in good shelter. There appeared then, overhead in wonderful beauty, *what had awed them from the distance in the early night*—a configuration of the banks marked visibly in the heavens. Furling sails and setting a light in the rigging, all hands turned in, for it lacked three hours yet of daylight.

By break of day the crew prepared to land and fill water, for on the Cay is stored some hundred thousand gallons of rain water in cisterns at the base of the lighthouse. Here occurred one of the most curious adventures of the whole voyage. It started with the "conch" light keeper, who, as soon as he discovered that there was a strange sail in his harbor, hoisted the blue British Board of Trade flag and came down to the edge of the sand to greet the crew, thinking at first that they were shipwrecked sailors in distress; shipwrecked they were, but not in distress, as he had supposed when hoisting the flag, which signified assistance for distressed seamen.

On learning their story, however, he began to regard them as possible pirates. The Oriental appearance of the *Liberdade* no doubt justified this idea, for with bright mahogany hull, junk sails and bamboo guards, she certainly must have made a fantastic impression upon his unaccustomed vision, for he was seen to rub his eyes as he blinked at the boat. The mate, with a bucket on his arm, had vaulted to the sand with an oar, only to be refused water. "Where are you from, and where are them doubloons?" was all that could be got out of him, as he looked the mate up and down with evident hostility. "Tell the captain to come ashore and bring his papers."

Seeing that the light keeper was suspicious of smugglers and wreckers (if he were not a reformed pirate himself), the captain shoved his "papers" into his hat, and, leaping into the surf, waded ashore. The document which he presented was the original *passe especial,* written in Portuguese, a language entirely unknown to the keeper, who, nevertheless, stared knowingly both at the parchment and the great seal attached thereto. The nature of the voyage was carefully explained to him, also the location of the "Island of Rio," as he persistently called Rio de Janeiro, from where the Brazilian papers dated. In his whole knowledge of Islands, that was one that this Sancho Panza had never heard of before. The captain made things as clear as he could to the "conch" of the Bahamas. However, the Brazilian flag was against them still, and the keeper, seemingly, was about to search for "them doubloons", but he finally gave the gunwales of his trousers a fitful hitch and said, "All right, take all the water you want; it is free." Suspicion allayed, he became friendly.

This patch of sand had been only lately swept by a hurricane, but the tall iron tower of the lighthouse showed no apparent marks of the conflict. Near the lighthouse were the quarters of the keeper, who, at the time the *Liberdade* stopped there, was enjoying a visit from his wife and three children from Nassau. These, together with the two assistant keepers, made up the total population of this island kingdom; the smallest kingdom the crew had ever visited, and by far the most isolated.

Two days of brisk sailing over the white Bahama Banks brought the *Liberdade* to Bemini. From there a mere push would send the crew to the coast of their own native America. They remained at anchor for a day for a last swim in these seas, and then launched out on the great Gulf Stream where they were swept along by its restless motion, making on the first day, before the wind and current, two hundred twenty miles. This was great getting along for a small canoe. Going at the same high rate of speed on the second night in the stream, the canoe struck a spar and went over it with a bound. Her keel was shattered by the shock, but, finally shaking the crippled timber clear of herself, she came on quite well without it. No other damage was done to the craft, although at times her very ribs were threatened before clearing this lively ocean river. In the middle of the current, she went along with a wide swinging motion, but on nearing the edge of the stream fell in with rips and a high cross sea. "Seas like that can't break this boat," declared Garfield, as a big one hit and rattled the boat. The wind in the meantime had chopped around to the northeast and came in dead ahead, which put some real seas aboard for the first time since leaving the coast of Brazil.

Early in the afteronon of October 28th, 1888, the crew made land and got into smooth water. Lying before them now were the hills of America which they had sailed so many thousands of miles to see again. Drawing in with the coast, they made out first the broad, rich forests, then open fields and villages, with signs of comfort on every hand. It was the land about Bull's Bay on the coast of South Carloina, and, with night coming on, Cape Romain Light came plainly into sight to the north. The wind falling light as they drew in with the coast, and the current being against them, the crew anchored about two miles from the shore, in four fathoms of water.

The first American vessel to hail the *Liberdade* was the pilot boat at Fryingpan Shoals off Cape Fear.

"Where are you from?" they cried, eyeing the Chinese rig.

"Rio."

"Rio Janeiro?"

"Yes."

"Great Caesar's ghost!"

The pilot boat, on the point of going into Southport, hove the *Liberdade* the end of a friendly line and towed her in to a snug anchorage. The good people were at first at a loss to understand the meaning of the name of the boat.

"Well I d'clar," exclaimed one, "freed the niggers and had no wah. Mister," continued he, turning to the captain after a pause, "mister, d'ye know the South were foolish? They had a wah, and they had to free the niggers, too."

"Oh, yes mister, I was thar. Over thar beyond them oaks was my house."

"Yes mister, I fought too, and fought hard, but it warn't no use."

Two pleasant weeks in Southport were enough to refresh the crew, who in the meantime stripped the boat of her fantastic bamboo sponsons which would not be of further use for the inland trip to winter quarters.

The following table gives the actual time at sea and the approximate distances in nautical miles from point to point on the courses steered:

	Days	Distance
From Paranagua to Santos.......	1	150
" Santos to Rio de Janeiro....	¾	200
(towed by *Finance*)		
" Rio to Cape Frio.........	2	70
" Cape Frio to Caravellas....	4	370
" Caravellas to St. Paulo.....	3	270
" St. Paulo to Bahia.........	½	40
" Bahia to Pernambuco......	5	390
" Pernambuco to Barbados...	19	2,150
" Barbados to Mayaguez.....	5	570
" Mayaguez to Cape Romain.	13	1,300
	53¼	5,510

Including all the distances of the ins and outs that were made would considerably augment the number of miles covered. To say, therefore, that the *Liberdade* averaged a hundred and three miles a day for fifty-three days would be considerably inside the truth.

From Southport a leisurely sail up the coast took the *Liberdade* to Norfolk and finally to Washington, D.C., where the crew moored for the winter. The final port of the *Liberdade* was the Smithsonian Institution in Washington, where she remained at anchor for several years, recognized with national as well as technical interest, as the smallest vessel on record to make such a long ocean voyage. The fact that the *Liberdade* was built on the deck of a wrecked ship and then sailed many thousands of miles home was regarded as a commendable example of Yankee resource and seamanship.

The author's voyage home from South America in the *Liberdade* led him to become vitally interested in the history of castaway boats, and the following accounts are the result of research while sailing in the waters where the events actually occurred. In no other way could they be adequately visualized. This statement of familiarity with locality, however, does not apply to the Arctic or Antarctic regions, in neither of which the author has had experience. The Polar regions, interesting as they may be, are not usually included in trade routes of the merchant sailor. It was, however, the merchant sailor's business to venture into many other dangerous but romantic places, among the coral islands of the Indian Ocean, or skirting the reefs of the Pelew Islands, or cruising about the Great Barrier Reef of Australia which was witness to Bligh's boat exploit, since pronounced to be the outstanding piece of seamanship and navigation in the annals of the sea. While on the ship *Northern Light*, it was the writer's experience to meet with just such a mighty storm off the Cape of Good Hope that disabled the *Hercules* and sent her ashore. The *Northern Light* had better luck and finally rounded the Cape after spending three months in Algoa Bay repairing ship for the continuance of her voyage to New York; in the meantime there was ample time to receive a very clear impression of the lore of South Africa, to learn the particulars of

Indiamen wrecked at Fish River, to visit the Kaffir kraals and to talk with the Kaffirs themselves.

While on three successive whaling voyages as harpooner, the writer had battles enough with sperm whales to enable him to fully realize the possibility of the destruction of the *Essex* by one of the sea monsters, full of wrath.

Herman Melville got the idea of "Moby Dick" for his great classic from the sinking of the *Essex* in the Pacific, and after the famous disaster he had many talks with Owen Chase, on Nantucket. The narratives of Owen Chase and the other survivors were published by Gilley, London, 1822, now a very rare book.

The chapter on the Wager Longboat was chiefly derived from the very minutely written journal of Bulkeley, the ship's gunner. It was the only account of the extraordinary proceedings from the time the boat was rebuilt on the rocks of the Gulf of Peñas, its eventful passage of the straits of Magellan and its arrival in Brazil, and by influencing public opinion, it served the purpose of saving Bulkeley from being tried for piracy on his return to England.

It was while the writer was on a voyage to New Zealand that he discovered the story of the Tawiti Castaway, which is a favorite with the North Islanders as a part of their colonial lore. The story reached England in 1862, when it appeared in the "All the year round" weekly, then edited by Charles Dickens.

The particulars of the Fenua-ura Castaways were first broadcast to the world in a letter written by Captain Pond of the ill-fated American bark Julia Ann, to the New York Herald in 1856. Pond was sore about the shabby treatment accorded both to himself and the other survivors by the French authorities in Tahiti.

For the facts relating to The Jeannette's Boats, the author is not only indebted to Captain De Long's journal in the "Voyage of the Jeannette" and to Chief Engineer Melville's "In the Lena Delta" but for personal aid graciously lent by Mrs. De Long herself, who is now (1938) a resident of New York. In the Watton home, within sight of the Soldiers and Sailors Monument, on the bank of the Hudson, may be found many sacred relics of the Jeannette expedition.

The completely successful dash made by Sir Ernest Shackleton and his crew of the little "James Caird" is a vigorous refutation of the old saw about "wooden ships and iron men." Here were iron men bread in iron ships. It is not the ship. It is the man. Here, revealed in this Antarctic boat voyage, were seamen of the same salty and indomitable type that could have been found with Drake, Hawkins, Anson or Nelson; equal on any point to the most heroic traditions of maritime glory for centuries past.

2

The Hercules Castaways

THE American ship *Hercules* set out on her voyage from Calcutta, March 17th, 1796, with rice consigned to the British East India Company in London. Due to their own shortness of tonnage, the Company was chartering foreign ships at this time to meet an emergency, for a corn famine in Europe was causing an acute shortage of food in England, and Johnny Bull was taking in his belt. Captain Stout, therefore, was urged to make all possible despatch with his cargo. He was glad of the prospect of soon getting out to sea, for he had occupied a lay-up berth in the deadly Hugli River for five months, waiting for a charter, with the consequent loss by disease of nearly the whole of his American crew.

The recruiting for the voyage was done at random in regard both to race and nationality—the polyglot flotsam of an Eastern seaport. The larger part of the new crew was made up of native Lascars who belonged

41

in India, and the rest were from all the maritime countries of Europe, making up a complement of sixty-four. To this mixed company Captain Stout, an example of humanity and tact, learned to adapt himself, and no very unusual event took place on the ship until the Cape of Good Hope was reached. An Irishman on board said: "There's 'rason' in everything but the duff, and not a raisin in that!" There is a reason for the bad weather in the vicinity of all great promontories, and the greater the promontory, the worse the possible disturbance. According to this natural law, the worst could be expected of the "Cape of Storms," for here the presence of two opposing currents of water, each sweeping around on its appointed course with great velocity, makes this southernmost point of Africa more difficult even than Cape Horn. The stream nearer Africa is known as the Agulhas; while nearer to the South Pole flows the Antarctic Drift, on its drive before the eternal westerlies of that terrestrial region. In the time of storm, the highest seas in all the world are to be fallen in with at the adjoining edges of these two ocean streams.

As the *Hercules* was being carried forward on her course in the Agulhas, she was met by heavy westerly gales which piled up a mountainous cross-rip: gigantic pyramidal mountains of water which raised their heads to the clouds to curl and roar over the ship. The *Hercules,* undaunted, hove to, to make the best of the onslaught, under "a mitten over a belaying pin, with the thumb brailed in." For six days she labored and strained. The gale kept increasing in force until the seventh day, when the contending forces of wind and water reached a terrifying climax. In this tremendous hour, nature seemed to threaten itself with dissolution.

At midnight, a sudden shift of the wind threw the ship in the trough of the sea, which struck her aft and staved in the whole of the stern frame, unshipped the rudder and started the wood ends at the stern post, allowing the sea to pour into the hold. Sea after sea boarded from aft to forward until the stricken ship came again into the wind; she was fast losing her buoyancy and showing a "logy" tendency to settle. The sounding rod showed four feet of water down below. Part of the crew manned the chain pumps which were in the 'tween decks and protected from the weather, while the rest broke out cargo from the run to get at the leak. To save the ship, bales of muslin, small sails, and everything at hand that could stop the inrush of sea water was packed into the opening. The pumps, with a capacity of fifty tons an hour, were worked like mad, the men in frequent relays making the wheels fly to cheat Davy Jones. It is a desperate feeling, that of hand pumping to keep afloat, with the water slowly rising in the well.

At this time the *Hercules* was a hundred miles from land. The storm abated, but the swell remained high and dangerous. Some of the Europeans, led by the carpenter, openly demanded that the longboat be put over the side, leaving the Lascars to their fate, but they were driven back to duty at the pumps, though the ship was sinking. Captain Stout, after bawling out the mutineers for their cowardice, set a party at getting a raft together for all hands, irrespective of race, to float off on, if necessary. Apart from the likelihood of sinking, the ship, due to the swelling of the rice, now well soaked, bade fair to burst apart and dump them all into the sea. A heathen Lascar broke away from the pumps and declared to the captain that he had a way to save the ship by making an offering to his gods. With perfect composure, he filled his turban with some of the rice, and, climbing the mizzen rigging with his offering held in his teeth, he secured it to the topmast cross-trees. All of the other Lascars now knew that the gods must be on their side, and their redoubled energy at the pump handles affected even the unbelievers.

In spite of hope, it was clear that the ship was doomed to destruction in one manner or another, and, after a consultation of the officers, it was agreed to reach the land, if possible, and run the ship ashore. In two days land was sighted at a distance of eighteen miles; the ship was worked slowly in with a hold half filled, but still keeping upright. To keep from capsizing, Stout might now have cut away his masts and taken to the boats and the raft, but he instinctively held on to his ship until the last possible moment, in the hope of saving it, as well as the lives of his people. In the morning, at a distance of two miles from shore, they let go the anchor, still with the hope of saving the vessel; but her stern was stove in in such a manner that it was decided to beach at once. Hoping to preserve some of the records, the captain placed the ship's register in the hands of the second mate, with orders to hoist out

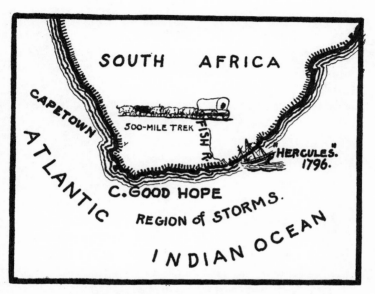

Map of the *Hercules* castaways

the longboat; to take his own chances, and to make a separate landing after the beaching of the ship. The second mate took with him three men and sufficient supplies for a cruise of several days, if need be; on shoving off, he said that he understood all of his instructions. He was a man to be depended upon.

As the land became plainer and the details of the sand hills came into view, the anxious gaze of the men on the ship met a sight which filled them with horror, for black natives, clothed in skins and well-armed with spears, were gathered on the shore, accompanied by large dogs. Immediately, the natives began to light fires among the sand hills to signal others in the back country. The prospect of being speared or torn to pieces by dogs was terrifying to the crew of the *Hercules*, who were now preparing to beach.

This location turned out to be the Kaffir coast of Cape Colony near the Great Fish River, where the British East Indiaman *Grosvenor* had been wrecked a few years before. The *Grosvenor* was from Ceylon, bound for England. Her passengers and crew, with very few exceptions, had perished in an attempt to journey on foot to Cape Town, five hundred miles around the trend of the coast. Some had met death by sheer exposure and fatigue; others, by wild animals and savages. The women passengers had been taken alive by the Kaffir chiefs to their kraals to meet a fate worse than death. Captain Stout knew all about the *Grosvenor!*

The wind was blowing inshore, which tailed the ship in at her anchor. They wanted to take it head on, since that would give them a better chance to select a soft spot on getting closer. A spring from the starboard quarter was bent to the cable, which was then veered out to bring the strain of the cable upon the stern of the ship and swing her head inshore. Hoisting the jibs and slipping cable and spring, the *Hercules* was started on her short course to destruction.

Within half a mile of the shore she struck on a cluster of sunken rocks. Here she pounded three or four minutes, until a heavy sea carried her over about a cable length nearer the shore, where she struck again and kept heaving in with the surf, which breached clear over the hull and washed overboard the raft which was intended to take off the crew. One of the Lascars took his own chance, jumped overboard, and climbed on the raft, to be capsized with it three times, but still clinging to it. After two hours of such struggling, he reached land, to be grabbed by the waiting Kaffirs. The crew on the wreck saw them whisk the man off behind the sand hills, where they supposed him to be speared, or "scragged," as they called it on the Cape. Nevertheless, twelve more seized spars, or anything else that would float, and took to the surf, to be thrown upon the land. No sooner were their feet on solid land than the Kaffirs seized them, as they had the first one, and hustled them behind the sand hills. When the Kaffirs reappeared upon the beach without any of their captives in sight, those on the ship very reasonably took it that their shipmates had been massacred, and that they were doomed to the same fate. Looking at the fires, they began to believe it better to drown on the spot, than to risk torture and death ashore. That end seemed better than submission to the savages. Some proposed to swim ashore together in a body, but they still feared the spears. Thus the night was spent in painful doubt concerning what was likely to happen to them in the morning, and they dreaded the rising of the sun on such a day.

When morning finally appeared, they looked toward the shore, but not a person was in sight. At length, about nine o'clock, the scene changed in a moment. All the people who had landed the day before were seen making toward the shore, beckoning and signalling for them to land. In a few minutes, every spar, grating and piece of timber that could be found in the wreck, was afloat and drifting inshore, each with one or more men clinging to it. The captain stripped off his shirt, put on a short jacket, seized a spar, and launched with it into the sea. He was dashed ashore unconscious and rescued by his people, before he could be carried out again by the backwash. When he returned to consciousness, he inquired about the longboat and was told that it had not yet come ashore, and that one man had perished in the surf. He tried to communicate with the Kaffirs, but could not make himself understood. Fortunately, there was present a Hottentot, who had lived with Dutch farmers, and could speak their language. The third mate was a Dutchman, and these two served as interpreters.

This conversational difficulty overcome, the gaining of the assistance of the Kaffirs, who proved to be friendly, became more of a probability. This place was at no great distance from the spot where the *Grosvenor* had been wrecked thirteen years before, and the captain learned from the Kaffirs details about the disaster. From the top of one of the sand hills they pointed out the place where the British East Indiaman had gone to pieces. One told how Captain Coxson had been killed by a chief while defending two white women, one of whom had died soon after being taken to the kraal. The other one lived and had borne several children to the chief.

"Where she is now we know not," they said, through the interpreters.

It was further learned that the Kaffirs knew about the "Colonies," as they called the new United States, which had been separated from England. As they were hostile to the English, they were inclined to welcome the Americans.

"We are friendly to the Colonies," said one, "and it will not be our fault if we are not always so."

This declaration sounded promising to the crew, who still, however, felt far from being in a position of safety, so accustomed had they become to native treachery.

The Kaffirs hovered around the rocks, salvaging whatever was washed in from the wreck, the white crew working with them until dark, when the Kaffirs retired, leaving the castaways to sleep under the sand hills, without covering and without food. The men decided, since the weather was boisterous and cold, to spend the night with some on watch and the others near the fire, trying to get a little rest. Instead, the

night was passed without a moment of repose for anyone. The sand, driven by the wind, filled their eyes,
ears and mouths, as they lay under the banks, and kept
them in misery. Neither did their suspicions of the
natives encourage sleep.

At length, day appeared and the Kaffirs returned in
great numbers, bringing a bullock which was killed in
a revolting manner. The warm entrails were greedily
devoured by the Kaffirs, and the carcass was given to
the famished crew, who feasted well upon it. Naturally, they supposed that the part not consumed would
be left them for a later meal, but the Kaffirs were a
hungry lot and saw no reason why they should not
finish the unused larger portion. They, like all savages,
were communistic, and when one of the tribe slew a
bullock for the use of his own kraal, the rest pounced
upon it, leaving the owner hardly more than the hoofs.

The meal over, the crew went down to the shore
from where the longboat was sighted at a considerable
distance. The *Hercules* was dividing very fast, and the
gale increasing. Many things were being washed on
the shore, which the Kaffirs were not slow in seizing;
among them was a sixty-gallon cask of rum, enough
to intoxicate the entire three hundred Kaffirs present.
Fortunately, the crew reached the cask first, and, on
the pretense of saving it, rolled it up the shore in such
a manner that the bung was stove in and the liquor
allowed to run out harmlessly upon the ground, without attracting the attention of the Kaffirs, who, on
coming upon the scene, smashed the empty cask for the

iron hoops. Iron, to them, was of the greatest value for pointing weapons.

In the general search along the shore, one of the Kaffirs came upon the ship's compass. What it was used for he could not imagine, but the brass bowl, the swinging card under the glass, and the gimbals on which it had been suspended in the binnacle, were objects of wonder. He carefully carried the compass to the chief, who took it to pieces and thoughtfully examined it. He looked upon it as some sort of an ornament, and smilingly hung the larger gimbal of brass around his neck with his own collection of rings. The captain, watching the Kaffir, remembered a pair of spare paste knee buckles which were in his pocket, and, taking advantage of the savage's delight in his new decoration, hung one of these glittering objects on each of the chief's ears. The chief, thus decorated, took on an air of increased importance. Again, through the interpreter, the captain indicated to the chief that he wished to depart to the nearest European settlement, and offered to amply repay a guide. A savage never likes to be hurried. The chief, to show his importance, paused, and then replied:

"When I have considered that matter, you shall be informed of my decision."

Such an uncertain response to a reasonable request was alarming to the crew, who had not placed full confidence in the Kaffirs, especially since the natives were seen to form into groups and to cast furtive glances at them. Appearances boded no good.

The second night was passed by the crew in the same

manner as the previous one: all lying on the sand and
keeping a fire with a watchman on lookout. As June
is a winter month, they suffered from the cold. The
men were warned not to irritate the Kaffirs in any
way, but, if attacked, to resist in a body and to defend
themselves as best they were able.

As soon as the sun rose on the third day, they
climbed the sand hills to look for the longboat, but
it was nowhere to be seen. Not a word passed this
day about the departure of the crew, and their anxiety
was greatly increased; the uncertainty of their condition and the continued silence on the part of the chief
seemed to indicate possible treachery. That night, in
spite of worry, most of the crew slept well from sheer
exhaustion.

The fourth day dawned, and the first thought was
for the longboat and the four men who were still at
sea, but she could not be sighted, and never again did
the men of the *Hercules* find her. The boat had disappeared in the storm.

In a short time, the Kaffirs advanced to the sand
hills, many of them with *assegais* and buffalo hide
shields, and others with clubs. Some of them wore
headdresses decorated with ostrich plumes. The chief
was conspicuous in a fine leopard skin *kaross,* and re-
splendent in his scintillating knee-buckle earrings, which
seemed to indicate a holiday mood. This proved to be
the case, for the white men received a friendly salute
of raised weapons, which was taken as an invitation to
follow them to the shore. Together, they ranged the
rocks in search of more wreckage. Unobserved by the

blacks, one of the crew picked up a handsaw and hid it in the sand to keep them from finding it; this was too valuable to lose, and was later to be of great use in cutting branches of trees for firewood.

To entertain his unwilling guests, the chief put on an exhibition of *assegai* throwing. The *assegai,* a spear pointed with iron, and with a four-foot shaft, is made of elastic wood, and on some occasions is poisoned. Natives go into action with a number of them clasped in the left hand, to be hurled at game or the enemy with the right. On beginning their mimic warfare, they fixed a block of wood on the ground for a target, and, retiring about seventy yards from where it lay, proceeded to illustrate their manner of fighting when in battle. A party of about thirty first ran to a considerable distance and then fell flat to the ground, so that they could not be seen. In a moment, they jumped on their feet, divided their party into two bodies, joined again, and ran in a compact body towards the target on the ground. Halting, they let fly a shower of *assegais* at the mark with an astonishing precision, which was very impressive to the crew of the *Hercules.*

On the day following, the Kaffirs appeared at a later hour than usual, as all the wreckage had been collected. Captain Stout had decided to use new tactics in dealing with the chief's procrastination. He announced that he was going away on the next day, and that he would need a guide. That worked.

"I shall give you two guides," said the chief.

Then the captain learned that the Hottentot inter-

preter and a Kaffir, who knew the country better than
he, had already been selected on the day before. The
chief was not such a bad fellow after all! Apparently,
a start for the next Dutch settlement was about to
begin: a trek of one hundred miles, following the
course of the Fish River and westward directly into
the country, with the hope of reaching by this route
the best drinking water. The water on the coast was
brackish, a condition which had caused the whites much
suffering (Kaffirs live on sour milk).

"I told the chief," said the captain in his narrative,
"that we had endured great distress for want of water
to drink, and begged to know where we could procure
some. 'I shall conduct you to a spring of water,' said
he. 'It is not far from this place, and if you like we
shall go there at once.'"

They set out immediately.

"The Kaffirs were gayly singing and dancing as they
went. My people were somewhat suspicious, but followed hopefully. After traveling about four miles to
the westward through a delightful country, we came
to a wood, in the depth of which there was a hollow
containing a stream of most delicious water, to which
the chief pointed. We all drank as much as we wished,
and, having satisfied our thirst, looked around us. The
place was most dismal, and my people were again
filled with fear, thinking they had been led there to
be massacred."

Recovering from some of their fear of the Kaffirs,
the men sawed off some tree limbs and built a fire for
the night, the natives retiring to a camp of their own.

On this night, the crew were free from drifting sand, and the trees protected them from the wind.

When morning came, they prepared for the long march. The natives helped to pack the provisions. Each man was to carry his own stock, consisting of four pounds of dried beef and some sea biscuits, which had been saved from the ship's stores. It was an allowance which would have to last, at the very least, for three days' march. The natives seemed to show regret at the departure of the white men. The captain, taking the chief by the hand, thanked him for his kindness, and assured him ample reward if the crew survived the long journey ahead. The chief, in turn, expressed his thanks and desired that the captain would trust the guides. Kaffirs and crew parted in a friendly way, in spite of all former misgivings.

The guides explained, at the beginning of their march, that on no account must they travel early, as the wild beasts rose with the sun and ranged the desert in search of their prey. A single lion or leopard was capable of destroying most of them. After eating breakfast in the morning, they waited uneasily for the sun to rise in the sky, and then set out in high spirits.

Not more than three or four of the party possessed shoes. They had one hundred miles to tramp over unknown country, ascending high mountains, penetrating woods, fording rivers; and they were to do it all, barefooted.

"As my feet were naked," said the captain, "like most of my people, one of them offered me an old pair of shoes, which I refused. My clothing consisted of a short jacket, which I put on to jump overboard from the ship, a table-cloth, which I found on shore, to wrap around my waist, a shawl over that; four shirts, all of which I had on, a pair of trousers and a hat."

The country they came to was fertile, with hills, dales and extensive plains, well watered. They came upon the tracks of beasts of prey. After searching the plain for water, at sunset a brook was discovered running through the corner of a wood, and here they decided to pass the night. The handsaw was again brought into use, and a fire was lighted by a guide striking a flint spark into a pitch tinder, which caught at the first stroke. The guides explained to the party that the spot chosen for sleeping quarters was a leopards' water hole, aand should they be attacked by the animals, there would be no escape. The only response made by the sailors to this warning was to build more fires, and finally to sleep in an exhausted state right where they were, leopards or no leopards.

On getting up, they found that there had been no leopards. But with the rising sun there came the morning salutation of the roaring of lions. They fled from the water hole without seeing a single lion, and at seven were again on the march. As they passed along, they crossed several dry river beds to ascend a great elevation, from which they had a wide view of the surrounding landscape. They beheld beautiful vales covered with long dry grass and copses of trees; in other directions, there were forests skirting mountains of various elevations. They lost much time in searching for water, but at last, late in the afternoon, they found

a small stream. This water, "not very good," prevented them from suffering with thirst. Near this place
they decided to spend the night. All hands turned to
getting fuel and cheerful fires were soon burning, sending out a grateful warmth to their tired bodies. No
wild animals had been encountered during the day, but
tracks of the elephant and of the rhinoceros were
frequently noticed. They were truly in Africa.

In the morning, all hands were able to answer
"Here" to the muster roll. Soon after sunrise, the
party was moving again. As they were to travel
through a wood of considerable extent, the guides
warned them to be on guard against wild animals,
which frequented the place in large numbers. They
escaped the lions, rhinoceroses, leopards, and elephants, but about noon they met a group of hostile
Kaffirs. On first sight, the guides explained that they
were very bad ones, but some of the Kaffir women
were kind and gave the sailors baskets of milk—baskets so closely woven as to hold water. The men of
the tribe were disposed to be insolent. The two guides,
alarmed at their appearance, fled to the banks of the
Great Fish River, two hundred yards distant, which
was dry, and, having reached the opposite bank, they
continued up the side of the ravine with all possible
speed, leaving the captain and crew at the mercy of
the enemy. The savages brandished their weapons and
appeared about to spear them all. One of the crew
had a knife in a sheath, which was slung over his shoulder. A Kaffir made a snatch at the handle, but the
owner, resisting it, made him loose his hold. This so

enraged the savage that he lifted his *assegai*, but from somewhere received a blow from another sailor on his "funny bone", which made it drop from his hand. To quote Captain Stout:

"This savage presented a picture of the utmost horror at that moment. He wore a leopard skin, his black face bedaubed with red ochre; his eyes inflamed with rage, appeared as if starting from their sockets; his mouth expanded, and grinning, his teeth gnashing with all the fury of an exasperated demon."

The crew escaped their tormentors and followed the path of their guides up the farther side of the ravine. They were told that they would all have been killed, had not the remainder of the horde been away hunting. According to the guides, they were Fitcani Kaffirs, a murderous tribe who used poisoned arrows, and, when on predatory trips, ate raw flesh to avoid discovery by making fires. On the other side of the mountain lay a wide plain with large herds of antelope and zebra grazing and drinking at the streams. Before night closed down, a camping place was picked and wood was cut, not only for the fire, but to make a rough stockade as a protection against wild animals. This fortification undoubtedly saved them from being trampled to death by a herd of elephants that brushed the stockade in the dark after the fires burned down.

The next day's trek brought the travelers to the edge of a small forest, and camp was again made inside a temporary defence. This night a lion found its way into the shelter and carried off one of the sleeping men without awakening the others. On following the tracks in the morning, they found the remains of the man, and discovered that the lion, which must have been a very large one, had taken the man by the head, crushing in the temples with its long fangs. Mercifully, death had been instantaneous.

The crew now fully realized their unprotected state in the wilderness, which had as many dangers as the sea. Fatigue and shortage of food were beginning to tell upon them. The water found on the trail was brackish, though the streams were fifty miles from sea, and it would not quench thirst. Many of the men dropped on the trail, footsore, and unable to take another step. The ablest pushed on with the intention of making a camp for the rest to come up to later, but the disabled men remained on the ground where they had fallen.

The guides assured them that they would reach a Dutch farmhouse the next day, and they did so, only to find that it had been destroyed by the Kaffirs in their late war with the Dutch. The march was then pushed on to the next farm and in three hours they were rewarded by the sight of civilization, when one of the guides roared out, "I see a Hottentot with a flock of sheep." It was the voice of the Kaffir, and the man he saw was attending a flock of five thousand sheep. The shepherd was, at first, alarmed by their appearance, but noting that they were mostly whites, held his ground until they came up. From him they learned that his master was a good man, who lived three miles away. Footsore, and at the point of collapse, the men threw themselves upon the ground, scarcely able to move. Out of their original sixty, thirty-six had been left astern on the trail. At length the captain rose, and said,

"Come on my lads, we are safely moored at last; and our people in the desert will soon be relieved."

Ten followed him and the guides to the house of Jan du Plieses, who proved to be a settler of the best class, humane and generous. He was about sixty years old, and had been a farmer and herder in Africa for many years. He lived in a clay cottage, thatched with native reed, and furnished in a simple way. His family consisted of six sons, their wives and children, together with a daughter, making altogether about twenty people. His stock was considerable, not less than twelve thousand sheep and a thousand oxen.

After recovering from their alarm, the entire household stood listening, astounded at the tale of the crew who had come a hundred miles barefooted, from a ship wrecked upon the seacoast. What was more astonishing was that they should have escaped from the particular tribe of Kaffirs they had been thrown among; for the Tambookies had a bad reputation as killers. The second tribe they had met with were even worse. Du Plieses was amazed that they had escaped with the loss of only one man. Besides the savages, he declared that the country they had traversed was so infested with beasts of prey that people could never travel safely save in well-armed parties. Their presence in his house seemed to him a miracle. The farm was in a stir with preparations to rescue the sailors left astern of the advance party. An eight-oxen wagon in charge of two of the sons, and accompanied by the guides, at once started out.

The captain's account of his treatment by the Tambookies greatly surprised and relieved du Plieses, for his mind had been poisoned by the tales of some of his depredating neighbors, and, since he himself had never gone on these incursions against the natives, he had no first hand knowledge of their real character.

On coming in sight of the house of Mynheer du Plieses, the sailors had found it surrounded by trees on which were hung the skins of lions, leopards, and other destructive animals killed in the vicinity. A rhinoceros, which his sons had just killed, lay in the yard to be skinned, and the meat given to the Hottentots on the ranch.

"These creatures," said the farmer, "are worse than any other animal, and do more damage to the planted fields. A lion will run away from a rhinoceros. I had proof of this two years ago, when I saw a lion entering a thicket at a distance from the place where I stood. In a few minutes I saw a second, a third and then a fourth lion; in less than an hour I saw nine lions enter the thicket. Never seeing so many lions together at any one time I became interested and watched. After waiting for an hour without hearing anything unusual and on the point of leaving, I had my curiosity gratified. A very large rhinoceros appeared and approached the thicket and facing it, stood motionless for about five minutes, when he tossed up his nose, and at last scented the animals that lay concealed. In an instant I saw him dart into the thicket, and out came the nine

lions, scared to death and scampering in different directions. The rhinoceros beat about the thicket in pursuit
of his enemies for a considerable time after they came
out; but not finding them, he broke covert and appeared on the plain. He then looked around him, enraged at his disappointment, and began tearing up the
earth with his horn, showing every sign of madness and
desperation."

The sailors slept under cover that night, and after
they had finished a good breakfast, the neighbors came
in and offered to quarter the entire company on their
respective farms until they had entirely recovered from
their hardships, when they would convey them to the
Cape on their annual trip by ox wagon. This seemed
too slow for Stout, who made offers for immediate
transportation, as he had gold enough in his belt to
defray the expense. Their arrangements were interrupted by a Hottentot calling out, "The wagon is in
sight." In it came with its Lascar cargo; the farmer's
sons had found them huddled together without hope
for relief, and perfectly resigned to their fate. The
thirteen Europeans had wandered and could not, then,
be found. These poor fellows had a series of adventures quite unlike the others and, after falling into
the hands of friendly Dutch farmers, finally succeeded
in joining their shipmates at the Cape before they left
for home.

The route of the coming land voyage was over the
ox-wagon trail which had been marked out by the
Dutch settlers from the Cape in search of new lands
to the east. From Swellendam, the trail followed the

general trend of the coastline about fifty miles inland from the sea, winding over grassy plains and in among long fertile *kloofs* between ranges of mountains; then on to traverse a hundred miles of barren *karroo,* and finally to plunge into the Kaffir Bergh region, to make the Great Fish River which was to become the eastern boundary of the Dutch colony. The pioneers advanced from settlement to settlement, the distances between them, limited only by the travel endurance of the oxen, progressing until the grazing lands became less restricted and more adapted to their needs. Adopting a semi-nomadic form of life, the Boers settled on widely scattered farms, some of vast extent, stocking many thousands of sheep and horned cattle. The Dutch were as thrifty in South Africa as in Holland; their establishments were models of domestic organization, deriving revenue from seasonal movements of herds from the pasture grounds to the main settlement at the Cape. These were usually annual visits.

There were now forty-seven castaways at the farm, and, by an arrangement with their captain, Mynheer du Plieses, together with his neighbors, provided them with sufficient ox teams and wagons to convey them to the Cape. On account of the forced marching necessary to make the thirty miles between settlements, an extra team of oxen was provided for each wagon, allowing the working team to outspan at half the distance. Preparation of the wagons was comparable to fitting a fleet of ships for sea. Hottentots were sent as drivers and to take charge of the cattle. Some of the neighbors' sons, very likely looking forward to an unexpected visit to town, went along, with their long guns, to guard against both savage and wild beast.

Starting at daybreak, the caravan reached the first neighboring settlement soon after dark. On this thirty-five miles they had perfect immunity from attack. Elephants were known to charge wagons and for such as these a son of du Plieses and the other gunners kept a sharp lookout and a ready trigger. On the next day's trek these were needed, for a rogue elephant, making an entirely unprovoked attack, charged the middle wagon. Du Plieses fired and the beast fell, only to regain his feet and stumble back into the thicket from which he had emerged. Thinking he was done for, du Plieses and two other boys, Prim and Mulder, went in after him. The elephant was on his feet and stalking them and, rushing upon Prim, the enraged animal first trampled and then tusked him while he was on the ground; that finished, he took the dead body in his trunk and tossed it high in the air, to come down again on the earth with a thud. The mad animal then returned to renew his charge upon the wagons. The terrified sailors scattered, some fleeing to a distance and others hiding under the wagon bodies. Apparently satisfied with the damage that he had done, the elephant disappeared in the woods. The people sorrowfully took up Prim and began to dig a grave, when the elephant suddenly made a reappearance to drive off the grave diggers and to again trample the body. Du Plieses was cool enough to get another shot at the animal, which brought him down for good. The interrupted interment was completed, and order was restored in the caravan. The elephant's skin and choice bits of flesh were looked after by the Hottentots.

During the five succeeding days, their land voyage took them from house to house, generally spaced at fifteen or sixteen miles distance from each other, where they were always treated hospitably. They found that the farmers lived the year around on mutton and game, but seldom enjoyed the luxury of a loaf. Although there was a scarcity of water in places on account of a drought, they saw on the plains springbok by the thousand, so thick that a single shot would sometimes bring down two or three, ensuring a good supply of venison. There were likewise zebras and ostriches in their path, and even the weakest of the men began to take notice of the beautiful country before them: mountains and valleys, woods, and then beyond more extensive valleys. One of these was so vast that it took them four days to pass through. The ridges stretch for seventy or eighty miles, parallel to each other, with rich pasturage between for cattle.

After twelve days of travel, the wagons reached the settlement of an old blind farmer, who possessed both a large family and considerable means. When he heard the story of the wrecked and destitute seamen, he was so overcome with emotion that he broke out his best jug of Cape Town brandywyn and gave them all a swig. In Stentorian tones the sightless patriarch bade his guests a royal welcome. There were too many to seat in the house, so the Hottentots were ordered to bring the carcass of a sheep, to provide pots, and to cook an outdoor supper. Curious to hear more about the wrecking of the *Hercules,* the host invited the captain to sup with the family. Of all the incidents, he was most impressed by their escape from the coast Kaffirs, who had the reputation of being so very deadly. The eating of the sailor by a lion, and the attempted destruction of the wagons by a rogue elephant were, to him, matters of more or less every day experience, but the escape of the crew from the Tambookies and again from the Fitcani Kaffirs, was to him incomprehensible.

When supper was ended, the patriarch told the captain that he was so pleased with their miraculous escape that he would celebrate it with a song, which he proceeded to do with such a vigorous and vibrant bass that the people, in and out of the house, burst into applause. It now became the crew's turn to sing. An American sailor complied with his best chantey and the entire crew, well lubricated by extra schnapps, came in on a thundering chorus, each in his own language. Such a concert was never before heard, and the merry old farmer nearly fell from his chair in a fit of laughter.

As the strange caravan advanced into a country of increased population, more and more farmers stood stolidly and regarded it with wonder. The settlements were now not more than two miles from each other. Many of the homes were beautifully placed, and the land, no longer used for the grazing of prodigious flocks of sheep and herds of horned cattle, was cultivated to produce grain and fruit in abundance. Such a land of plenty our mariners had never before seen, and they were reluctant to go farther.

After twenty days of ox-carting they arrived at the village of Swellendam, the seat of the landorse, an official of importance in the colony. The landorse took charge of the whole outfit and the oxen were outspanned for the last time, before making their return trek to Kaffir Bergh. The sailors were hospitably quartered until arrangements could be made at the Cape for their departure.

The landorse thoughtfully gave the captain a letter to General Craig, the British commandant who had just hauled down the Dutch flag at the Cape, a political event that Stout did not yet know of. The landorse had no misgivings, however, and assured the American that the general was a courteous man and one likely to accord to him good treatment. The remaining distance to the Cape was a hundred and twenty miles, and this Captain Stout, accompanied by a guide, accomplished in six days, resting each night under a hospitable roof. His last host, before entering Cape Town, detained the captain for two days and saw no reason why he should not stay for two months; but Stout tore himself away in the line of duty and reached Cape Town on June 20th, 1796.

General Craig was much interested in the report of the loss of the *Hercules* and her cargo of grain, which was so greatly needed in England where there were bread riots, in protest against armies trampling down the crops in continental Europe. Stout, in turn, was amazed at what the general had to say:

"The political changes in Europe are affecting the destiny of South Africa; Robespierre and his commune have been guillotined to extinction; the armies of the French Republic are everywhere successful; they have invaded Holland and driven out the Prince of Orange, the hereditary stathouder of the Netherlands; he fled to England; as a trustee of Cape Colony he authorized the British government to assume control of the Cape temporarily to prevent its seizure by the French, who already had a foothold here. We are now holding the Cape in trust for the Prince of Orange but it is difficult to make the Dutch understand the situation. The French must be kept out."

General Craig sympathized with the crew and ordered them to be conveyed from Swellendam to his headquarters.

From this point on, the story of the *Hercules* castaways becomes indistinct, but, since the Cape was a clearing port for ships between the West and the East, it is very safe to assume that the faithful Lascars were returned to India; the British fleet may have had berths for the Europeans. At all events the American captain and his compatriots returned home, where their neighbors and seagoing cronies were eager to hear them spin this twister, as sailors' yarns are called.

3

Lady Hobart's Boats

A STRIKING instance of unpreparedness in a boat get-away was shown in connection with the foundering of the *Lady Hobart*, when, in 1803, she rammed an iceberg on a dark foggy night, and sank within an hour. The ship, rated as a government armed packet, with a large complement of men as well as a passenger list of seven, to say nothing of mails and dispatches, sailed from Halifax on June 22nd bound for England. The *Hobart* was in command of Captain Fellowes, who was accompanied by his wife. On the passenger list were two other women, Lieut. Col. Cooke, Captain Thomas, R.N., and two naval lieutenants. After clearing Sable Island, Captain Fellowes, to avoid possible French cruisers, hauled to pass over the northern part of the Grand Banks of Newfoundland, well into the dangerous ice fields.

Four days out from Halifax, Fellowes sighted a large schooner under a French flag, standing towards them with her decks full of men. From the stranger's manner of bearing down upon them, it was concluded that she knew the war in Europe had been reopened and that she mistook the *Hobart* for an ordinary enemy brig. Fellowes cleared for action, fired a shot, and the Frenchman struck his colors. The prize, sent back to Halifax in charge of the two passenger lieutenants, proved to be the privateer *l'Aimable Julie,* of Port Liberté. The French commander, Citizen Rossé, together with Citizen Goflin, his mate, and a boy, were taken on board the *Hobart* as prisoners to be carried to England. The main body of French prisoners were transferred to two British schooners which happened along, bound in to Halifax. This incident of capturing the Frenchman at the very start of the voyage proved the *Lady Hobart* to have been a well manned and well organized packet.

There was no mistake about the iceberg. It was a real one, towering over and above the ship, more than twice as high as the masts. As they were running free and making eight knots, a top speed for a vessel in 1803, they struck the iceberg hard, pitching the watch below out of their hammocks by the impact. It was one o'clock in the morning, dark, with a high sea running. No more unlucky a time for a disaster could be imagined. Since they were on the weather side of the berg, they received the full violence of the backwash which boarded the ship at the waist and swept the decks from side to side. The seas tumbled down the open main hatch, threatening to fill the hold. The pumps were manned and a gang was put at the hatch to bale with buckets. The backwash had force enough to thrust the ship against the wind, causing her to haul off and strike the overhanging berg a second time broadside on, and then to stern off. The *Lady Hobart* bounced like a ball against the ice, showing how well ships of oak were then constructed.

All hands tumbled out on deck and, with perfect seamanship, did what they could to keep the vessel afloat. They did not lose their heads; there was no indication of a panic. In a quarter of an hour they did an incredible amount of work by cutting the bow anchors away, sliding the guns overboard, and hauling two sails under the ship by the way of collision mats to keep the water out. But the hole in the bow was deeper and larger than they knew; the fore chains were soon level with the water; the ship was sinking.

If all accounts are true and undistorted, there was an unwarranted hesitancy on the part of the officers of the *Hobart* to abandon the ship. Their deliberate actions seem to indicate that they were more afraid of their necks than they were of the sea. Fellowes and the naval captain lost much valuable time in discussing the proper disposal of the mail and dispatches. Deciding that there was no space in the boats for such heavy and cumbersome packages, they actually took time, in the midst of a boiling sea, to comply with the war regulations which provided that mail be ballasted with iron and sent to the bottom by itself, without waiting for the ship to take it down.

Except for the fact that no detail was told off to water and provision boats when the ship first struck the

berg, the discipline was perfect. Provisioning the boats
should have been the first duty of the steward, with
the cook and cabin boy as assistants. The entire crew
were so drilled in routine that they could not visualize
themselves leaving a ship at sea under any circumstances. It wasn't done! By the time that the mail and
dispatches were meticulously consigned to the deep, the
fore deck, together with the ship's launch lashed bottom up, was submerged, with only the quarter deck
above water. The sea was now breaking completely
over everything. The two remaining boats, the cutter
and the jolly boat, were shoved over the side to take
the people off. The three women leaped into the cutter
first, followed by the men passengers and then the
crew.

While the boats were yet hanging on they were provisioned in a hit-or-miss manner by the crew running
below and hastily picking up and throwing in whatever
could be found handiest. This is difficult to believe, but
a careful perusal of Captain Fellowes' statement points
very cleary to the fact. No water breakers were provided for the boats as part of the regular equipment,
such as present-day law requires. The principal supply of water for the cutter was a five-gallon jug
tossed in at the last moment by Seaman Tipper, who
was afterwards cited by the commander not only for
his thoughtful conduct but also for pouring the rum
out on the deck in order to replace it with drinking
water at the scuttle butt. No British tar had treated
rum so casually before, and the act was considered an
indication of a betterment in the service, for Captain

Fellowes included quite a moral dissertation on this act of Seaman Tipper in his formal report to the Lords of the Admiralty.

As the stern of the ship came level with the sea, Captain Fellowes and the master jumped into their respective boats, and hardly were they in when she suddenly gave a lurch to port and went down head first. The boats narrowly escaped being drawn down in the vortex. At the moment of the sinking they were surrounded by a school of whales, which was an added danger. There was great likelihood of the whales striking and damaging the boats, and the frequent instances of boats cut in two by a single stroke of the mighty flukes kept coming to mind.

When day dawned, the little flotilla faced a desperate chance. The nearest land was three hundred miles away. The wind was against them, blowing directly from the point they wished to reach. It was still stormy and the sea was rough. In the cutter, twenty feet long and six feet wide, were eighteen souls: the three women, Captain Thomas, Citizens Rossé and Goflin, the master's mate, steward, carpenter, and eight seamen, with Captain Fellowes in command. This load brought the gunwale almost down to the water. The jolly boat, in charge of Master Bargus, was fourteen feet long and five feet wide, and carried eleven men (Lieut. Col. Cooke, the bosun, sailmaker, and seven seamen), as well as the bulk of the stores, the quadrant, and the spyglass. Each boat had a compass. The provisions mustered by the two boats consisted of forty or fifty pounds of hard bread, the

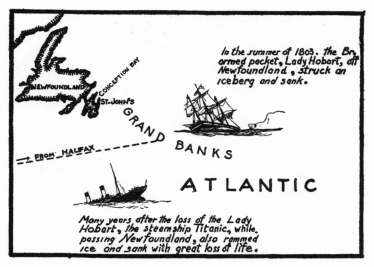

In the summer of 1803, the Br. armed packet, Lady Hobart, off Newfoundland, struck an iceberg and sank.

Many years after the loss of the Lady Hobart, the steamship Titanic, while passing Newfoundland, also rammed ice and sank with great loss of life.

NEWFOUNDLAND
CONCEPTION BAY
ST. JOHN'S
GRAND BANKS
FROM HALIFAX
ATLANTIC

Map of the *Lady Hobart* wreck

While the boats were sailing before a strong breeze,
he leaped into the sea and sank instantly. (p. 76)

five-gallon jug of drinking water before mentioned, a smaller jug of water, part of a small barrel of spruce beer, a demijohn of rum, a few bottles of wine, a small tin mug and a wine glass. The deck lantern, with a few spare candles, had likewise been thrown into the boat, and the cook had had the foresight to secure his tinder box and some matches which were kept in a bladder, thus enabling them to steer at night.

Soon after daylight, the cutter made sail and, with the jolly boat in tow, stood close hauled to the north and westward in hope of reaching the coast of Newfoundland. With the prospect of at least seven days before making land, it was at once understood by all hands that the allowance of hardbread and water must be cut down to the lowest amount that would sustain life. They all agreed to leave the five gallons of water untouched as long as possible. Arriving at this understanding, one of the women read the prayer imploring the Almighty for deliverance from the perils of the sea, the men uncovering during the service.

The next day there was less wind, but it was found to their dismay that sea water had damaged the biscuits, and it was at that moment that they first realized the full horror of their situation and their nearness to starvation. A thick fog came on followed by a heavy rain. Unfortunately, they had no means of collecting this rain water to relieve thirst. Their crowded and exposed condition was rendered more distressing for all were thoroughly wet, as no one had been permitted to take more than a great coat or a blanket, in addition to the clothes on his back. At noon, after their biscuits and rum, one of the women again read prayers for them.

On the third day, the sea became calm, which gave the men a chance to work the oars. There was still fog and sleet and the air was raw and cold. They were now passing through the central fog region of the Banks, which is the most dense of all fog regions on the Atlantic coast. At noon, Bargus reckoned that they had progressed one hundred and four miles, leaving two hundred and forty-six to go. The jolly boat, having only three oars, was taken in tow, the men doing what they could at the oars to help themselves along.

The fourth day found them facing a hard west-southwest gale with high confused sea, thick fog, and the spray of the sea freezing as it flew over the boats. All felt a painful depression of spirits. The want of nourishment and the continued suffering from cold rendered them almost incapable of exertion. Some had their feet swollen from salt water and the confined space. Drinking water in the jug remained untouched. The cutter, overloaded and deep in the water, became endangered by the boat in tow and was obliged to cast her off for the safety of each. The jolly boat contained most of the stores, which would make a long separation from it a very serious problem. We are not told how the smaller boat managed to weather the gale, but the cutter made a sea anchor of the foresail, bending a bridle to each end of the yard to accommodate the warp. It held the boat well and broke the oncoming sea. Some of the crew cried out for water but the jug was not opened. The cold and wet made it possible for them to endure the draught of burning rum served instead. This rum drinking was most severe on the three Frenchmen, who were not accustomed to spirits. One hundred and forty-eight miles still to go. All hands were losing vitality from lack of sustenance, and the heroism of the woman afforded the crew the best examples of patience and fortitude.

Extreme cold and hard rain came on during the night of the fifth day. Few in the boat were able to move on account of the constant exposure. To the joy of everyone, the jolly boat hove in sight and she was again given the towline. The party on board her had feared that the cutter had perished during the awful night. A readjustment of the provisions was made and both boats bore off to the north and west. Apathy was growing among the men, and Captain Fellowes felt it his duty to give a small allowance of water to the Frenchmen and some others who were suffering the most. Some of the men foolishly drank sea water which resulted in fearful cramps of the stomach and bowels.

On the sixth day, the French commander committed suicide by jumping over the side. For some days past he had been increasingly despondent and could not be cheered. Captain Fellowes had learned to like him and was greatly affected by his death. Regarding himself as the accidental cause of Rossé's misfortune, Fellowes had endeavored to make the position of his prisoner as easy as possible. At first, the hope of being speedily exchanged had quieted Rossé's mind, but his fortitude forsook him, and the raw spirits, to which he was un-accustomed, drove him into a delirium that hastened his end. While the boats were sailing at a good speed before a strong breeze, he leaped into the sea and sank instantly. Had he floated, they could not have rescued him under the conditions. The other Frenchman, also delirious from drinking the raw rum, was lashed down to the bottom of the boat before he could attempt self-destruction.

The misery in the boat was beyond description. The sea continued to break over them so constantly that those who were able had to bale without stopping, to keep from sinking. However, bailing the water out of the boat with buckets was welcome exercise, keeping fit those who could do it. In the stern of the boat they were so huddled together that it was difficult for any-one to put his hand into his pocket, and the greater part of the crew lay in the water upon the boat's bottom.

Dawn brought them no relief but light, and those who had secured a few hours of interrupted sleep awoke to a consciousness of utter wretchedness. To add to the misery, a very heavy gale came up from the southward with so tremendous a sea that the most careful steering was necessary to prevent the boats from broaching to and foundering. In scudding before it, every combing sea was expected to drown them all. Towards night the storm abated. They had nearly run down the distance which they had supposed themselves from land, but the weather was too thick to see far. For their encouragement, they passed several patches

of rockweed and then the wing of a sea bird known
to belong to the coast of Newfoundland. A sharp lookout was kept, for a few began to have hallucinations
about land, breakers, and the firing of guns. Suddenly,
a tern appeared and, circling about, tried to alight on
the mast, which was taken for a good omen.

They had every reason for thinking that land was
close. The few who were able to move were called
upon to get out the oars, for the likelihood of a wind
off-shore in the morning urged them on to make the
last effort to save their lives. With the greatest care,
the bread and water in the boat could not be made
to last two more days. For six days and nights they
had now been constantly wet and cold, their only sustenance a quarter of a hardbread and a wine glass of
fluid in each twenty-four hours. The men who had appeared totally indifferent to their fate now summoned
up all their reserve force, and as many of them as were
capable of moving from the bottom of the boat took
to the oars.

At dawn of day the fog thickened so that they could
not see beyond the boat. During the night the cutter
had been forced to cast the jolly boat off to make them
do their share of the pulling, and now the two boats
were out of sight of each other. Soon after daylight,
the sun shone for the second time since they had
quitted the wreck. During the entire period of seven
days, there had never been an opportunity of taking an
observation, either of the sun, moon or stars. The fog
rising, they beheld the land a mile away. At the same
moment, the jolly boat came in sight again and inshore

a schooner was standing off towards them. The cast-aways went wild with various forms of ecstasy; in their exhausted state, some laughed, some cried, some looked at each other with a stupid stare as though doubting the reality of what they saw; several were in such a state of lethargy that they took no notice. Extra grog, made very weak with the last of their water, was being served out as the schooner came within hail. Soon they were all on board and the two boats taken in tow to the nearest fishing village, which was reached at four in the afternoon.

In this village of Island Cove in Conception Bay, they lived for three days, slowly recovering from the fearful adventure. The most infirm were then taken in the schooner to St. John's, forty-three miles away, with the remainder of the crew following on in two boats. Here they received first aid from the garrison and were hospitably entertained until in a fit state for transportation to Halifax.

4

The Essex Castaways

THE ship *Essex* sailed from Nantucket, August 12th, 1819, on a whaling voyage to the South Seas. She was a stout three-boater of two hundred and fifty tons, and carried, for a whaler, a very small complement. But paucity of numbers in the crew list was compensated for by efficiency. The majority of the ship's company were Nantucketers, relatives and neighbors, engaged on a three year cruise on a share basis. Captain James Pollard was in command, and lowered his own starboard boat. The mate, Owen Chase, lowered in the larboard boat, while Mathew Joy, the second mate, had the waist boat. Whaling is fishing on a large scale, and the so-called lucky fisherman is the one who makes an intensive study of his fish, big or little, and their feeding habits. Whales, like all animals, follow the food supply and wherever this food is to be found, there are also the hunting grounds. These grounds are scattered about in many seas, and are well known to the whaling skipper.

On the voyage out, the *Essex* cruised with some success over the Western Island Grounds, the St. Helena Grounds, Tristan da Cunha Grounds, and the Patagonia Grounds. In the following January, after rounding Cape Horn, the *Essex* arrived at Santa Maria Island, on the lower coast of Chile. Santa Maria was a calling place for New England whalers, where they laid in wood and water and exchanged news or "gammed" with other whalers about the conditions of the grounds in which they had cruised. These communications were received through a post office, which at Santa Maria consisted of a box nailed to a tree. At this "whaler's post office" letters were deposited and collected by ships, both coming out and homeward bound, and sometimes did not reach their destination until years later. This method of contact between ships on the different grounds over the world and the people at home was peculiar to American whalemen. The *Essex* was to drop outgoing mail, as well as to receive news of other Nantucketers who might possibly have preceded her into the Pacific.

Along the coast of Chile was a good cruising ground, where by the end of the season the *Essex* had added enough to her catch to make upwards of a thousand barrels of oil. This was good work and all hands felt jubilant, for in a third of her time out the *Essex* was half filled. After going into the port of Tumbez, on the Guyaquil River, to replenish wood and water, the *Essex* stood off for the Galapagos for the usual sup-

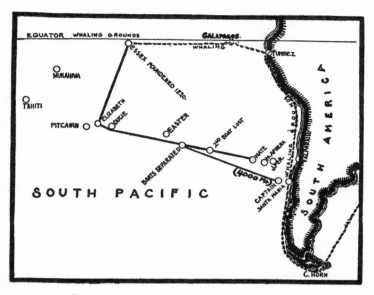

Destruction of the whaleship *Essex*

ply of turtles, which both buccaneers and whalers were accustomed to lay in at that group of islands, to the ultimate extermination of the useful turtle. Anchoring at Hood's Island, they remained seventeen days, obtaining three hundred turtles weighing upwards of eight hundred pounds each, and at Charles Island, sixty more were taken. With these aboard, their future supply of food was assured. One might add that before throwing them into the pot the sailors rode the turtles in a reptile handicap race on deck.

Surmising, from the lack of whales at the Galapagos, that they had not yet migrated in that direction, Captain Pollard decided upon striking boldly into mid-Pacific. Arriving on the Equatorial Grounds, the *Essex* set her mastheads and soon began to raise spouts. On November 20th a reef of spouts was raised on the lee bow about eight o'clock in the morning. It turned out to be a school of large whales, blowing and playing leisurely upon the surface, all traveling in the same direction. The ship's wheel was put up to take the school "head and head"; all hands were called; and the electrifying order, "Get the boats ready," rang out from the masthead. The crews of the boats sprang to their line tubs, spliced lines, bent on head-irons, and breathlessly stood by for the next order, "Hoist and swing." It was the longest reef of spouts yet seen on their voyage. The whales were feeding on squid and had just returned to the surface for air, after a prolonged dive for the giant mollusk which is their principal food. A school of sperm whales, having been down for nearly an hour, usually remains on the surface for at least half an hour before again diving. If a ship cannot come upon them while they are up, she will take their direction when they "go flukes" to sound, and try to be nearer when next they come to the surface. Such is whale hunting. The *Essex* managed to range half a mile to the fore of the slow moving school. They backed her main yard to remain stationary while the boats lowered away to take the whales "head and head." In that way, all of the boats were sure to get fast.

The *Essex* was short-handed for a "three boater," having only twenty men. As six men were required to man each boat, only two could be left on board as "ship keepers" when the boats were down and away. This duty of "keeping ship" and of sometimes following the boats when they were fast, devolved upon the steward and the cabin boy, Owen Coffin, who was the captain's nephew. With the exception of six Negroes on board, the complement of the *Essex,* as remarked above, was composed of relatives and neighbors from Nantucket, the boats being in charge of the captain, the mate, and the second mate, respectively.

As the boats pointed up to the reef of oncoming spouts, the "headers" of each of the three boats picked out his own whale, from among the largest ones, which could be selected by their more ponderous way of snorting and rolling in the water. Head and head the boat could slide alongside of the oncoming snout, heave the irons, and sheer off from the smashing blow of the flukes. When the mate struck his whale, the unusual happened, for he drew a fighter, which, instead of lunging ahead on feeling the iron, stopped short, milled around, and kicked it out, and with his tail instantly smashed the boat into kindling wood, leaving the crew to float on the wreckage. The mate chopped the line with his hatchet to avoid the possibility of being dragged to the bottom. The captain and the second mate did not have time to see what had happened to the larboard boat, for they themselves were each fast to a whale and being towed away on a short line at lightning speed.

The steward and the cabin boy, unable to swing the main yards to pay the ship off to go to the mate's rescue, let go the topsail and to'gallant sheets to ease the ship out of irons and gain steerage way toward the stove boat and the crew floating on the oars. As soon as the mate and his crew regained the deck, they first sheeted home to follow the other two boats, and then started to break out the spare boat on the after gallows frame.

While the men were clearing away the spare boat, a very large sperm whale was seen to break water about a hundred yards from the weather bow, at first lying quietly with his head toward the ship, spouting lightly on the surface. Then he turned up flukes and sounded. In a minute he broke water again, the ship's length off, and made directly for her. Both were then making the same speed, and the men on board felt no alarm until they saw that the whale was coming on with increased velocity. "Hard up your wheel!" roared the mate, but the ship paid off too slowly to avoid the attack. The whale struck under the fore chains, and brought up the ship as suddenly as if she had struck a rock, knocking some of the men down on the deck. The unexpected shock rendered the mate and crew speechless for some minutes; in the meantime the whale passed under the ship, knocking off a long section of the false keel, which came floating up alongside.

Badly stove, the ship began settling by the head, and all hands on board went to the pumps. The whale, in the meantime, went into a flurry of rage, a convulsive brain storm terrible to look upon: leaping, turning, writhing, threshing about in the water, beating it with his mighty flukes, thundering upon it with all his force, and all the while snapping his enormous jaws together as though consumed with wrath and fury. The men at the pumps were too hard at work to watch the whale closely, but they saw him start for a point about a mile ahead of the ship. After a few moments had elapsed, one of the men shouted: "Here he is, he's making for us again!"

The great cachalot was now directly ahead and bearing down upon the ship with twice his ordinary speed. The foam flew in all directions from his swath through the sea, which was churned by his mighty flukes. On he came in malignant fury to smash his floating antagonist with a single one hundred-ton blow. His huge head, a perfect battering ram, was inclined half out of the water. The mate made one more desperate effort at putting the wheel up, but the already waterlogged ship, down by the head and more sluggish than ever, had fallen off only one point, when the whale, leaping at her with demoniac energy, delivered a blow which effectually staved in the bows of the *Essex,* bringing her up again, all standing, and putting her in a sinking condition. Those on board could feel the huge bulk scraping beneath the bottom of the ship for a second time, and then, the damage done, the beast went hurtling off to windward, apparently unhurt.

By the time the boat had been carried to the waist, the ship filled with water and started to go down on her beam ends. There was no time to lose. The boat was shoved from the planksheer, all hands jumping into her at the same time as they launched clear. The boat was scarcely two lengths off when the ship careened to windward and settled down into the water. After shoving off, not a word was spoken by anyone for several minutes. All hands were stupefied by the rapidity of changing events, for not ten minutes had elapsed between the time of the first attack by the whale and the total annihilation of the *Essex*.

While the boat was being carried along the deck to be put overboard, the steward, with great presence of mind, had secured some nautical instruments, for he was aware of their life-saving value thousands of miles out at sea; ship's compasses, quadrants, and tables of latitude and longitude were stowed in the boat before anything else.

While the *Essex* was being demolished by the bull whale, the captain and the second mate were at a considerable distance, each in deadly conflict with a whale, lancing and getting it dead. While passing a short warp through the fluke of a dead whale for towing to the ship, one of the Negroes in the second mate's boat, looking off into the distance, suddenly exclaimed: "Massa Joy, where ship?" Men in the captain's boat were asking the same question: "Where is the ship?" As usual, when running with a whale, compass bearings of the ship were taken by the boats while flying along, for sometimes the sail was lowered under the horizon before the whale stopped or turned. The whales had stopped running before the *Essex* was hull down, but now, suddenly, she had disappeared altogether from their sight.

In alarm the two boats cast loose from their whales and jumped on their oars on the compass bearing on which the ship had last been seen. Soon they met the mate's boat pulling slowly towards them. There was still no ship to be seen. The captain pulled close to the mate, but was so overpowered with apprehension that for a few moments not a word was spoken either by himself or the mate. He slumped down on a thwart and stared blankly at the spot on the sea where his ship should have been.

"My God, Mr. Chase," he gasped at last, "what is the matter?"

"We have been stove in by a whale, Sir."

The three boats pulled to where the ship lay floating on her side. With the boat hatchets they cut away the shroud lanyards, then reached under water to hack at the masts, which at last gave away, allowing the ship to right in the water so that the crew could get on the deck to salve gear and stores.

It was nearly noon when Captain Pollard took one

of the quadrants from the mate's boat to observe a meridian altitude of the sun to get his latitude. He put her in 0 degrees and 40 minutes south latitude and 119 degrees west longitude. The nearest land, according to the calculations, were the Marquesas, fifteen hundred miles to the southwest. Of the Marquesas Islands they knew nothing except that they were inhabited by treacherous savages from whom as much was to be feared as from the dangers of the sea itself.

By removing the booby-hatch, access was had to an after store-room where a hogshead containing six hundred pounds of sea biscuit was found unspoiled by sea water. This was the best find, except the water, of which a whaler always has plenty stored in casks to keep them in fit condition until they are wanted for oil. Sufficient water was hauled out of the hold to fill as many water breakers—sixty-five gallons in each boat— as were safe to put in the small boats, together with the two hundred-pound quota of bread. Two Galapagos turtles were put in each boat and some firearms, bullets, a small canister of powder, a box of percussion caps, a couple of files, two rasps, and two pounds of boat nails (to be of great use).

In the afternoon the wind came up to blow a strong breeze. Salving was belayed for the day and preparations made for safety at night. A towline was made fast to the ship, and to the other end of it one of the boats was moored fifty fathoms to leeward; another boat was then attached to the first one, eight fathoms astern; and the third boat a like distance from her.

During their first sleepless and strange night in the

boats, the men reflected upon the happenings of the day and endeavored to realize by what unaccountable design this sudden and most deadly attack had been made upon them. A whale had never before been suspected of premeditated violence; in fact, whales were proverbial for insensibility and inoffensiveness. Every fact convinced them that it was anything but chance which had made him come at them; he had made two separate attacks upon the ship, at short intervals, both of which, according to their direction, were calculated to do the most injury by being made ahead, and thereby combining the speed of the two objects, for the shock. Resentment and fury were clearly indicated. He had come directly, as if fired with revenge for the suffering of his three companions which had just been struck by the boats. Sperm whales, though unwieldy in outward form, have great sympathy for each other, and a whale often swims directly for a comrade just killed by the whaleman's lance and noses him about as much as to say: "Old chap, what is the trouble?" Their sense of direction under water is marvelous, and methods of communication with each other perfect and sometimes pathetic.

In defense, their usual mode of attack is to come up under the whaleboat and bite it in two or to smash it with a stroke of the flukes, tail. This whale knew that either of these methods would not do for a great ship, and he knew the strength which lay in his head and his hundred tons of bulk to give it impetus for making a smashing blow. The structure of the bull sperm whale's head is admirably designed for the sinking of a ship like the *Essex;* the most prominent part is as hard and as tough as iron; a lance or harpoon would not make the slightest impression. The officers agreed that it was diabolical intent on the part of the whale. The destruction of the *Essex* was the most extraordinary happening in the annals of whale fishery.

Next morning dawned upon a wretched company. The weather was fine, but the wind blew a strong breeze from the southeast and the sea was very rugged. At sunrise they pulled up to the wreck and climbed on board to rig the boats for a long voyage the destination of which was not yet decided. Light spars were gathered for boat masts and spirits; light canvas was stripped off the yards for boat sails and the day was spent in cutting and fitting them. Each boat was fitted with two masts, to carry a flying jib and two sprit sails made each with a double reef band, as blows were expected. With great difficulty the boats were each fitted with a raised top side which gave them six inches more free board. For this purpose some cedar boat boards, which whalers always carried to rebuild boats, were utilized. Cedar was sometimes high priced in Nantucket, but it was always put on board by the prudent owners, not without admonishing the skipper to be careful, therefore, in the chase. Without this extra free-board the open whaleboats could never have survived the seas, for with starvation the men became too weak to bale efficiently and keep the boats from filling. After holding on to the wreck for another night and finishing the rigging and sails on the boats on the next day, the flotilla was ready to start to whatever destiny awaited it.

The wreck now began to work, the deck to give away, and the thousand barrels of oil in the hold, which was keeping the wreck afloat, began to stave and to spill out the oil upon the sea, making a wide slick for the boats to lie in. Captain Pollard decided that standing by the wreck was a waste of time. So did the *Essex,* and with a shudder she sank from sight.

Captain Pollard called a council of his officers to decide upon the course to be taken. The decision was against the Marquesas. The wind to these islands was fair, but fear of cannibals made them direct the course towards the mainland of South America. By sailing close to the wind to the southward and out of the limits of the trades, they there expected to fall in with westerly winds to blow them to the coast of Chile. It was a stupendous alternative, four thousand miles against fifteen hundred, with slow starvation on the way. The three whaleboats about to undertake this voyage were not husky sea boats; they were of the kind modeled and built expressly for the purpose of hunting whales from a ship; really large hunting canoes, twenty-five feet long, slender and double ended with planking less than half an inch thick. They were pulling boats designed to be swift under oars in the chase. A ship, while on a cruise, carried from three to five of these boats on the cranes at the davits, ready for instant lowering when whales were sighted. From much practice, whalemen became expert boatmen, fearless hunters of the mightiest beast in nature. The mate's boat was the smallest, with six men; the other two had seven men each. A pound and a quarter of sea biscuit and a pint of water was the daily standard allowance set for each man during the voyage.

The boats soon showed a marked tendency to leak during the long and exhausting voyage. The mate's boat started a plank. At the risk of the lives of the crew the boat was heeled over sufficiently to get at the place and nail it up. One night the captain hailed: "I've been stove by an unknown fish." A grampus (a small kind of whale) had been following the boat for some time and had made an unprovoked attack, striking on the bow and breaking in the thin cedar. The boat began to fill fast. The bread, water, and turtles were put into the other boats, and the stove boat kept afloat until daylight when a patch of canvas was adjusted.

The pint of water a day did not satisfy thirst. To alleviate its pangs, the men, one after another, dropped over the side of the boat to wet their skins. It was thus discovered that there were barnacles on the bottom of the boat. Ravenously they scraped them off, but they made very poor eating. The bathers became so weak that the others in the boat were obliged to drag them back in over the gunwale.

A week after leaving the wreck, a turtle was killed in each boat and the men waited with impatience to suck the flowing blood of the animal. A small fire was made in the shell of the turtle in which the meat was cooked, entrails and all. The stomachs of some of the men revolted at the sight of the blood, but most of them did not stop to think anything about it. The food was stimulating and took their minds from the horrid prospect of death by starvation. Another fear was that of a possible separation during the night and a pistol was sometimes fired as a signal to keep them together.

The second week a gale of great violence set in, and the men in the boats prepared themselves for destruction, although the rain striking their bodies relieved the pangs of thirst to some degree. It was found that the rain water dripping from the sails was salt from much previous drenching by sea spray. The night to them became dreadful. The appearance of the heavens was dark and dreary; the blackness which spread itself out over the face of the deep was dismal. The heavy squalls which followed each other in quick succession were preceded by sharp flashes of lightning, which, striking the sea about the boats, appeared to wrap them in flames. The seas rose to a great height and every wave threatened to be the last that would be necessary for their destruction.

An unaccountable good fortune kept the boats together during that night. The gale abated, the masts were again shipped, a little sail was made, and the boats headed on the proper course. Flying fish, striking the sails at night and falling into the boats, were eaten alive.

Another plank started from one of the boats. It was fastened by clinch nails driven from the inside, one of the men diving under the boat with a hold on. In this way were the boats kept from falling apart upon the sea.

After four weeks of blind sailing to the southward, land was unexpectedly sighted. Shaking off the lethargy of the senses, the crews took on a fresh hope. The land was a small island with cliffs fully fifty feet high, covered with vegetation, but proving to be of little more use to humans than a temporary resting place, as it was to the tropic birds that nested in its rocky crevices. The island was of an elevated coral formation with wide projecting shelves of coral, washed by the sea. By landing on the protected side of the island, the crews, by lively work, were able to run in on an incoming breaker over the shelf, and after leaping out and holding on against the back wash, they managed to drag their light boats out of the reach of the next breaker. It was neat work, only to be safely done by accomplished surfmen. On landing, the mate killed a large fish held in a pool among the rocks and all hands ate it raw before doing anything else. Then, their strength overtaxed by the effort and excitement of landing, the men threw themselves on the ground for some time, before feeling strong enough to work inland in search of water.

For a week no water was found; not even little pools of rain water remained in the holes. Tropic birds were plucked out of their holes in the rocks for food. The birds made no attempt to fly and took very little notice of the hunters. Fires were made with flint and steel and the birds roasted for eating. An edible grass was found which could be chewed with the meat. The bread supply in the boats was untouched during this stay upon the island.

Water was at last discovered one day at low tide in a very unexpected place, a spring that trickled out of a seam in the rocks at the base of the cliffs. The spring was covered at high tide, but, when it could be reached, provided sweet drinking water. The men all drank their fill, some of them none too wisely, considering the condition of their stomachs and throats. After rolling about stupidly on the ground for a time, the unwise ones recovered, and could walk about. They had been cramped up in the boats for thirty days, and it took some time to get the muscles of the legs in working order once more. After satisfying the violent cravings of hunger and thirst, sleep fell upon them until the following morning.

Since the finding of water, the party thought better of the island; if the spring kept running and the birds held out, there now seemed to be no reason why they should not stay there as long as they chose to remain. In the meantime some vessel might pass. Time could be improved by mending their boats and putting them in better order for sea voyaging. As the men became stronger and regained their land legs, parties were formed to explore the island. In the tangled underbrush among the rocks were found some caves formed by nature. In one of these a gruesome discovery was made: eight human skeletons, in all probability the remains of castaways like themselves, who had perished for want of food and water. The skeletons were side by side as if their once animate owners had deliberately lain down to die together. The sight was disconcerting enough to the white men, but when the six blacks were told, they were filled with superstitious dread.

Near the dead men's cave was a tree with the name ELIZABETH cut in the bark; whether that was the name of a ship which at some previous time had stopped at the island and left a record of her visit, or whether it was the name of the ship on which the unfortunates had been wrecked, it was impossible to discover. But since the island is now called "Elizabeth Island," the former conjecture is very likely correct. The men thought they were on Ducie Island, but that was impossible, for Ducie is an atoll but two miles in diameter, and does not answer to their description of the island upon which they had landed.

On Elizabeth Island each man sought for his own daily living on whatever the sea or the shore could furnish, and every day, during their stay, the entire time of every man was occupied in searching for food. This was found to be growing scarcer daily, and it was also noticed that at low tide the supply of fresh water in the trickling spring was gradually diminishing. The cause of the fate of the eight men in the cave began to grow more vivid, as scarcity became more apparent. The foragers found in a few days that everything edible on the island had been picked up, and often after a day's search they would return to camp with empty stomachs.

When the search for food became fruitless, prudence turned their attention to the boats which they hauled up and prepared for sea. Remaining on the island presented a more dubious prospect than the chances of surviving in the boats on the ocean, for when sailing there would be some progress towards the mainland while the provisions lasted. The ever present chance of meeting with a passing ship would be increased. Another examination of the Bow-ditch was made and it was finally concluded to set sail for Easter Island, one thousand miles distant, a little to the southward of due east. The prospects of weathering Easter were yet doubtful, for the winds were northerly and easterly. All the information that could be gathered about Easter did not throw any light upon its extent, productions, or inhabitants; but at any rate it was a thousand miles nearer the mainland than Elizabeth, and could not be any worse.

December 26th was the day set for the departure of the boats; Chappel, Wright and Weeks decided to remain, leaving seventeen to venture to sea with almost certain death before them. The body of the men could make no objection to the decision of the three voluntary marooners, as it lessened the load of the boats. Should the boats arrive safely on the mainland, they could send relief to the island by some ship bound across the ocean.

Even before the boats left, the three marooners began to build a hut of tree branches, thatching it with reeds to shed rain. The captain wrote letters to be left on the island, giving facts of the fate of the *Essex*, and stating that the three boats had set out for Easter Island. These leters were put in a tin case, which, in turn, was enclosed in a wooden box and nailed to a tree on the west side of the island, near their place of landing. On sailing (December 27th) each boat was provided with a flat stone and a quantity of wood with which to make fires in the boat for cooking fish or birds that came their way; there was no premonition of the future, and the straits to which they were to be driven. At low tide the boat breakers were filled at the spring under the cliff, and the start was made, but not without once more circling the island to find a few more birds on the rocks. At six in the evening the boats had faded from the sight of the three men on the beach.

Two weeks after leaving Elizabeth, Joy, the second mate, suddenly died from an ailment, thus not meeting his end by absolute starvation. With a palm and needle, Joy was sewed up in his blanket, a large stone was tied to his feet, and the boats having all been brought to, his body in a solemn manner was consigned to the deep. Joy's death threw a feeling of gloom over the survivors which continued for many days.

January 12th there came a gale of wind with a rough sea which separated the mate's boat from the other two. The three were destined never to come together again. The boats were now reaching the longitude of Easter Island but missed it by being headed off by the wind. It was yet two thousand miles to the mainland!

There was water to drink, but the starvation allowance of sea biscuit was reducing them all to a state of extreme debility, which affected mind as well as body. In desperation, Peterson, one of the Negroes, pillaged the bread chest which the mate guarded with a pistol.

The Negro was detected and accused, but the mate did not have the heart to shoot him in spite of the clamorings of the rest.

A large shark, also ravenous, attacked the boat several times; it tried to reach the gunwale, snapping at the steering oar and trying to bite it in two, and manifested such fearless malignity that the men in the boat became afraid of it before it gave up. A school of whales came up and blew about the boat during all of one night; one, diving under the boat, threatened to capsize it and end the story right there. With all of their late experiences, the men were no longer fearless of whales.

On the 20th, Peterson died; he refused his allowance after being caught at pillaging the bread box. He said that he was ready to die and begged the mate to tell his wife of his fate, if New Bedford was ever reached. Peterson's body was committed to the sea and made to sink. The crew were now in a state of almost complete dissolution and hardly able to crawl about the boat. Stark madness looked out of each sunken visage. The mate tore the leather from his steering oar and chewed it up ravenously. Finally there was not a man in the boat with strength enough even to steer with the oar. The boat was allowed to drift as is would. A breeze came up and an effort was made among them to trim the sails so that the boat would sail itself by the wind.

Eighteen days later, Cole died of convulsions, his companions horrified at the sight of the writhing man in the bottom of the boat. His corpse was kept all night. Hunger was soon to drive them to the necessity of cannibalism. While two of the men were getting ready to cast the body into the sea, the mate told them to stop, for it might save shooting another man. The mate's proposition held; instead of burial, the limbs were separated from the body and the flesh cut from the bones; after which the heart was taken out and devoured. Strips of the flesh were hung up in the rigging to dry. Some of it was roasted over a fire to be eaten during the day. In this manner did the crew dispose of their fellow sufferer. The recital is that of the deeds of maniacs rather than of sane humans. There was no telling to whose lot it would fall next, either to die or to be shot and eaten like the poor wretch who had just been dispatched. Humanity must shudder at this dreadful tale.

The next morning the flesh had become tainted and had turned to a greenish color; it was cooked at once to prevent it from becoming putrid. Too weak to handle an oar and steering by sail alone, the men left in the boat contrived to live on the revolting meat, cut up in small pieces and eaten with salt water. In a day or so the survivors became recruited sufficiently to enable them to steer and to make a better course towards the mainland.

In six days this flesh was consumed and there remained but two sea biscuit in the chest, which were powdered and made to last four days. All reckoning had been lost, but they were yet three hundred miles from land. Then a high island came into sight, which might be reached in two days; this was Mas Afuera, close to Juan Fernandez.

At sunrise on the following morning a sail came in sight, a speck on the horizon. There was a good whaleboat breeze and the course was shifted to head the sail off. The boat sailed the faster of the two vessels and the sail was soon hull up. The larger vessel took in sail. They were seen. The whaleboat was hailed; who were they and from where? Responding, "From a wreck," the boat was taken alongside and hoisted on board. The boat's crew found themselves on board of the British brig *Indian*. They certainly made a deplorable picture: sunken eyes, bones starting through the skin, ragged clothes stuck about sunburnt frames that no longer looked human; their very appearance was revolting.

A week later the *Indian* arrived at Valparaiso. On March 17th, the American whaleship *Dauphin* came into the same port with Captain Pollard and the survivors of his boat's crew on board. The *Dauphin* had picked them up not far from St. Mary's Island.

After becoming separated from the mate's boat in the gale, the captain and the second mate, in their respective boats, continued to make what progress they could towards Juan Fernandez, as it was agreed to do in case Easter Island was missed. The navigators half expected to be blown to the southward of Easter, and, after passing the longitude of that island, contrary winds and extreme hardship were against them.

Provisions in the second mate's boat became exhausted first and ten days later Shorter, a Negro, died.

His body was cut up, shared between the two boats, and eaten. Then another Negro died in the second mate's boat, followed by the death of a third in the captain's boat. The bodies of these two men were the only food of the survivors. These were roasted to dryness over fires made in the sand in the bottom of the boat.

A day later (January 29th) the two boats separated; it was on a dark night and there was not sufficient power to manage the boats to keep them together steering by sail only. Nothing was ever again heard of the second mate's boat, but from what happened in the other two it is not difficult to form a conjecture regarding its fate. In all probability, crew and boat consumed themselves to extinction.

Two days after the separation, the men in the captain's boat looked at each other with horrid thoughts in their minds, but kept silent; looks told what must be done. The musket was loaded and ready. Lots were cast. The fatal one fell upon the cabin boy, Owen Coffin, the captain's nephew. The captain started forward with the gun: "My lad, my lad, if you don't like your lot I'll shoot the first man that touches you." The emaciated boy hesitated a moment or so, then laid his head on the gunwale of the boat and said: "I like it as well as any other." Lots were cast again to choose the executioner; the lot fell upon Ramsdale and the cabin boy was soon dispatched.

A Negro was the next to die. Now only the captain and Ramsdale were left. Each of these two was contemplating the eating of the other, when the *Dauphin* hove in sight. They had been sixty days at sea and were picked up four thousand miles from the wreck of the *Essex*.

There was an American frigate in Valparaiso, possibly the *Macedonian,* when the *Essex'* boats were brought into port and the commander requested that a British ship, the *Surrey,* just leaving for Australia, stop at Elizabeth Island to take off the three men there, if they were yet alive.

On the morning of April 25th, 1820, the three men on the island were in the woods as usual searching for food and water, when they heard the report of a great gun. It was unmistakable. A ship was making a signal for them. Crawling out into an opening, they saw a ship close at hand, and knew that they had been sighted on the rocks. Down went a boat with strong arms to pull it ashore. But the surf was heavy and the rocks dangerous for a boat like the *Surrey's* launch. Chappel, the strongest of the three on the shore, jumped in and swam to the boat, and was safely pulled in. Wright and Weeks made their way out on the rocks as far as they could and were picked off as the boat became able to veer from a grapnel and back in between the highest breakers. Soon all were aboard and off for the ship, after a stay of four months on Elizabeth Island.

5

The Lord Eldon's Boats

1834

THE *Lord Eldon* was a British East Indiaman, bound in 1834 from Bombay to England with passengers and merchandise. On the passenger list were four women, an infant four months old, and two invalid men. The ship was loaded with baled cotton which, compactly stowed in the hold by means of the stevedoring operation known as "screwing," was a dangerous cargo, for, with the exception of soft coal, damp cotton is the most inflammable of cargoes, by reason of spontaneous combustion. In tropical regions this danger is very great, though very little understood or provided against. Marine underwriters now require that thermometer readings of the lower holds of ships loaded with either soft coal or cotton be taken twice a day, which is conveniently done by lowering the thermometer down a tube at each hatch. Any student of marine disasters knows that fires are generally the result either of carelessness or a blunder. The law of cause and effect is no truer anywhere else than it is upon the sea.

The *Lord Eldon* was not more than a week out from Bombay, when smoke was seen to curl out of the fore hatch. The tarpaulin had probably been lifted at the corner and a hatch raised to ventilate the hold, as is customary on all ships in fine weather. The cotton was discovered to be on fire. Without first spreading alarm, the hatches were battened down tight and the deck scuttled in places to pour water down upon the smothered blaze. In this way the furnace under the hatches was kept under subjection as long as possible. Soon after eight in the morning, the fore part of the main deck became so heated that the men could no longer walk on it; all hands were obliged to retreat to the quarter deck.

Finding it useless to fight any longer, Captain Theaker notified the passengers and all hands to prepare to abandon ship. The longboat and the two quarter boats were hoisted and swung out over the side ready to lower into the water. The wind was light and the sea smooth, except for the long undulation of the swell which never ceases. All the boats were fitted for sailing and carried a full navigational equipment, including the ship's chronometer which was in the captain's boat. No mention is made of the quantity of stores placed in the quarter boats, but in the longboat, which was to carry twenty-six persons, there were 216 gallons of water, most of it held in a large puncheon, twenty gallons of rum, biscuits and preserved meats for a month. This ample provisioning was made under careful direction in a situation of terror, and it was done to relieve the prospect of great suffering in the boats. For this foresight credit is due Captain Theaker.

By one o'clock in the afternoon, the entire fore part of the ship was ablaze, the flames leaping out of the hold to lick up sails, shrouds and spars. The ship had been kept before the wind to allow the heat to drift ahead, but now the wheel was put down and the main-yards backed for lowering. With no loss of life the entire company, in three boats, shoved off to clear what was, by this time, a floating inferno.

The two quarter boats took the longboat in tow to a distance of a mile to wait for the *Eldon* to blow up, for there was a large quantity of gunpowder in her magazine. As piracy by Europeans was then common in the Indian Ocean, which was frequented by rich traders to and from the Orient, all merchant vessels were obliged to sail armed for defense against attack by the sea robbers. The "Jolly Roger" might be expected to heave in sight at any moment. All Indiamen carried eighteen-pounders, small arms, ammunition, and an organization very similar to that of a regular man-of-war. In fact it was customary, when bound out from England, to join a convoy at St. Helena, for the rest of the passage around the Cape of Good Hope and to India. The harpies, in fast sailing schooners, often followed even the convoy to seize a laggard in the fleet. After plundering, it was the method of the pirates to force all hands into the hold, batten down the hatches, scuttle, and send them all to the bottom.

Fine people were those pirates—very noble and very brave!

The little flotilla lay and watched its ship slowly burn to the water's edge. It was long after dark before the work of the fire was entirely done and there came an explosion which shook the sea. The boats were located a thousand miles to the southeast of Cape Comorin, India, which put them four hundred fifty miles from Diego Garcias, in the Chargos Archipelago; six hundred miles in a southwesterly direction from Mango Island in the Seychelles; and a thousand miles from Rodriguez which bore nearly south. The distance to Port Louis in the Mauritius was a hundred twenty miles farther, and in direct line with the dangerous and uninhabited coral islands at the southwest end of the Nazareth Bank, where the *Cabalva* had been wrecked twelve years before.

The southeast trade wind put Diego Garcias directly to windward; why Captain Theaker did not swing off for the nearer point of Mango Island is hard to explain, for he must have known of its position. From his other acts it is clear that he was a man of excellent judgment in navigation, so there can be no doubt of his wisdom in deciding to head for Rodriguez. According to sailing orders, the three boats took up their course, and in the daytime spread out so as to increase the chance of raising a sail. In the night, the smaller boats were guided by a lantern hoisted to the masthead of the captain's boat.

The freshening trades and an increasing sea made it necessary to rig a tarpaulin weathercloth on the cutter. The carpenter, who at first was on the long-boat, went on board of her with some tools, nails and battens. He lashed a bamboo ridge-pole, four feet high, between the mast and a stanchion at the stern. The tarpaulin, battened to the weather gunwale and stretched to the ridge-pole, added much to the safety of the boat, for it kept the sea from breaking over the weather side, but even at that it took four men constantly bailing to keep her from filling.

On the fourth day, the small boat in charge of the chief mate split a plank and began to fill. The car-penter was transferred to her to meet the emergency but his efforts to repair the leak were without result. The crew of ten was ordered aboard the longboat, which was already loaded down beyond the limit of safety. In the longboat with the captain were the four women, the baby, and the two invalids; the added company made thirty-six on board, which brought the boat's freeboard down to eight inches. That night, the following sea increased to "rough" to break over the stern, and, according to their narrative, "wetting the poor women to the throat." A man can stand the gaff but he hates to see a woman suffer. Nothing was ever mentioned about the baby which seems to have come through all right. After shipping the heaviest of the seas, with the passengers completely terrified, the captain called out cheerfully: "That's nothing; it's all right, bale away, boys!" For nearly forty-eight hours he stood on a thwart to watch the sea and give com-mands to the helmsman. Afterwards he declared that he had not expected the boat to survive the night.

When morning broke, they had more cause for cheer, the weather having moderated and the sea being less boisterous. Some shift was made for the women by rigging a curtain to give them whatever privacy was possible in a boat of such limited dimensions. They needed it more than ever in their drenched condition, but by all accounts, or by the lack of them, they set a good example and asked for no more comfort than the men.

The regular daily ration was divided into three small meals of biscuit with meat or jam. A greater mercy was that there was no "allowance" of drinking water, there being sufficient, with ordinary economy, to last a month. The sailors had their daily tot of rum. "We had plenty of cigars," to quote the account, "and whenever we could strike a light, had a smoke, which we found to be a great luxury." Of these, the ladies did not partake and so they were declared to be "the most wretched."

On the evening of the thirteenth day, on running their distance down, they began to look for land. The captain, with great consideration, warned them not to be over sanguine, for he was not sure of his chronometer after its late rough usage in the boat. However, it proved to be right, for by midnight the loom of high land appeared through the mist. The boats were then brought into the wind and hove to, to await daylight, when Rodriguez was sighted, six miles away.

The boats were first seen by a native fisherman, who came out to pilot them in, little understanding their history. Through the reefs he guided them, and they made a safe landing fourteen days after they had been left in open boats upon the sea to watch the burning of their ship.

6

Beer and Cold Raw Shark

(The Heroes of the *Cabalva*)
1818

TWO and a half months from London, the East Indiaman *Cabalva* made her way around the Cape towards
China. The East Indiamen at that time favored the
northabout route to China instead of the more circu-
itous but safer route, by the way of the South Indian
Ocean and Java, which was later adopted. In taking
the northern course to the Straits of Malakka, the
Cabalva entered a sea which was as badly infested with
dangers to navigation as any in the world. North of
the Mauritius is a broken chain of coral reefs extending, with some interruptions, for many hundreds of
miles to the Malabar Coast of India, and these dangers were in the track of the *Cabalva*. Captain Dalrymple was both a popular commander in the service

and an experienced navigator who was well acquainted with his route.

The weather was fine and with a fair wind the ship cleared the Mauritius. Double lookouts were then posted at night; a man on each cathead and also a man on each fore yardarm to watch for land or breakers. The ship was proceeding under shortened night canvas as was then customary on Indiamen, without regard to weather conditions. With them there was no hurry and no driving. At sundown, in came all the light sails which remained stowed until sunrise when everything was set again, weather permitting. On this particular night, everything was serene, and a moonless, starlit darkness hung over the expanse about the ship. Except for the mate, pacing the quarter deck, the man at the wheel, and the lookouts, the rest of the watch on deck were allowed to take it easy by lying about amidships, but ready to spring upon their feet at a call.

About the middle of the morning watch, a cloud of tern and frigate birds, the kind that are known to live about coral reefs, flew, with shrieks of alarm, through the ship's rigging, some of the birds striking the lookouts on the fore yardarms. These birds feed upon fish that shoal around the reefs, and the ship, pressing on, had frightened them out of their rest upon the water. A seaman who knew anything at all about reef birds would have recognized at once the warning signal, and brought his ship to, to await the dawn. Nature was doing its best to give a warning, but of this Mr. Franken, officer of the watch, took no more heed than an amused notice. He was headed for a reef, near at hand, and did not know it. But he was soon to learn.

Just before daybreak the watch was aroused by the startled cry of a yardarm lookout: "Breakers ahead!" Franken ran aft, shouting to the quartermaster: "Hard aport!", and leaped upon the wheel with him to spin it down; even while they were doing this, the ship was grazing a submerged rock which stopped her way and prevented her from coming into the wind. Fifteen minutes sooner, the alarm would have saved them. The first shock came when the heave of a swell lifted the doomed ship over a ledge and let her fall with a mighty thud which could have shaken out the masts. A lookout on the yardarm was hurled from his perch overboard to drown. The jarring of the hull tossed the sleeping men below out of their hammocks and up onto the deck. They had never hit the deck so suddenly before. Tumbling up the ladders and out onto the main deck, they fell in with the wildest confusion. There was the shouting of speaking trumpets, the splintering of wood, and the thunder of breakers roaring in from seaward, to curl over the ship. A calm and serene night in a moment had been turned into one of chaos and horror. Axes were called for and the work of cutting away the masts begun, to ease the ship while pounding out her life.

At dawn, the cutter was launched over the rail and reached the water right side up. Manned by several officers and a crew, the boat pulled away for a low stretch of reef which had just become visible. Captain Dalrymple and Franken remained on board to clear all hands away. It is due to Franken's account that we know the facts connected with this wreck. Working his way to the fore part of the ship by clinging to the bulwarks, he found that she was lying across a sunken rock, her back broken, with only her poop and forecastle above water. Looking towards the reef, he saw another boat, larger than the first, with about thirty men in her, which, on going into the breakers, struck a rock and filled. This decided Franken to make an attempt at launching the big longboat to run the breakers. The longboat was heavy but there was ample man power left on board to handle her. The captain and twenty men climbed into the boat, but, before clearing the wreck, it was stove, and everybody found himself in the water and in danger of being killed by floating spars. The nearest visible rocks lay not over 150 yards away. The space between the rocks and the wreckage was filled with helpless, floating humanity struggling with the giant combers, all expecting at any moment to be dashed lifeless against the rocks. Of the company split out of the longboat, some (including the captain) regained the ship, some made the reef, while others drowned. There were ninety men yet on the wreck and the captain heard some of them in his cabin having a brawl over his private wines; the imminence of death could not deter them from carousing.

The longboat was patched and launched once more, only to be stove again, drowning five. A raft was next formed of the spars which had caused the damage to the longboat, and onto this Franken managed to pull the half-drowned captain. On this precarious float there were twenty-two people who drifted into the breakers. There was no way to keep it end on to the surf or to prevent it from swinging broadside to; on getting into the combers it was picked up, and capsized to fall on the helpless men who were hurled upon the rocks. When the survivors were counted, the captain was missing. On this rock the raft's crew found a number of others, stripped entirely of clothing and shivering in the wet. Sharing the rock with the castaways were the bruised and whitened corpses of a number of their late shipmates. All told, a hundred and ten were still alive, about twenty having drowned. The purser, the doctor, the lone passenger, and the officers were saved.

As the tide receded, the reef rose out of the sea and on it was strewn all manner of wreckage. The *Cabalva's* cargo had consisted of miscellaneous trade merchandise consigned to the Far East, and included specimens of almost everything made in England. On the rocks were scattered, therefore, in ironical profusion, bales of brightly colored cloths, printed muslins, cretonnes, dimity; casks of ale, cases of watches, Spanish dollars, perfumery, scented soap, and fancy goods of every description. Impelled by the wet and a salt-water thirst generated among the breakers, the men fell to ripping open the bales of cloth to cover their nakedness, and then, staving in some of the beer casks, most of them became gloriously drunk and forgot entirely the troubles of the sea. In every direction on the reef could be seen sailors, gayly clad in colored prints, many recklessly fighting over handfuls of watches and Spanish dollars, as though the latter were of any value at all in such surroundings. Some of the more sober ones, happening to realize that the tide would rise again to cover the reef, again lashed the raft together in preparation for floating off. In their drunken condition, most of the men must surely have been drowned if the tide inundated the rocks, for they no longer had wits enough to man a boat.

However, the sure prospect of a returning tide had a sobering effect on all but the very worst cases and a trek was at once started for higher ground. By wading, barefooted, over the sharp coral for three miles they reached a sand island which was less than 200 yards in length, and only six feet above sea level at high tide. In the event of a hurricane, this new refuge would be swept off clean in short order. As the day advanced and the tide rose, water covered the rocks upon which they had first landed. The sea lifted everything floatable on the reef and scattered it again on the sand bank where they now were. To the great relief of the sober ones the tide did not entirely cover the island they occupied.

At low tide the next day, searching parties were sent over the reef, now partly dry, to salvage provisions. The best find was the longboat loaded with provisions and equipment and with the fifth officer, a lame man, aboard. Some of the searching party waded out to the wreck in the hope of finding breadstuffs, for the ship was known to be well stocked with hardbread in watertight casks. These could not be found, but a number of live pigs and sheep, some cheese and a breaker of water were reclaimed. Another fortunate find was the ship's cutter, unharmed, which was to be their means of escape from the reef. Before shoving off from the wreck, they came upon a shipmate lying in a drunken stupor beside a cask of brandy in a cuddy. He did not know that he had been shipwrecked. They formed a comical procession as they filed back to the camp with pigs and sheep, to say nothing of the bibulous one who had to be carried on a stretcher. That same day, the chief officer scented a plot which some of the men were fomenting to steal the cutter for an attempt to reach the coast of Africa, which they vaguely understood was somewhere to the westward. The foolhardy plan was nipped before any harm was done.

On the third day some organization of the camp was undertaken by the officers. Two-thirds of the crew were useful to themselves and were disposed to heed reasonable orders; the rest were a mutinous, lazy, drunken and quarrelsome set. A sufficient number of tents, made of canvas and muslin and stretched over ridge-poles, were erected to house every one. The officers' tent was the largest, a sort of headquarters of the island. The sandy floor was covered with folds of muslin. A wooden chest in one corner housed the sextant, quadrant, sailing directions, Norie's *Navigator*, and other precious gear. Under the floor cloth was buried the liquor. From the ridge-pole hung muskets and side arms. The Canton passenger lived with the officers, a regular nabob, the possessor not only of a shirt, shoes and trousers, but also of a hat, a coat and a snuff box.

The rest of the crew were a mutinous, lazy, drunken,
and quarrelsome set.

CARGADOS CARAJOS SHOAL
AND
WRECK OF CABALVA
1818.

MADAGASCAR, 500'

"BEER ISLAND"

COCOS ISLAND
MAIN CAMP

SHELTERED WATER

DRY AT LOW TIDE

SHOAL

BOAT VOYAGE TO
MAURITIUS, 240'

THE CABALVA BROKE
IN TWO ON STRIKING
AND THE ENTIRE CREW
WERE WASHED HALF NAKED
UPON THE REEF AT NIGHT.

INDIAN
OCEAN

He was heard to remark, however, that he did not appreciate his good luck.

The mutineers took themselves out of the way by wading some distance to another hump of sand to set up a camp where they could feel secure from reproof. This camp was made of a semicircle of beer casks set upon end. Inside this shelter were rigged some muslin tents, each placed in such a way that the sailor could lie and guzzle beer with the least effort to himself. Each man was girded with as many weapons as he could find, pistols, cutlasses, even carving knives, and some wore broad belts filled with Spanish dollars. Franken paid a visit to the mutineers and was good-naturedly entertained. He called the camp "Beer Island," an appellation which stuck. He found a number of the men in need of medical attention; one had a shattered arm resulting from the explosion of a musket, and there were plenty of black eyes and flesh wounds. They had a plentiful supply of shark and beer. They reported that their foretop-man had been elected as chaplain and read prayers every night; that they spent their days drinking, sporting, fishing and fighting. Franken regarded the Beer Islanders sadly and wondered if they were worth salvage. Nearly the whole of their sand bank was submerged at high tide, making of it an extremely dangerous position, but a trifle like that did not worry the dull-eyed sots as long as their beer held out. At night the Beer Island camp was marked by a driftwood fire which died down as the roisterers fell asleep, while in the main camp a fire was kept blazing all night as a distress signal intended to attract the attention of a possible passing ship.

Sewell, the chief officer, saw to it that the provisions were protected against theft and ruin. The store list was augmented by the dozen pigs and the five sheep taken out of the fore end of the wreck. There was a small quantity of beef and pork and some cheese, but neither biscuits nor water. This last deficiency was eased by the finding of a deposit of rain water under the sand in the middle of the island, a pocket in the coral. The sheep were fed upon a bale of hay, washed ashore, while the pigs prolonged their days upon the island by showing a fondness for beer grounds, scented soap and pomatum. "I don't know about the scent, but they'll get bloody well fat, any'ow," observed a sailor watching them feed on their unusual diet.

It was finally decided to recondition and fit a boat to go for relief. The carpenter and his mates found tools and materials to repair the cutter, while the sail-maker discovered himself to be in possession of his kit of palm, needles and twine. Thus he started on a suit of sails for the boat. The bosun skillfully laid up long strips of muslin into rope for the cutter's running gear. The officers worked out their position and calculated that they were 250 miles, northeast by north, from Mauritius. They planned a boat voyage best favored by the wind, and the one to Mauritius was decided upon. On the fifth day, after great effort in overcoming obstacles, the cutter was pronounced to be ready for sea, and the names of the chosen crew were posted on a board for everyone to read. Franken was chosen to command, and from the account which follows, he was every inch a sailor. With him were Ayres, the ship's purser, and eight picked seamen. An adequate stock of provisions was stowed aboard.

For navigational equipment they had a quadrant and a Norie but *neither chart nor compass,* for none were saved from the wreck. However, they knew that Port Louis, Mauritius, was southwest by south and 250 miles away. The course of southwest by south was ten points off the trade wind, which kept a direction steady enough to be depended upon. All they had to do in the daytime was to keep the wind two points abaft the port beam and they were headed for Mauritius. The navigational problem, long and carefully discussed, was to run the latitude down, close to the wind, and then to sail on that parallel until reaching Port Louis. For compass directions it had been computed that the true western amplitude of the sun was west-north-west, with the consequent eastern amplitude of east-south-east. If the sky should be clear at night the south direction would be very nearly indicated by the Southern Cross, while Antares, Venus, Mars, and the half-moon would indicate their east and west directions.

The cutter sailed at five in the morning. There was a heavy sea driven up by violent squalls, for which this region is notorious. They started out with close reefed main and mizzen, but later had to take in the main and heave to under the mizzen. The weather moderating, they took up their course again, which by the bearing of the stars was south-southwest. They logged five knots.

On the second day out the sun rose clear, and by its amplitude the course of the boat was southwest by south. A meridian altitude gave them a latitude of 18-30 south. By watch time, which was set to that on the sand bank, they had made five minutes difference of longitude bu that was not to be depended upon because both of the watches had been wet. They kept as close to the wind as they could under the conditions of wind and sea, but at night broke off to southwest by west, according to the bearing of the Southern Cross. Franken began to fear that he would be unable to weather Mauritius at all, but instead be obliged to make at last the island of Bourbon, as it was then called.

The break of the third day filled them with hope when they sighted Flat Island on the weather bow. This was not far from Mauritius. But there was hard work for them in squally weather and a high sea which drove them twenty miles to leeward of Port Louis. The cutter could not beat to windward, so they doused sail and pulled on the oars. A ship coming out of the harbor marked the line for them and by night, after working both sail and oars, they came inshore to anchor with a ballast bag in nine feet of water. The cutter was close under the land but with no idea of how far it was to Port Louis. The sea was smooth and throughout the night it rained in torrents.

At daybreak on the fourth day they weighed to pull four miles along the shore and to discover the harbor, which they reached at eight o'clock. When the *Cabalva* cutter arrived in Mauritius, to quote Franken: "Our

appearance must have been strange and ludicrous."
Accustomed to it though he was, he was probably
right in surmising that they did, at least, look like a
cross between an escaped circus and a band of comic
opera pirates. Out of the ten persons in the boat, only
one had a hat; the rest wore turbans of muslin or
ladies' fancy caps made of leather and trimmed with
fur, which had been made to stick on the head by
splitting them up behind. Three had jackets; the rest
wore their sand bank mantles of bright printed cloth
with holes for the naked arms. Three had trousers
but there were no shirts, no stockings, no shoes among
all the party. Their feet and legs, and indeed, every
part of their bodies, were completely sodden with rain
water; in addition to which, their faces and arms had
been exposed to the scorching rays of a nearly vertical
sun; so that, upon the whole, they had much more the
appearance of savages than of Europeans. The inhabitants brought them bread, coffee and fruit, in short,
whatever could be wished for, and many of them invited the castaways to their homes. The purser went
ashore immediately to report to the Company's agent,
while Franken made the boat secure and had everything taken out of her. On the news of the loss and
position of the *Cabalva,* not a moment was lost, for
the *Magicianne,* frigate, and the *Challenger,* brig,
were dispatched within an hour to the scene of the disaster. Two days later they both arrived at the reef
with their pilots aboard.

The day of the rescue being Sunday, the sailors were
at prayers when the frigate first came into view, but

the bosun, who always kept an eye on the horizon while he worshipped, spied the distant sail and the service was never finished. The work of getting them off was safely carried out and they were all mad with joy, even the Beer Island gang, who swore that they would never go to sea again.

7

The Oroolong Schooner

ON July 21st, 1783, the British ship *Antelope,* three hundred tons burden, with a complement of fifty, left Macao, China, bound homeward by the Cape Horn route. This would take the ship through the South Sea Islands instead of by the way of Java and the Indian Ocean. For that reason, Captain Wilson, the commander of the vessel, shaped his course eastward and southward from China, through the Ballintang Channel, with the intention of passing to the east of the Philippine Islands and to the north of New Guinea, in clearing the Malay Archipelagos.

Near the Philippines, he was struck by a typhoon, caught in the southern semicircle, and had his ship hurled against the Pelew Islands, which are surrounded by a fringing reef for fifty miles from north to south, making of them a menace to navigation, and causing the destruction of many a China trader. With her decks swept of livestock and everything else that could be set adrift, the ship labored in great seas under close reefs, to be driven at the mercy of the storm. On a dark night, breakers suddenly appeared under the lee bow, and at the next moment the ship was fast.

It took less than an hour's grinding against the coral to punch a hole through the ship and to fill the hold to the lower hatchways. Masts were cut away to relieve the ship and to get rid of dangerous top hamper, which was left floating alongside. Knowing that they were liable to encounter hostile islanders, the next orders were to secure gunpowder and small arms. A cask of hard bread was lifted out on deck, the boats hoisted out, provisioned and all hands mustered aft upon the quarter deck to wait for daylight.

At dawn, they found they had been thrown upon a barrier reef which was heaving up high columns of spume as far as the eye could reach in either direction—a most terrible sight to those in distress. The storm abated, but the swell of the sea continued for days afterwards. Over the top of the reef and beyond the lagoon, they could make out an island to the south. When the sea moderated, preparations were made to abandon ship in good order. Two boats, loaded with stores, were sent by a passage through the reef to the island, which was five miles inside; meanwhile, the men left aboard commenced to lash the floating spars together to make a raft.

The heave of the sea made the work both difficult and dangerous, causing the loss of one valuable life: that of Godfrey Minx, who, because of his zeal in clearing wreckage from the mizzen chains hanging onto the spars in the water, slipped off and was drowned. In the afternoon, the boats returned from shore, reporting that the stores were secure on a landing place where there was a good harbor, plenty of drinking water, and no inhabitants in sight. Five men had been left on shore to guard the stores and to put up a tent.

Having finished the raft, they loaded it, as well as the two boats, with as many stores and provisions as they could take on, and at the same time leave room for the people who were to be taken off the wreck. When all was ready, the crew, including sixteen Chinese, were ordered into the boats and onto the raft to go ashore. The boats took the raft in tow towards the passage into the lagoon, but the swell of the sea was so great that they repeatedly lost sight of each other in the troughs. Those on the raft were obliged to lash themselves down to avoid being washed overboard, while the shrieks and "hi-yas" of the panic-stricken Chinese, unaccustomed to the perils of the deep, rendered the situation still more awful and blood-curdling.

On pulling into the lagoon, between the reef and the shore, they came to an anchor in order to hold their own against a strong tide, which tended to sweep the cumbersome raft in the wrong direction. The captain pulled ashore in the yawl and found the tent ready, with a spot of ground cleared for the stores. A fire for cooking and drying clothes had already been started by discharging a pistol to light the matches.

By this time it was dark, and, on returning to the raft, the captain heard the men in the pinnace who were, themselves, now pulling in the gloom towards the cheerful blaze on the beach, and hailed them. Those on the pinnace, feeling hilarious over the prospect of a warm supper after all their hardship, answered his hail in a manner so unusual that the captain thought that real savages had invaded the lagoon; he had reason for this surmise, for he had learned from the guard on the beach that they had found a native fireplace which showed recent use. Turning his boat on her oars, he pulled for the shore at once, fearing attack. All anxiety was relieved by the arrival of the pinnace at the beach, when the crew, on finding that they had been mistaken for aborigines, had their first laugh since the wreck. Cheered by a meal, all hands piped down, and set an anchor watch against a surprise attack by natives. Their sleep, however, was disturbed by the booming roar of the breakers outside the reef, for another gale had come up during the night and threatened to dash the wreck to pieces before it would be possible to recover from it the necessaries for life on the island.

Next morning, still very stormy, an attempt was made to tow the raft across the lagoon and into the bay, but the tide was still too strong to manage it. To save time, the sails and the provisions were lightered ashore in the two boats, until a spell of slack water allowed the raft to be towed in and beached.

In the afternoon, the weather improved sufficiently to permit the boats to reach the ship; they did not return until late at night, with the men reporting that,

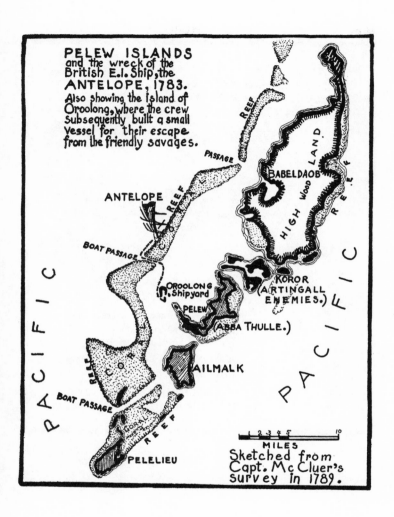

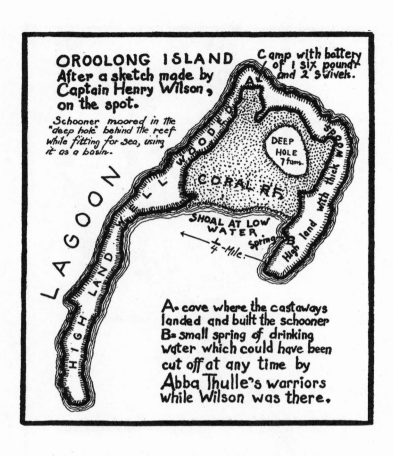

OROOLONG ISLAND
After a sketch made by
Captain Henry Wilson,
on the spot.

Camp with battery
of 1 six pound'
and 2 swivels.

Schooner moored in the
"deep hole" behind the reef
while fitting for sea, using
it as a basin.

DEEP
HOLE
7 fams.

CORAL RF.

SHOAL AT LOW
WATER.

¼ Mile.

Spring B

A. cove where the castaways
landed and built the schooner
B. small spring of drinking
water which could have been
cut off at any time by
Abba Thulle's warriors
while Wilson was there.

in their opinion, the ship could not last until morning. But the ship held, contrary to their expectations.

The next morning was too windy to visit the wreck again; so they set to work drying provisions and putting up better tents made from the sails brought ashore the day before. At eight o'clock Captain Wilson, who was on the beach with Tom, the Malay interpreter, saw two canoes with dark men in them, coming around the point and into the bay. The sudden appearance of the natives gave such alarm that the crew on the beach took to their muskets, which were loaded and ready. As there were comparatively few of the natives, Captain Wilson ordered his men to lie low until they found out what was going to happen. They knew that the natives had seen them, for they halted, and, talking together, kept their eyes on that part of the island where the English were.

The natives, unarmed and apparently not hostile, advanced cautiously towards the beach. When they were near enough, Tom, the interpreter, hailed them in his own language. At first they did not seem to understand. They stopped their canoes and one of them asked, also in Malay, who the strangers were and whether they were friends or enemies. Tom replied that they were friends and Englishmen, who had lost their ship on the reef.

On learning this, the natives stepped out of their canoes and waded to the shore, where they were greeted by the captain in a manner which allayed their suspicions. The spokesman who had answered from the canoe was a Malay who understood Tom's dialect.

The Malay told the English, through Tom, that they were on the island of Oroolong, in the kingdom of Abba Thulle, a good and kindly man, whose people were not to be feared. The Malay further explained that a canoe out fishing had sighted the wreck of the great ship which was full of people, the like of which they had never before seen. In terror at seeing the destruction of the vessel, they turned and, putting on all sail, hastened back to the king's island of Pelew to tell him the astonishing news. He had at once dispatched his brothers, Raa Kook and Ara Kooker, both high officials, in the two canoes, to go to the wreck to find out what had become of the people, and to help them if they could. Theirs was an expedition of mercy. The formal introductions over and the way paved for mutual confidence, the visitors were invited to breakfast, which was just then ready. The guests did not care for the hot tea, but liked the rusk, which the steward produced for them as a special favor.

The two Pelew chiefs were fierce and wild in appearance, their men no less so, with crisp and bushy black hair bound straight up by a red band around the head. They were dark copper-colored, medium tall, muscular, compactly built, well proportioned and entirely naked. The natives thought the white men had been born with their clothes on, for they had never seen any such coverings on a human body before. On recovering from the first spell of reticence, they felt the white men, jerking on shirts and trousers, to see if they were not extra folds of skin which would come off. To them, the whole thing was very amusing and they gave free vent to mirth while chattering among themselves.

Their sharp eyes took in everything; the bullet fired from the pistol to light the fire did not escape a sharp glance. It was picked up, examined, and identified as something entirely foreign to their own experience and culture. Later, they were to discover more about bullets.

The islanders requested that one of the English visit their king, and finally, Mathias Wilson, brother to the captain, agreed to go with them to explain to His Majesty their plight in becoming shipwrecked on his domain, and to request permission to build a sea canoe large enough to carry them back to their own country. At noon, one of the canoes left the bay with Mathias, Tom, and the Malay on board. The other canoe, with four persons, among them Raa Kook, remained with the English as self-appointed hostages until the others returned. Captain Wilson paid honor to the king by sending gifts: a roll of blue broadcloth, a canister of tea, one of sugar candy, and a jar of rusk, which was added at the suggestion of the king's two brothers, who no doubt had an inkling of what might be received with the greatest favor.

The next morning two canoes appeared, in which were Tom, the Malay, Ara Kooker, and one of the king's sons. They announced that Mathias was on his way back in a slower canoe and informed Captain Wilson that the king offered them a welcome and assured them of his friendship; they had his permission to build a great canoe on any part of the island, and he and his subjects would help all they could. This gracious message cheered the castaways.

Raa Kook, of a genial disposition, presented his nephew to the captain and officers and seemed to enjoy the boy's astonishment.

During the morning, two boats were sent out to the wreck, where were discovered about twenty canoes drawn up alongside the ship and a large number of natives on board, who, with an inclination to pillage, stole two large copper kettles from the cook's galley. The thieves were surprised by Raa Kook, who, in an excited harangue, told them it was tabu and quickly dispersed them. As he was the admiral of the king's navy, not one disputed his authority, and after that they kept their distance from the strangers' belongings.

Meanwhile, the people at the bay were highly amused by Ara Kooker, an entertaining savage with an unusual talent for mimickry. He facetiously described the conduct of Mathias, who, it seemed to them, had been in great fear, while at the king's residence at Pelew Mathias soon appear to give his own version of what had happened. Here we have his narrative:

"On the approach of the canoe in which I went to the place where the king lives, a vast concourse of natives ran out of their houses to see me come on shore. The king's brother (Ara Kooker) took me by the hand and led me up to the town, where a mat was spread for me upon a square pavement and I was directed to sit down upon it. In a little time the king appeared, and being pointed out to me by his brother,

I arose and made my obeisance, after the manner of
Eastern natives. He paid no attention to it. I then
offered him the gifts and he received them in a very
gracious manner. Ara Kooker then talked with him
a good deal, evidently to acquaint him with our disaster and our number. After this the king tasted the
sugar candy; he seemed to like it and gave some to
several of his chiefs. They liked it. He thereupon
directed that all of the presents be carried to his
house. A crowd of natives had by this time surrounded
me, who were very curious and eager to examine my
clothes and person. It now began to be dark. The king,
his brother, myself and several others retired to a
large house where a supper of boiled yams and shell-
fish was served. They all kept up a talk that I could
not understand, but very likely it was about us. I was
then taken to the king's brother's house for the night
where mats to sleep on had been laid down." Not a
very exciting narrative!

A short time after this, the English were informed
that the royal outfit was on its way, and in less than
an hour they saw a great number of canoes turning the
point which formed the harbor. The king stopped as
soon as he got within the bay and directed one squadron of the canoes, all armed, to retire, thinking, apparently, that so many warriors would alarm the
strangers. He then advanced with the rest in platoon
formation as far as the tide would allow, when it was
signified to the captain by Raa Kook, who seems to
have been master of ceremonies, that he should go
forward to meet the king. This the captain did, on the

shoulders of two of his sailors, who carried him clear
of the water to the king's canoe; he was invited to
enter, and the two formally embraced each other. The
king made signs that he wanted to land. The captain
was carried by his crew, while the king waded ashore
after him.

On landing, he looked about with an air of suspicion, which soon vanished. Raa Kook advanced and
spread a sail on the ground for the king and his chiefs,
who squatted in the form of a square. His other attendants, numbering three hundred, formed a circle around
them, squatting down in such a position that they could
spring up in an instant. Captain Wilson offered the
king some tea, which he did not like, and then tried
a few ribbons, with better success. Abba Thulle was
quite naked and without any ornament, even a bone-
ring on his wrist. He carried a hatchet of iron over
his shoulder.

The captain related the nature of their misfortunes
by means of the two Malays, and repeated his request
to build a ship to carry them home. The king courteously told them they could build it where they were,
or on the part of the island where he lived. He said
the ground where they were became unhealthful when
the monsoon changed in the course of two moons, and
that with the change of wind to another direction, the
men might become sick. The captain, pointing to the
ship's surgeon, responded that he had a man of medicine with him, whose business it was to cure sick people
of their diseases, and that another place would be too
far from the wreck.

The officers and men were then paraded before the king, who called Mr. Benger (chief mate) the *"kikory rupak"* because he was second in command, supposing the captain to be the *"rupak,"* or king of some country. Abba Thulle was informed that Captain Wilson had a mighty sovereign and that he was only a captain. The king quickly learned the term "captain" and then called Mr. Benger *"kikory* captain" to signify his real rank. With a savage's respect for symbols, the king then inquired for the captain's badge of superiority; Wilson was wondering what to show when the mate, with quick wit, slipped him a ring which he put on his own finger and displayed to the king, who said it was very like their own mark of dignity.

This interview over, came a tour of inspection with Raa Kook as guide. They examined the tents, and nothing escaped their sharp notice. They even observed the difference between the English and the Chinese, apparently regarding the latter as distinct inferiors. The king also inquired about the food and was presented with a ham and a goose as samples of what the white man ate.

The firearms interested Abba Thulle more than anything else in the camp, and he wanted to know how they were used. Mr. Benger put the sailors through a drill on the beach and concluded it by firing three volleys. At the report of the muskets, the natives set up a hooting and hallooing almost as loud, to show their astonishment. To the further wonder of the natives, the mate brought down a bird on the wing. Raa Kook, who was possessed of an astute mind, told the king that the English used these fire tubes of great noise against their enemies, of which there were many in the distant seas, and that they were often at war with each other, just as he was at war with his neighbors. All of this information, later developments revealed, set the king to thinking.

The ship's two Newfoundland dogs had been taken ashore, and these were new to the visitors, who had never seen a dog before. In fact, the only quadruped they knew was the rat. They were so excited and delighted by the barking of the dogs that they barked with them, keeping up such an uproar that the poor dogs had to be confined.

A loud and prolonged yell from one of the islanders gave the English a scare, but it proved to be only a signal for the king's departure. All rushed to their canoes, and the king, with the greater part of the natives, took his leave. Raa Kook and the king's son, with a few attendants, stayed all night; two more tents were set up for their entertainment, one for royalty and the other for the commoners.

Captain Wilson remained with Raa Kook and his party for several hours, conversing through the interpreters to conceal his apprehension that it was the show of muskets that made his visitors appear to be friendly, and, before turning in, he set a guard. The natives in the distant tent, according to their custom, sang a song in honor of their hosts. The sounds, dissonant and harsh, were so like a war cry that the English, thinking it to be a signal for an attack upon them, sprang for their arms. They soon realized their error and, at their ease, followed the strange music with interest. A chief gave out a line of verse, which a company next him took up and completed. The last line was repeated and then it was taken up by the next party, who also sang a verse. When their song was finished, they wanted the English to sing and a lad named Cobbledick obliged them, much to their amusement. The fame of the lad's singing reached the ears of the king, who never met the boys afterwards without asking for a song.

Captain Wilson was interested in the Malay's history and requested Tom to get it. They learned that his name was Soogell, and that he came from the Dutch island settlement of Ternate in a piratical Javanese proa, which was wrecked upon the Pelews, just as the *Antelope* had been. He was the only survivor because he could swim well, and had managed to cling to the coral and to make his escape, while the junk and all the rest perished. Soogell knew some Dutch and a very few words of English. His own tongue was so like that of the Pelewites that they soon grew to understand one another. He was treated well by them, but he wanted to return to his own country, which was five days' sail, he explained, to the southward of the Pelews.

In the presence of white men, his nudity made him sensitive, and he asked for some clothes, which were provided for him. At the same time, an officer's uniform was offered to Raa Kook, who was commander-in-chief of the king's forces, but it proved too cumbersome for him. He first walked around in the uniform exclaiming, "Raa Kook, *Englees,* Raa Kook, *Englees."*

An unpleasantness was to come up. A chief took a fancy to a cutlass hanging up and made motions to the captain that he would like to have it. The captain was unwilling to part with it, but thought, on the moment, that it was best to comply. When Raa Kook saw the man with the cutlass, he took it from him and returned it to Captain Wilson, who thought no more about the incident until Soogell came ashore and reported that the king and his brothers were greatly offended by the offering of the cutlass to an inferior instead of to one of them. To make amends, some presents were sent to the king and his two brothers, but without much hope of bridging the impasse which had so unwittingly occurred.

Abba Thulle made the first move. In the afternoon he came around from the back of the island where he had spent the night, and Captain Wilson went out in the yawl with Tom, to meet him. Abba Thulle was gloomy. While the Englishmen were anticipating a demonstration of wrath, they discovered where the trouble lay. The king wished to borrow some firearms without seeming to demand such a favor. With great confusion, Abba Thulle went no further than to hint at what he wanted. A neighboring nation of Artingals had injured them, he said, and they intended to retaliate in a few days; would Captain Wilson also lend him a few sailors to shoot the Artingals!

Though Captain Wilson had great compunction regarding the infliction of gunfire upon a people with whom he had no quarrel and about whom he knew nothing, he immediately, for reasons of policy, complied with Abba Thulle's proposition. No sooner had the interpreter made the captain's answer clear than the king brightened up, became cheerful again, and created the captain a brother *rupak* to show his gratitude. He also ordered his chiefs to bring to his new allies from his extensive plantations all the yams and fruit that they wanted. He further assured the captain that his subjects were entirely at the Englishman's service to help him build the great canoe which was to take him back to his own island. The king then retired to another part of the island, saying that he would return next morning for the men.

There was no lack of men to volunteer for the adventure, but only five of the youngest were selected by the third mate (Mr. Cummins), who was to head the punitive expedition to Korro. They were placed together in a canoe among a large fleet, which left Oroolong for the sail southward. In five days the English warriors returned, after putting the Artingals to flight in terror, and so greatly to the king's satisfaction, that the end of the island of Oroolong, where they resided, was given to the English for their service. Orders thereupon were given to rig a flag pole to set a Union Jack.

The shipyard was now as busy as a bee hive. The fifty-ton schooner had been started, and the hands turned to with a will at the prospect of an early escape back to China and then home. They were in an ideal place to build a small vessel, for the interior of the

island was rich with the best timber, to be had merely
for the cutting. A buttressed tree of great height was
chopped down and wrought into a keel to a finished
length of forty feet. Crooked roots were formed into
frames and knees. The size of the vessel was limited
only by the man power present to bring it into shape,
and one of fifty tons was considered sufficiently large
to accommodate the crew for the 1500-mile voyage
to Macao. Many necessary things were secured from
the wreck to go into the new vessel, which, when
completed, was really a part of the old one: frame
saws for ripping the logs up into scantling and plank;
axes and adzes to hew; a fine grindstone to sharpen
the tools (the king took special notice of this grindstone and of the way that it would reduce a steel tool
to a fine edge, for he had never seen a sharp axe
before). There was a good supply of hardware in the
way of bolts and spikes; for treenail fastenings, which
were principally used, there were the proper augers at
hand. When the vessel was in frame and the planking
started, a steam box was rigged for the fore hoods to
be bent around the bluff bow.

The king watched all of these operations by the
white men with the interest of a progressive monarch.
His own people were the builders of the finest canoes
in the South Seas, canoes which were capable of making
voyages to other islands as far as five hundred miles
away, but here was something for his craftsmen to
emulate, that they might attain still greater superiority over his neighbors in sea skill. He ordered
twenty of them to work with the white men and to

learn what they could, with the intention of building a similar vessel when the English had gone.

On the 31st of August, Captain Wilson paid a formal return visit to the king's home at Pelew. Mr. Devis, a passenger, Dr. Sharp, the surgeon, and Harry Wilson, his son, accompanied him. The English went in the yawl, while the natives, headed by Raa Kook, took a canoe. At one o'clock they reached the king's island, and, upon landing, fired six muskets to make the best possible impression, and fixed their colors in the ground. Raa Kook then conducted them to a house to await the arrival of His Majesty. The natives thronged into the house to see the Englishmen, until it was announced that the king was about to arrive. When he entered, the captain embraced him, as at the first meeting, and presented him with a few trinkets, which were very graciously received. Abba Thulle proposed to conduct them to the town, which was a quarter of a mile from the landing place.

The English, to appear imposing, carried their colors before them. They passed through a wood, then came to a fine causeway made of large broad stones, laid in the center to make easy walking, and edged with smaller ones at the sides. This led them into the town, which was in the form of a large paved square surrounded by houses. In the center stood a house larger than the rest, which was assigned to the English. In it were a number of women of superior rank, wives of the *rupaks,* who received them politely and presented them with coconuts and sweet drink. The only dress worn by the women consisted of a piece of mat, or the dyed husks of the coconut, nine or ten inches deep, fastened round the waist. Some of these aprons were very neatly made and ornamented with red and black beads. Abba Thulle's daughter, Erre Bess, gave the captain's son Henry a present of a very neat one for his little sister to wear in England. (The only approach by the men towards clothing was to paint their bodies in bright hues, with yellow predominating, which they did at festivals.)

Shortly after their arrival, the king retired to bathe, which he always did privately, for, among the Pelewites, the etiquette of the bath for both sexes was rigorous. At the same time, a message was received from Queen Ludce, inviting the guests to her home, so they all repaired thither. This lady received marked deference from all the king's subjects, and apparently was the favorite wife of Abba Thulle, who resided almost constantly at her house. She appeared at the window accompanied by Raa Kook, and sent them a broiled pigeon, a gift which was held in the highest esteem, for wild pigeons were rare and it was consequently unlawful for anyone but *rupaks* and their wives to taste them. After satisfying her curiosity by this visit, the Englishmen were conducted by Raa Kook to his house, where they met with a most gracious reception, and had an opportunity to observe this man in his home. They were greatly impressed by the behavior of Raa Kook and his wife to their children. These last he fondled on his knee and caressed with all the marks of parental affection. The night was far advanced when the visit ended and they returned to their house.

Raa Kook procured plenty of mats for them to sleep on, built fires to keep off mosquitoes, and ordered attendants to sleep outside to protect them from the curiosity of other natives.

Next morning, they were conducted by Raa Kook to the queen's house for breakfast, where they found the king awaiting them. They breakfasted on yams and fish, and, after the meal, Dr. Sharp and Mr. Devis set out to visit a child of Ara Kooker's, who was sick. Dr. Sharp approved of the native treatment for the child, and Ara Kooker was very grateful for the visit. During the day, a council was held, decisions being reached by a majority vote, similar to the European method of deciding political questions. As a result, that same evening the king again requested Captain Wilson to lend them ten men with firearms, to assist in another battle with the neighboring Artingals.

Mr. Devis interested the king and the women natives by drawing their portraits. The first subject, a young woman, ran away in confusion. However, the king approved of the sketching and immediately commanded two other women to stand as models for the artist. They were delighted with their own pictures, chattering and laughing over them. The king then tried his hand, causing much merriment by his efforts. Nevertheless, he showed a genuine appreciation of the Englishman's work.

Captain Wilson and his companions were taken one day to see how the natives built their canoes. They showed him a canoe, just captured from an enemy, with as much pride as if it had been a man-of-war.

Here were native men making darts, hewing trees, etc.,
while the women attended to household affairs, such as
cooking, preparing the meals, and caring for the
children.

Days passed pleasantly. The schooner was now quite
advanced, and everything looked bright. On the 17th
of October, Abba Thulle brought his youngest daughter for a visit to the English camp. He conducted
her through all the cove, explaining the use of everything with much care. He also brought with him one
of his wives, Ludee, a very beautiful woman, superior
to any the Englishman had yet seen. She had with her
eight or ten females, escorted by Raa Kook. The captain entertained the party in his tent by serving a meal
of fish and rice sweetened with molasses.

Abba Thulle brought with him the agreeable news
that the chief Artingal had been at Pelew with offers
of peace, which had been concluded. He acknowledged
that the English muskets had procured peace for him
with all his neighbors, and requested that Captain
Wilson would leave him ten muskets when he sailed
from the island. This Captain Wilson said he could not
do, as he might meet enemy ships on his way home
and would need them. Abba Thulle then inquired as to
how much powder they had on hand, but Captain
Wilson, wishing to keep secret the smallness of his
supply, hesitated in replying, and the king tactfully
changed the subject. The captain assured the king that
the English would soon return with larger ships to
avenge any insult offered the Pelew natives during
their absence. In turn, Abba Thulle informed Captain

Wilson that he had come to get the guns from the wreck, which were to be placed at Pelew or at Oroolong, as the English pleased. Captain Wilson had previously consulted his officers on this subject, and ordered them to be taken to Pelew, with the exception of one, which they might need for the schooner. This was done the next day.

The king, with all his atttendants, lodged for the night at the back of the island. He had not been gone long when he sent for Captain Wilson in order to present him with ten large fish, part of a catch made by the natives. Of these, the captain accepted only four, enough to serve all of the crew, as no fish will keep over five or six hours in that climate. Next morning, the English heard the sound of singing in the woods. It was Raa Kook and a company of attendants, with six dried fish as a present to them.

That morning the king appeared with three Artingal people, late enemies, and showed them all the wonders of the camp, especially the firearms with which they had been subdued. Later they visited the camp again, and the Pelewites seemed to exult over the ignorance of their new allies. The English gave another exhibition of shooting a bird on the wing. On examining the dead bird, a bullet hole was found, and the Artingals observed that the same kind of a hole had been found in their own people, and that was what had killed them.

The vessel being now nearly completed, the launch ways were laid down and well greased. After caulking, there was neither pitch nor rosin to pay the seams.

This want they supplied by burning coral stone into lime, then sifting it, and mixing it with grease to make a chinam cement.

Meanwhile, Madan Blanchard, one of the sailors, requested to be left behind when the schooner departed. At first, this request was not taken seriously by the captain, but later, when he tried to dissuade Blanchard from the idea, his effort was without success. Blanchard really wanted to stay. Therefore, when Abba Thulle came to view the launching, the captain signified to His Majesty that in return for all his hospitality, they would leave one of their comrades to shoot the guns.

Blanchard spent that night with the king and was well entertained. All of the crew regretted parting with him. It was difficult for them to understand the motive which could urge him, a young man of twenty, to forsake the class of mankind among whom he had always lived, and to be separated from civilization forever. Abba Thulle, Raa Kook and their chiefs, however, considered it a very great advantage to have as a permanent resident one who understood the use of the firearms which would be presented to them on the departure of the vessel. The king was grateful beyond measure, and promised to give Blanchard two wives. He was also to be made a *rupak,* with a house and a plantation, and it seemed unlikely that he would have to work again as long as he lived. Unfortunately, Blanchard could not read nor write, and therefore would be unable to keep any record of his life at

Pelew, which might, by lucky chance, fall someday into English hands.

Next morning, the English made ready for the launching; the wedges were rammed and the blocking split asunder. The vessel became a live thing, hanging on the dog shores, ready to be tripped. About seven, the king and his chiefs were sent for to be present at the launching, and the captain said to Abba Thulle: "What shall be the name of this great canoe?"

"Let it be *Oroolong*," cried the king, "that you may long remember this place."

And *Oroolong* she was, as she was successfully launched to the joy of all hands on the beach. To the Englishmen, the event meant home, wives, children, which now seemed near. They all danced about and shook hands together with great enthusiasm. The Pelew friends caught on to the idea and displayed a real interest in the Englishmen, to whom they had become greatly attached. These were friends, from whom they had learned how to vanquish their enemies and much besides, who were now about to leave them. But they saw that the white men were very happy and realized that their future comfort depended upon this event; so they, too, joined in the celebration. After a jovial breakfast, everything was carried on board, and in the afternoon, the flood tide coming on, the vessel was hauled into the basin, a deep place with four fathoms of water.

Captain Wilson told Abba Thulle that he intended to sail on the next day. This news was not pleasing to the king, for he had sent word to the neighboring *rupaks* that the English meant to sail on the day following that one mentioned by the captain. The neighbor chiefs were to come to Oroolong the next night to bring coconuts and yams and to bid the Englishmen farewell. This information made the captain still more determined to set sail in the forenoon of the next day, for he did not care to be surrounded by such a great number of canoes filled with savages. He was fully aware of the generally treacherous nature of the South Sea Islanders, and was not sure but that the vessel looked sufficiently good for them to keep. Dissembling, for the second time, he apologized profusely to the king for his haste, saying that in his country it was an evil omen to delay a day after a sailing date had been decided upon.

Although the king showed great disappointment, he invited the captain and his officers to dine with him on shore, and after dinner he signified his intention of investing the captain with the Order of the Bone Bracelet. Upon the captain's acknowledgment of the honor, the Bone, with great solemnity, was drawn over his left hand by oiling it, for the ring was too small to go over otherwise. The king then addressed the captain, telling him that the Bone should be rubbed bright every day and preserved as a testimony of the rank he held among them, and that it should never be torn from his arm unless he was killed in battle.

As a further proof of Abba Thulle's confidence, he proposed entrusting his second son, Lee Boo, to the care of the captain. The king's object in doing this was to permit the young man to acquire some of the knowledge which he saw the English possessed in high degree, and so to render him more useful to his native country in the future. Raa Kook also wished to accompany them, but this request was refused by the king, on motives of policy. Ara Kooker, the humorist, who seemed to have set his heart on the Newfoundland dog, so warmly begged the captain for his favorite, that the latter could not refuse him. The king wished the English to leave their launching ways, saying he would go to work on the same place and build a great canoe similar to theirs. The subject of shipbuilding caught his most serious attention, as it was of national importance and required the patronage of a prince.

The king's permission was asked and obtained to paint an English pendant on a tree near the cove, with an inscription on copper to be placed nearby, as follows:

THE HONOURABLE EAST INDIA COMPANY'S SHIP
THE "ANTELOPE"
HENRY WILSON COMMANDER
WAS LOST UPON THE REEF NORTH OF THIS ISLAND
IN THE NIGHT
BETWEEN THE 9TH AND THE 10TH OF AUGUST
WHO HERE BUILT A VESSEL
AND SAILED FROM HENCE
THE 12TH OF NOVEMBER, 1783.

Captain Wilson explained the meaning of this to Abba Thulle, who was greatly pleased with it; having explained it to his own people, he assured the English that it should be carefully guarded there in remembrance of his visitors.

The king requested the captain to give him at that time the promised muskets, and the captain was inclined to do so. However, his officers demurred and advised holding these arms until the moment of their departure. The king argued that their former enemy, the Artingals, after the departure of the English, would again attack them, and without the English muskets they would be no match for them. Abba Thulle, quickly observing their hesitancy, was much agitated on sensing that his sincerity was doubted. "Why should you distrust me?" said he. "If my intentions had been hostile, you would have known it long ago, for you were completely in my power. And yet, at the very last, you suspect me of bad designs."

So eloquent was his plea that they sent on board the schooner for all the arms that could be spared, and on the boat's return, presented him with five muskets, five cutlasses, and more than half a barrel of gunpowder, with flints and ball in proportion. Once more, harmony was restored and Abba Thulle seemed to forget his friends' suspicions.

Lee Boo, the king's second son, arrived in the evening from Pelew, under the care of his elder brother, and was presented to the captain and then to the officers. His manner was so prepossessing that all were delighted with the prospect of having him with them as a companion. Dr. Sharp was assigned to be *sucalic* (friend) to Lee Boo, and the young man stuck by him at all times.

As to Blanchard, Captain Wilson admonished him as to his conduct among the natives: to be watchful of the arms and ammunition that would be left behind, and to assist in defending the Pelew Islanders against their enemies; not to fail in his religious duties, and to keep Sunday as a sacred day. The captain begged him not to go naked, and that he might have no excuse for doing so, all the clothes that could be spared from the schooner were left with him. The captain also urged that if he accepted the king's offer of wives, he should have them also dress more like his country-women. Asked by the captain if he had any request to make for his future comfort, Blanchard begged to be allowed to have one of the ship's compasses, and the masts, sails and oars belonging to the pinnace, which was to be left behind. This request was granted. But why did Blanchard want an equipped ship's boat and compass?

Wednesday morning, November 12th, 1783, an English jack was hoisted at the masthead of the *Oroolong,* and a swivel-gun was fired as a signal for sailing. This was explained to the king, who ordered all the provisions on board which he had brought for their voyage.

A great number of canoes surrounded the vessel, loaded with presents. When ready for sea, a boat was sent ashore for the captain, who then took Blanchard and the men of the boat into a hut that had been erected, where they knelt in prayer. At eight o'clock, the captain went on board, attended by Abba Thulle, Lee Boo, and Blanchard. As it was doubted whether the vessel would be able to get over the reef, it was resolved to land the six-pounders and to leave the jolly boat behind. To replace her, Abba Thulle took great pains to procure them a proper canoe.

Blanchard now got into the pinnace in order to take the schooner in tow, and parted with his old shipmates with as much composure as if they were to meet again after a short absence. He shook hands with them as indifferently as though they were to sail down the Thames on a coasting voyage. The vessel proceeded towards the reef, surrounded by a great number of the natives in their canoes. Every man had brought a present for his friends, "The Englees." Several canoes went before the vessel to point out the safest channel, and others were waiting on the reef to show them the deepest water. Owing to all these precautions, directed by Abba Thulle, the reef was cleared without mishap.

The king now came alongside and gave Lee Boo his blessing, which the youth received with great respect. He next embraced the captain, visibly affected, and then cordially shook hands with all of the officers, crying, "You are happy because you are going home, but still I am unhappy at your going." Raa Kook remained with a few attendants to see them safely over the reef, but was so dejected that the vessel had gone a long way before he at last thought of returning to shore. As he had been their very best friend, the captain gave him a brace of pistols and a box filled with cartridges. Raa Kook could hardly speak with grief. He endeavored to converse with Lee Boo, but was unable to do

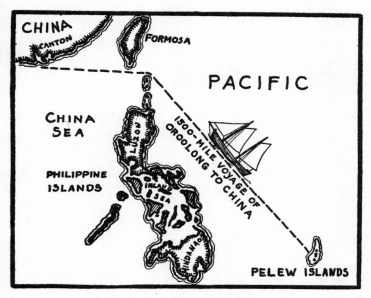

Voyage of the *Oroolong*

so. Thus terminated the Englishmen's connection with the natives of Pelew, after a residence among them of three months.

The English were now on their way back to China and proceeded on their voyage with the cheerful hope of being restored to all they held dear. Not far from the Island of Formosa, they fell in with several Chinese fishing vessels, and soon afterwards anchored near the highland called the "Ass's Ear." Having engaged a pilot to conduct them to Macao, they arrived there in two days. The Portuguese governor paid the Englishman great attention, and sent on board plenty of provisions for their needs. Captain Wilson, Lee Boo, and the officers had lodgings appointed for them on shore. Mr. Benger took charge of the schooner. A dispatch was forwarded to the company's general supercargo at Canton, apprising him of the arrival of the *Antelope's* crew on the schooner at Macao.

Lee Boo was amazed at all he saw in Macao, the great size of the Portuguese ships, the houses, rooms, furniture, ornaments, and especially the great mirror in which he saw himself full length. For the first time, he saw his complete person. He thought it was another person, laughed nervously, and looked again, not knowing what to think. It was remarkable that in all his confusion his behavior was always polite and discreet. He observed also that he himself was a curiosity, and good-naturedly allowed himself to be examined, describing the tattooing of his hands, and appearing pleased with all the attention paid him. On meeting some poor begging women with children tied to their backs, he gave them all the oranges and other things he had about him. But he would give nothing to young men beggars. "Let them work!" was his observation.

In due time, Captain Wilson received advices from the company's godown at Whampoa, providing for his transport at once to England. The *Antelope* party took passage for Whampoa (Port of Canton) in a company's ship, leaving Mr. Benger to take care of the *Oroolong* and to dispose of her. This he was able to do for seven hundred Mexican dollars, which was considered a good price for the schooner. Each member of the crew was given his share of the profits from the sale. Captain Wilson thanked them for their heroic conduct under difficulties, and promised to present them to the company in England as seamen entitled to particular regard; he had no doubt that they would be sufficiently rewarded. The captain took Lee Boo with him on the East India Ship *Morse,* while, from time to time, the others were put on different ships which were leaving Whampoa for home.

The prince of *Oroolong* made a sensation in London, and lived in Captain Wilson's house until he died of smallpox. The company was so agreeably impressed with his story and sad fate, that orders were sent to Bombay to dispatch the *Panther* and the *Endeavour* to convey the news to the king at Pelew and to make a survey of the islands. Captain John McCluer, on board the *Panther,* was in charge of the expedition. He was a commander in the Bombay marine and a hydrographer of high reputation.

On the arrival of the ships, Abba Thulle went out

to meet them. He received the news of Lee Boo's death with fortitude, saying that it was to be expected, and that he never had doubted the good faith of Captain Wilson. He was disappointed not to see Wilson, but was glad to hear that he was alive and prosperous, and that he commanded a much larger and finer ship than the *Antelope*. The king said, from his canoe, that Raa Kook, Ara Kooker, Blanchard, and many old warriors, friends of the *Antelope* crew, had been slain in battle. The war had been started by the Artingals' theft of the *Antelope's* copper plate from the tree where it had been fastened by Captain Wilson; they thought it was a talisman, and that by running off with it they would be able at last to beat the Pelews. The king, unhappily, could not give a good account of Blanchard, for he had gone completely native and worse, until he lost the respect of the king and of all the Pelewites; islanders always despise renegade whites. In the end, however, Blanchard expiated his sins, whatever they were.

Two former midshipmen of the *Antelope,* who were now with McCluer, directed the shore party to the cove where the *Oroolong* had been built. The ways were now overgrown with rank vegetation, for no attempt had ever been made by the Pelewites to again use them for building.

Some livestock was landed from the ships as a present to the king, who understood their future value to his people. He was surprised and bewildered by the boatloads of muskets, munitions, grindstones, axes, saws, shovels, and much other hardware that was de-

livered to him on the beach, and he was greatly embarrassed because he could give nothing in return. Abba
Thulle was made to understand that no return was
expected, as these things had been sent from England
in gratitude for his great humanity and kindness to
the shipwrecked crew of the *Antelope*. The king replied that his services were very trifling, for the English had been wrecked so far from Pelew that he was
prevented from aiding them as much as he desired.

Captain McCluer ordered the *Endeavour* to China
on duty, while he stayed with the *Panther* to make a
survey of the islands. He explored Babelthuab, in the
center of the group, and, climbing the highest peak,
saw both extremities of the chain of reefs. Captain
McCluer's surveys and notes, made in 1793, are the
basis of those in use today.

While on this scientific duty, McCluer did not ne-
glect the social side of life at Pelew. After being made
a *rupak,* he became Abba Thulle's son-in-law by marry-
ing Erre Bess, and taking over lands for a large plantation. In McCluer, Abba Thulle had a strong ally,
just now to be needed in another war with the Artingals, who were not yet aware of the presence of the
English in those waters. The *Panther's* longboat was
equipped with two swivels and manned by ten men
armed with muskets, to descend upon the enemy. Before firing, the king sent an ultimatum which was hastily acceded to by the Artingals, upon sight of the
forces. A peace pact was made on a permanent basis,
the English fired a salute of rockets which burst harmlessly in the air, and concluded the demonstration with

an offer of presents, to show that they did not come
to the Artingals as natural enemies. The presents were
graciously accepted, and thereafter the King of Pelew
was acknowledged as undisputed sovereign of all the
islands.

McCluer had other explorations and surveys to
make with the *Panther,* which kept him away from
Pelew for two years, when he returned to find Abba
Thulle dead. The *Panther* sailed back to Bombay, but
without McCluer, who resigned command of his ship
to spend the remainder of his days on the islands.

He was left there with the longboat and a quantity
of supplies, but in fifteen months he tired of solitude
and resolved to go to Ternate, "to hear the news."
Falling in with head winds he turned about and went
to Macao, where he purchased a small vessel by means
of a bill of credit drawn on the Presidency of Bombay.
In this vessel, manned by the five men who had sailed
with him to China, he returned to Pelew for his family.
With these, he sailed for Calcutta. In the Bay of Ben-
gal he met the Bombay frigate and lightened his small
vessel by sending some of his people by her. With the
rest, the intrepid adventurer continued on towards
Calcutta but (1794) was never heard of again.

8

The Saginaw's Gig

IN 1870, the U. S. S. *Saginaw,* Captain Montgomery Sicard in command, was detailed to sail from San Francisco to the Midway Islands in the Pacific, to supervise the construction of a coaling station for the use of American steamers on their passages between the United States and the Orient. The Midway Islands were expected to answer the purpose when the improvements were made. To do the work of deepening an existing shallow channel through the reef, a contract had been awarded to an experienced submarine engineer, and the *Saginaw* had been brought into service to transport men and material. Captain Sicard was to superintend, and to report monthly on the progress made.

The *Saginaw* found, on anchoring in the so-called Welles Harbor in Midway, that there was barely room in it to swing the ship. The island was a desolate looking place, the eastern end covered with brown alba-

U. S. S. *Saginaw*
Built in 1859

tross, and a few seal lying asleep on the beach. The white sand drifted about with the wind like snow. The next day a schooner arrived with the contractor's supplies and lumber for a dwelling and a scow. The scow was to be used by the divers in their outside work of blasting out the channel. During the first month the work both ashore and afloat was steadily pushed. The contractor's house was set up, and the diver's scow completed and launched. In addition, a thorough survey of the reef and bar was completed.

During the next six months, while the blasting of the channel was in progress, the *Saginaw* made several trips between the Midways and Honolulu, the chief port of the Sandwich Islands, a distance of eleven hundred miles. On the last return of the *Saginaw* to the Midways, she took on board the contractor's workmen, with their tools and stores, to transport them back to San Francisco. During their seven months' imprisonment, they had found their job anything but easy, and they were all glad that the appropriation had run out, though the channel through the bar was but one twelfth blasted. Instead of the fifty thousand dollars granted by Congress, it would have taken nearly a million to make a channel wide enough for large ships to enter safely. The blasting operations were carried on intermittently, as the weather permitted. For two months, constant gales beset the harbor entrance where the men were working. When those westerly gales blew, the sea broke all over the lagoon, and no work could be done. The proposal to form an anchorage for large ships in a lagoon which could be approached only

in smooth water, and in a region abounding with similar coral reefs, was a questionable undertaking.

With her homeward bound pennant hoisted to the
main, and the contractor's party on board, the *Saginaw*
sailed from the Midway Islands on Friday, October
29th at four in the afternoon, bound for San Francisco.
As soon as she reached the open sea, the captain
ordered the ship to be headed westward and the pressure of steam on the boilers to be reduced, it being
his intention to sail along before the light easterly
breeze under topsails. He expected to reach Ocean
Island at daylight, in order to examine it for possible
wrecks and castaways, for which it had acquired an
evil reputation. This was a duty required of all war-
ships when cruising in the vicinity of dangers to navigation, and such inspections were often well rewarded.

Since its discovery by an American whaler, Ocean
Island had never been accurately plotted, as whalers
never knew exactly where they were, nor did they care,
so long as plenty of whales were about. The reported
position of the island, therefore, needed to be verified
by careful observations and a reliable chronometer.
Thus the *Saginaw* was officially and humanely justified
in squaring her yards. Ocean Island is fifty miles west
of the Midway Islands, of similar formation, and is
supposed to be the last link in the chain of dangers extending a thousand miles from the Sandwich Islands.
It was on this reef that the British ship *Gledstanes*
(1837) and the American ship *Parker* (1842) were
wrecked.

On the departure of the *Saginaw* from Midway,

officers and men were fatigued after unusual preparations for sea. Securing the contractor's outfit and transporting it to the ship was hard work which had to be done in a hurry. There was none of the general homeward-bound hilarity among the crew and no disposition to skylark. After the bugle sounded "out lights" at nine, the steady tramp of the lookouts and their half-hour hail of "all's well" were the only sounds that disturbed the quiet of the dark night. The sea continued smooth, and the ship was on an even keel, making three knots.

At three o'clock, a sudden concussion was felt over all the ship, making her people think, at first, of a collision with another vessel. There was immediate commotion on deck. The shock was an easy one at first, followed by others of increasing force, which caused the ship to tremble in every timber. The long easy swell that had been lifting them along gently in the open sea was now transformed into heavy breakers which reached and swept over a coral reef, each wave lifting and dropping the quaking ship with a frightful thud, threatening to knock out her masts and stack. It was her death struggle with rocks. The engines were put astern. The fierce pounding of the jagged rock broke through the hull and tore up the engine and fire room floor, the water rushed in and reached the fires; the doom of the good ship was sealed.

Nothing could be seen of any land. Thinking they had struck some uncharted reef, the crew got their boats over the side opposite the sea, and waited for daylight. As the night wore on, wind and sea increased.

The ship, which had first struck the reef bows on, was gradually swung around until she was at first broadside to the reef, and then farther, until the after part, to which the crew were clinging, was lifted over the jagged edge of the wall of rock. She was finally twisted around by the sea, until the bow pointed directly seaward, with hull balancing at the edge of the reef. Thus the ship see-sawed from stem to stern, with each coming wave, for an hour or more, until the forward part broke away with a loud crash, and disappeared into the deep water outside.

All that was left of the ship now heeled over towards the inner side of the reef, the stack soon went by the board, and the mainmast was made to follow it by simply cutting away the seaward shrouds. Over this mast they passed to the reef. They took ashore three of the smaller boats; the launch had been smashed up in the night while being lowered, by some mistake, on the seaward side.

The first gray streaks of dawn showed them a small strip of land in the smooth water of a lagoon. A line was formed by the men across the reef, and everything that could be rescued was passed over the side and from hand to hand to the boats in the lagoon, for transfer to the island. The sea had robbed them of the larger part of their provisions, for the bread and clothing storerooms had been in the forward hold. They stood waist deep in water, feet and ankles lacerated and bleeding, stumbling about the sharp and uneven coral rock, until five in the afternoon. The order was then given to abandon ship, which was carried out without the loss of a single life.

At nightfall, after fourteen hours of hard labor transferring provisions and material to the beach, all hands, wet, tired and hungry, were piped down to a supper, which was sorry enough, but not without its jests for sauce; sailors will laugh at anything. One of the most care-free was the Negro mess room steward, who, when the ship struck, was in double irons for some offense. In the subsequent confusion, the key had been lost. He sat on a skylight and whistled "Way down upon the Suwanee River," until his manacles were severed with a cold chisel. He did such good work salvaging stores that his sentence was remitted, which he took to be an event of major importance.

Until means of escape from the reef could be planned, the ninety-three castaways lost no time in establishing a camp, which was strictly disciplined and governed. It soon looked like a village. The tents holding their meagre stock of provisions had to be set upon high posts with inverted pans over them to keep the contents away from the rats which swarmed over everything. These rats were probably the numerous descendants of forebears, landed from other wrecks, such as the *Gledstanes* and the *Parker*. After the marauders had devoured a much valued box of macaroni, a double sentry had to be placed over the stores at night, but with orders not to kill, with a view to the possible usefulness of the rats as future food.

As the two good old sailors' standbys, hard tack and potatoes, gave out, more reliance was placed on the

stray hair seal on the beach, but even these were seasonal animals, likely to migrate at any time. Another
source of meat supply was the gooney, a kind of albatross that nested on the island. The modus operandi
adopted by the galley detail for the capture of these
birds was to invade with a club the bushes where they
nested, from the weather side, as they could rise only
head into the wind. But gooney, though hard of mas-
tication, was declared to be ahead of seal, which had
to be parboiled all night before being fried in the
morning. They all fell to with a right good will, but
the tough all-meat diet was tougher on the white man's
stomach, the men perceptibly losing weight and
strength by reason of malnutrition.

Fuel for the cooking-fire was found in the old and
dried timbers of the *Gledstanes,* which were strewn
about the beach in sufficient quantity to last a long
time. The fire, started by their only dry match, was
kept constantly going. This memorable match was in
the possession of Mr. Baily, the chief diver, and a
civilian. This brings a curious naval regulation to our
notice, for they all lighted their pipes at the smoking
lamp, which was in charge of the master at arms. It is
remarkable, though, that not one of the after guard
had a dry match. Later, part of a barrel of sperm oil
and a lantern were saved, thus guaranteeing a supply
of lighting material for the fire, which could then be
put out at night, saving much fuel.

The problem of fresh water was the principal anxiety of the castaways, until it was relieved, later, in an
almost miraculous manner. Their original supply had

consisted of the few breakers, filled for emergency, which came ashore in the boats. Rain was not to be counted on. Several wells were dug in various parts of the island, but found to be too brackish.

It was finally decided to improvise a distilling plant, with the bones of the *Gledstanes* for fuel. A small portable boiler, owned by the contractors and used by them for hoisting lumps of coral onto the scow, was found lashed to the after deck of the wreck; suspended between two boats, it was landed upon the beach. There were also, in one of the wheelhouses of the wreck, some heating coils, which were just right for distilling. These the engineer's force successfully rescued after much hard labor, for the sea was washing through the wheel-house with terrible force. The precious boiler was set up on the beach to make the steam and connected with the distilling coils by a piece of canvas hose. The inner end of the coils was joined to a length of speaking tube as a return to the beach. By this arrangement the steam passed under the cooler water of the lagoon and was condensed as it returned to a bucket on the beach. The first sight of the little stream caused much joy among the castaways and a great fear to be lifted from their thoughts. At supper, on this day, they had their first mug of coffee. Soon, they added to their fresh water a supply of fifty gallons, caught in a rain storm, and served out an extra cupful to every man. The storm threw up a rough sea, which drove some large sea turtles to seek shelter in the lagoon, and these the crew turned on their backs to prevent their escape.

Before long, huge breakers washed the mainmast into the lagoon. It was soon towed to the landing place, where it was anchored. It was to be erected and used for a lookout station, as well as a means for flying a distress signal, should a passing vessel be sighted. However, there was not much hope of rescue from passing ships, for the presence of these coral reefs constitutes such a menace to navigation that they are avoided. Vessels generally pass far to the north or south of them.

The captain's idea of sending a boat to the Sandwich Islands was revealed by an order to the senior officers, in which he directed each one to file with him an opinion on the feasibility and necessity of such a trip; each written opinion to be without the knowledge of the others. Soon afterwards, the gig was carried well up on the beach and set in a cradle, to be made ready for the long voyage to the Islands. It was the intention to raise her sides a few inches, to construct a light deck overall, and to fit her with two masts and sails. In the deck there were to be four small square hatches, with covers in case of bad weather, in which the men could sit and pull oars.

Lieutenant Talbot, the executive officer, had volunteered the day after the wreck to make the attempt to sail to the Sandwich Islands, and several of the crew had asked to go with him. In fact, so many volunteered that it was found necessary to take the pick of those most likely to stand the exposure, for, although they knew that such a trip had been made by the crew of the *Gledstanes,* they also recalled that it had taken them five months to build a seaworthy vessel, while the men of the *Saginaw* would go in what was practically an open boat.

While Captain Sicard was in favor of the gig, he also planned to send the cutter back to Midway Island to post a notice. In addition to this, he planned to build a schooner big enough to take all of them away from Ocean Island. Timber for the prospective schooner was selected and piled up, as the wreckage from the *Saginaw* was washed over the reef and into the lagoon. While towing in some of the floating timbers, they came upon a large fragment of the hurricane deck, which was exactly the right material for the planking. The hurricane deck was three inches thick, but they had a single bucksaw which could be converted into a frame ripsaw with one man above and one man below. The blacksmith thought that the nails extracted from the old timber would be ample for the fastenings. In the contractor's crew was an experienced boat builder who was to take hold of the schooner job as boss.

A detail had been told off to raise the observation mast. A hole had been dug at the highest point of land, near the captain's tent, and the mast rolled up to it, with guys ready to hold it upright. A small derrick was rigged to support the mast nearly in balance. The heel of the mast slid into the hole, and the top was elevated by the guys, until the mast stood on its foot and was secured upright. All hands were piped to dinner, and no sooner were they at mess than one of the guys parted and the mast fell. Luckily, it was not injured, and the captain said, calmly, as though it were an every-day occurrence, "Well, men, we must do it again."

While they were standing about the hole, and the captain was directing preparations for another effort, one of the men, noticing the water at the bottom, scooped some of it up in a shovel and raised it to his lips. His eyes snapped, his face went white and broadened almost into a grin, and he seemed for an instant to hold his breath. Then his color came back, and with a wild shout of gladness, he exclaimed, "Boys, fresh water, by God!"

And so it proved, soft and pure, although within twenty feet of the salt water at the beach. Examination showed that there was quite a pocket of this filtered rain water, and that the point where they had excavated was evidently where the island had originally commenced to form on solid ground. They noticed, too, during the afternoon, that the water in it rose and fell with the tide of the ocean, in the lagoon, without mixing. This was explained by one of the officers, who had before seen such conditions, as being due to the difference in density of the two waters, and the fact that the small rise and fall of the tide, which was only about twelve inches there, did not create an inrush and outgo sufficiently strong to force a mixture. With this newly discovered supply of water, however moderate, they were now able to dispense with the boiler, which had begun to give trouble from rust and leakage.

The mast was again raised and care taken to prevent a repetition of the accident; stronger guys were led to heavy, deep-driven stakes. A topmast was added, and a "Jacob's ladder," to the cross trees.

Work on the gig was progressing fast; the top-sides were finished and the deck now on. Her spars, rigging, and sails had been made with all the care that experienced hands were capable of. Lieutenant Talbot was ordered to take command, and, acting under instructions, he selected four volunteers to accompany him on his enterprise, and got ready to sail the gig to Honolulu, a fifteen hundred-mile sailing distance, for relief of the *Saginaw* party.

The writer saw the boat, not long since, rolled up on her beam ends, under a stairway in the Museum of the U. S. Naval Academy at Annapolis, where she is still to be seen, bearing the scars of her battle for life. I found her to be a boat of the whaler type, but with very fine lines; not adapted to heavy seas or weather, but rather for easy pulling in smooth water.

Curator Kraft kindly furnished me with some particulars, and the dimensions of the boat, which are as follows: length, twenty-five feet; breadth, six feet and three inches; depth, two feet and eight inches, this latter having been increased during rebuilding on Ocean Island, by the addition of an eight-inch top strake on the gunwales. The gig, as I saw her, could not properly be called a decked boat, for the light shelter made over the top was pierced by four square openings, each over a thwart, so that the oars could be pulled if necessary. Chocks were fastened to the decks to support the rowlocks. The hatches were covered with canvas covers for wet weather, the one over the steering cockpit having a hole in it and a reeving line to draw it tightly about the helmsman's body when heavy spray swept over the boat while sailing.

Out of material at hand an entirely new set of spars and sails was made, entirely disregarding the regulation rigs for navy boats. She was schooner-rigged, with a little flying gaff-topsail set from the deck, and a flying jib set from a short bowsprit. But the sail which was to be their best standby was the stoutly made square sail with two reefs. Steering was by a long tiller reaching to the cockpit. The boat was provided with a chronometer, a ship's compass with binnacle, marine glasses, and a barometer. The most remarkable item of navigational equipment was the sextant, made by Engineer Herschel Main, out of the face of the *Saginaw's* steam gauge, together with some fragments of broken mirror and bits of zinc. He marked the arc of zinc with the point of a fine needle, and upon testing the sextant, Talbot pronounced it to be accurate enough to navigate with. Another officer drew a duplicate of the official chart of that part of the Pacific, and still another copied all of the necessary tables from the Nautical Almanac, for Talbot's use on his boat voyage.

In the light of the fate of the boat and its crew, it is of interest to note the store list which was provided on the basis of half rations for thirty-five days. This included: 10 breakers of drinking water (probably 10 gallons each), 10 days' rations of hard tack in canvas bags, 5 days' rations of hard tack sealed in tins, 2 dozen small tins of preserved meat, 5 tins (5 pounds each) desiccated potato, 2 tins cooked beans, 3 tins boiled wheaten grits, 1 ham, 6 tins preserved oysters, 10 pounds dried beef, 12 tins lima beans, 5 pounds butter, 1 gallon molasses, 12 pounds sugar, 4 pounds tea, and 5 pounds of coffee. A small "cooking apparatus" for burning oil was improvised and furnished.

Talbot's crew of four were picked for physical fitness, and it is related in this connection that a rivalry between two of the volunteer applicants was settled by a wrestling match, the winner making for himself a place in the relief boat. When ready for the water, the gig was surrounded by men and carried bodily into the lagoon, and anchored off to be loaded, as well as to receive the last finishing touches. Engineer Butterworth put the last one on by standing waist deep in the water while she was afloat, to screw rowlocks to the gunwales.

On Friday, November 18th, the day set for the departure, all hands were mustered on the beach. The sailing of the boat had the solemn atmosphere of a martyrdom. With bared heads, the crew listened to a prayer of the Episcopal ritual read by the captain. When sailors pray, there is something to pray about. The men who were to imperil their lives for their shipmates waded off to the gig and climbed on board. They were: Lieuteant John G. Talbot, Coxswain William Halford, Quartermaster Peter Francis, Seamen John Andrews and John Muir. As the gig gathered way and headed for the outlet to the sea, three rousing cheers broke the gloom, and the tiny sails faded from sight. That evening, Captain Sicard invited Mr. Read, to whom we are indebted for this story, to walk with him around the entire island; while doing so, his dark expressive eyes often turned to the spot where the gig had disappeared from sight. As they separated in front of his tent, the captain said in a tremulous voice, "Good night, Paymaster; God grant that we see them again."

On Thanksgiving day in the island camp there was albatross on the tarpaulin-covered table instead of turkey. The gig had been gone a week, and there was no expression of thanks at the mess table until one of the officers, having finished the extra cup of coffee served in honor of the day, said, "Say, fellows, let's be thankful that we are alive, well, and still with hope."

Work was steadily pushed on the schooner. The keel was hewed out of the *Saginaw's* topmast and blocked up on the beach. They turned to ripping the old deck plank in two with their old bucksaw and one handsaw, and, while it was slow work, they could see their boat plank ahead of them by the time the frame would be ready. The schooner was to be forty feet long, of centerboard, flat-bottomed type, and the captain had settled on her shape and dimensions after experimenting with a small model, in company with the contractor's carpenter, who had had experience in boatbuilding.

Every afternoon, when the work was suspended for the day, the subject of Talbot's whereabouts was the first note of discussion; as though it had not been in their minds all day long. As the possible failure of Talbot's effort began to enter their calculations, greater effort was exerted to provide for another avenue of escape. And with gradually weakened strength, owing to lack of sustaining food, the carpenter's gang, in particular, found the labor exhausting.

The captain ordered the cutter to be fitted also for a voyage to the Midway Islands, there to erect a sign to serve in case the Navy Department should send a relief vessel in search for the *Saginaw*. Twice every day a lookout climbed the rope ladder on the mast, to search the shipless horizon, sometimes with such a strain of nerves and hope that phantom vessels crossed his vision. The loneliness and solitude of the vast expanse of water surrounding them was, to the castaways, beyond expression. They might easily have fancied that beyond the line of the horizon there existed only infinite space.

In the camp, the rats, first small and timid, were now growing larger and bolder. They were not interfered with, for they began to loom up in importance as a food supply. The seal, on the contrary, were growing fewer in number, and the albatross also were soon expected to leave when the hatching season was over and the young had been taught to fly.

On January 1st, 1871, Talbot had been away forty-three days, and it seemed unlikely that he should have reached the Sandwich Islands before the food was exhausted. There was a lingering hope, however, that some delay in starting relief for them had occurred, or that the expedition had reached some island other than Oahu, where Honolulu is situated, from which communication with Oahu might be limited.

On this New Year's night they threshed out the

whole situation in an earnest discussion between the sanguine and non-sanguine members of the crew. It is doubtful if anyone but the marine sentry at the storehouse saw the birth of the new year, or cared to see the new year come in. They wanted no more holidays to chronicle there, except the one that was to liberate them from Ocean Island.

Three days later, at half past three in the afternoon, the paymaster says he was working on the schooner, helping Mitchell, one of the carpenters of the contractor's party. He was handing Mitchell a nail, when he noticed that the latter's eyes were steadily fixed on some point to seaward. He paid no attention to the proffered nail, and his continued gaze induced the paymaster to turn his eyes in the same direction. He, too, saw something which held his gaze. They were very careful about reporting what they saw, or what they thought they saw, for on the occasion of the last false alarm an order had been given out that no one should again alarm the camp before permission from the captain had been obtained. Far off to the northeast and close to the horizon was a faintly outlined cloud, and as they both watched, with idle tools in their hands, the cloud seemed to grow in size and density. Very soon Mitchell spoke in a low voice, as though not wishing to give a false alarm: "Paymaster, I believe that is the smoke of a steamer," and, after another look, "I am sure of it." And then arose a shout that all could hear, "Sail ho!"

The order concerning alarms was forgotten in Mitchell's excitement, but, as the captain stood nearby,

his face beaming with his own joy, no notice was taken
of the violation. The lookout was manned, and a watch
kept on the steamer until her smokestack came into
view. At first she was not heading directly for the
island, and it was feared that those aboard had failed
to see the signal of distress waving from the mast,
and that she was about to leave the castaways, stricken
with despair at the thought. When the steamer arrived
at a point nearly to the north of them, the lookout saw
her change her course until her masts were in line,
and then he shouted the fact to those below, for it
was now evident that she was bound for Ocean Island.

The steamer was soon in view from the ground.
All hands gave vent to long pent up feelings; rough
looking men, many of them witness to the shock of
storm and battle, laughed, sang, and danced, embrac-
ing each other with tears of joy running down their
cheeks. The stores reserved for the schooner were
broached, and a full supper was spread on the mess
tables. There was unlimited salt pork, flapjacks, and
beans, finished off with coffee, the feast being interrupted continually by someone's rushing out of the tent
and back again, to report the movements of the
steamer. By the time they had finished supper she was
very near, and was recognized as the *Kilauea,* a vessel
belonging to the king of the Sandwich Islands. She
came within half a mile of the reef where the *Saginaw*
was wrecked, and, dipping her flag, slowly steamed
away in a southerly direction. This maneuver was understood, for, as it was getting late in the day, the
rescuers were evidently intending to return the next

day, thus avoiding the danger of a night near the reef. Captain Sicard ordered a fire to be kept in good blazing order throughout the night, as a beacon.

The *Kilauea* appeared at daybreak and anchored near the west entrance of the lagoon; very soon afterwards her whaleboat landed. Captain Long (retired whaler) received three rousing cheers from the crew, as they stood at attention. Captain Sicard went down alone to receive him, and after a cordial greeting, they conferred together for a few minutes. Together they approached the crew, and Captain Sicard held up his hand as a signal for silence. He uncovered his head and said in a tremulous voice:

"Men, I have the great sorrow to announce to you that we have been saved at a great sacrifice. Lieutenant Talbot and three of the gig's crew are dead. The particulars you will learn later; at present, Captain Long is anxious for us to remove to the *Kilauea* as quickly as possible."

He bowed his head and a low murmur of grief passed along the line. From a cheering happy crowd they were in an instant changed to one of mourning. All the dreary days they had passed seemed to fade into nothing in the face of their great sorrow.

According to the official reports made afterwards, Lieutenant Talbot had indicated his intention to sail into the North Pacific, by the wind, until he was well clear of the northeast trades and in the settled westerlies, and then to run before the wind until he could lay Honolulu with the northeast trades when he entered them again. The sailing route would thus be increased to fifteen hundred miles, but in the favorable winds the estimated time for the voyage was thirty-five days. The gig seems to have followed that route, but for the actual facts, scantily rendered, from the time of sailing from Ocean Island, to the landing on Kauai, we are indebted to the deposition made by Halford, who was the only survivor. Of dates, courses and runs during the voyage, no record is to be found.

On the run eastward they encountered strong west winds, blowing gale force, most of the time, the seas washing down into the hatches and drenching the boat. The gig ran before it under square sail, double reefed, so long as it was possible without broaching to and foundering. Six times she hove to under sea anchors which were repeatedly carried away. The first to be lost was the regular one, and that was replaced by another made of three oars lashed together in a triangle. The third sea anchor was made of the remaining two oars lashed together crosswise, and over this was fastened a square of convas. When the last drag broke adrift the boat was nearly swamped, but they succeeded in reaching what they supposed was the longitude of Kauai, which they determined to make instead of Honolulu. They were, however, as was afterwards proved by their landfall, about a degree and a half to the west of this position, for the rough condition of sea and weather had made the navigational instruments in the boat of little use.

Here are two yarns by Halford illustrating life in the boat, and they had better be passed along without comment: "We were scudding along before a gale of wind before a reefed square sail. A nasty sea was running at the time. I was standing in the hatch, steering, had the reeving string of the cover nailed around the combings, drawn tight under my armpits to keep out the sea as it washed over the boat, when I felt a shock. The boat almost capsized but I felt the next sea lift her over. I looked astern and saw a great log, forty or fifty feet long and four or five feet in diameter, water-logged and just awash. We had jumped clean over it. It was touch and go with us."

And here is another: "One night I had relieved Peter Francis at the tiller and he had crawled forward on the deck. Somehow or other he got overboard; luckily we had a strong fishing line towing astern all the voyage but never got a bite till it caught Francis and we got him aboard again. It was a bright moonlight night."

They suffered greatly from wet, cold and want of proper food, for their ten-day ration of hard tack in canvas bags, as well as the tea, coffee and sugar, were soon spoiled by the sea water. Almost at the very first some accident deprived them of means of cooking, for they "lost all light and fire." Regulation flint and steel were in the boat but no tinder or dry wood, but near the very end they succeeded in making fire with a lens out of the glasses. "Of the stores," Halford says, "the desiccated potato, mixed with fresh water, saved us from actual starvation. Then when our provisions had run out entirely, a large sea bird came and landed on the boat and looked at me as I stood at the tiller. The other four at this time were very weak from want of food and from dysentery; they were more dead than alive. I caught the bird, tore off the feathers, cut it up in five pieces, and we all had a fine meal. It was raw but it tasted good. About thirty-six hours after this, just at daybreak, I was sitting at the tiller, I felt something strike my cheek. It was a little flying fish. I caught it, and soon a school of them came along, several dropping on deck. I captured five or six of them, and they gave us the last meal we had on the gig. At daylight I saw land."

It was on Friday, December 16th, they sighted Kaula Rock, a barren islet, six hundred feet, sheer up and down, near the southern end on Niihau Island. They stood north by east with Niihau in sight all day. During that night and on Saturday night they stood northeast by north, and on Saturday night, headed southeast. Sunday morning the wind allowed them to head southeast with the island of Kauai in sight, and on Sunday night they were off the Bay of Hanalei, on the north coast. Then they hove to with the head to the northwest, the wind having hauled to the westward. At eleven P.M. the entrance to Hanalei came in sight and the boat was kept off to steer in that direction until the sky clouded over and the darkness shut off the land.

After keeping off and heaving to several times, the boat was kept off to run for the entrance until she ran into shoal water, and was suddenly boarded over the stern by a breaker. Lieutenant Talbot immediately hauled into the wind when another breaker capsized the boat, which rolled over twice before finally right-ing up. Only Halford was left to cling to the boat as she washed to the beach and grounded. Halford landed with the water breast high and took with him the tin case of dispatches telling of the loss of the *Saginaw*. The breakers that the gig ran into were those of a fringing reef extending about a quarter of a mile off-shore on each side of Hanalei, since well located on the chart. But what struck the crew the hardest was their sad physical condition, which had reduced them to an extreme point of non-resistance. Sea-wear, starvation and sickness had done their work and it must be kept in mind that on top of all this it had been seventy hours since those few raw flying fish had been divided among them.

Upon the arrival of the news of the disaster to the *Saginaw*, at Honolulu, the government steamer *Kilauea* had been at once dispatched to Ocean Island. On the way back to Honolulu, two of the *Saginaw's* men were overheard discussing their misfortunes with reference to the superstition connected with sailing on Friday. "What better proof," said one of them, "would you have of its being an unlucky day than in the case of the *Saginaw?* She sailed from the Midway Islands on a Friday, and two days afterwards she lay a total wreck among the breakers of Ocean Island. The gig that went for help also started on Friday, and what was the result? Four out of the five brave boys who manned her came to an untimely end—how Halford escaped is a mystery to me; but I guess he'll think twice before starting on another voyage on Friday!"

9

The Fenua-ura Castaways

ON the 7th of September, 1855, the American bark *Julia Ann* sailed from Sydney, Australia, bound for San Francisco, with fifty-six people on board, men, women and children. Twenty-seven days out, a bright lookout was kept for low land all day, and the vessel had a press of sail on in order to pass certain dangerous shoals before night. At sundown no land could be seen from the royal yard, and Captain Pond, a careful navigator, judged that they were thirty miles beyond the shoals. However, in compliance with his usual custom of precaution when in the vicinity of reefs and islands, he charged the mate at eight o'clock to keep a good lookout during the night.

In half an hour, the alarming cry of, "Hard down the helm!" was heard. Men were thrown to the deck by the violent striking of the ship, and in a few minutes she was thumping hard. On deck the scene was terrific. It was blowing a trade gale, and a high sea was running. The vessel was in the breakers of a coral reef, with no hope for the ship, and very little for the lives of those on board. Captain Pond kept sail on the vessel to force her as high as possible on the reef, and then cut away the masts to relieve her from the immense strain. To save the lives of those on board was the next care, but the prospect was gloomy enough.

The sea was making a complete breach over the ship, for she had fallen on her beam-ends, seaward, and threatened to break up at any moment. There was no land in sight, and not a dry rock visible upon the reef. One of the quarter boats was stove on first striking. An attempt was made to secure the only remaining boat, but it soon broke adrift from the davits and plunged headlong into the sea. The second mate and three of the sailors jumped overboard after it. The boat was stove and turned bottom up, and they were all thrown upon the reef together. Owens, the second mate, was so badly injured that he was incapable of further exertion.

Volunteers were now called for to make an attempt to reach the reef by swimming with a small line. One of the sailors stripped instantly, and the log line was attached to his body. He succeeded in swimming to the reef under the lee of the vessel. By this means, a larger line was hauled to the reef and made fast to the rocks. A small one for a hauling line was also rove, and then commenced the perilous task of getting the women and children upon the reef. A sailor, in a sling upon the rope, took a woman and a child in his arms, and was

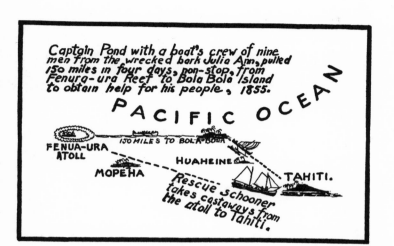

Captain Pond with a boat's crew of nine men from the wrecked bark Julia Ann, pulled 150 miles in four days, non-stop, from Fenua-ura Reef to Bola Bola Island to obtain help for his people, 1855.

PACIFIC OCEAN

FENUA-URA ATOLL
150 MILES TO BOLA BOLA
MOPEHA
HUAHEINE
TAHITI.
Rescue schooner takes castaways from the atoll to Tahiti.

hauled to the reef by those already there, then hauled back again by those on board. The process was an exceedingly arduous one, and attended with much peril. But it was their only means of rescue, for, even if the boats had not been destroyed, they would have been useless in such a surf among the rocks.

In the meantime, the vessel was laboring and thumping in such a fearful manner that it was almost impossible for anyone to cling to the iron railing upon the quarter-deck; one or two persons had already been hurled seaward by the awful throes of the ship. The passengers collected in the after cabin, where they were compelled to remain, though the sea breached in and half filled it, until, as their names were called, they could be passed ashore on the rope. There was no confusion; up to the last, all were subservient to orders. But events now rapidly drew to a crisis.

The vessel had fallen off from the reef to more than double her former distance. The rope attached to the rock was stretched to its utmost tension, and the hauling line had parted for the third time. The crew were all on the reef, and, after repeated efforts to regain the vessel, they were compelled to abandon the attempt. Two large families still remained on board, with the captain and the mate. Five people had already been drowned, and it was with the utmost difficulty that anyone could be kept from being washed away. Those remaining on board were urged to get to the reef on the rope before it parted—it would be a desperate chance, but their only hope for life. The women and children were unable to manage it; even the men shrank from the yawning gulf as from certain death. However, the captain and the mate determined to take the risk. Throwing themselves upon the rope, they reached the reef just as the vessel broke in two, and the stern, relieved from the pressure of the cargo, the fore-part hanging seaward, righted itself, and was thrown high upon the reef. This gave the remaining passengers the chance to escape easily on floating spars.

The scene on the reef can better be imagined than described. It was about eleven o'clock at night when all were landed, up to their waists in water, and with the tide rising. The moon was up to shed her faint light over the dismal scene; and the sullen roar of the breakers sent an additional chill through the people, plunged into such sudden misery. The bell at the wheel, at every surge of the sea, seemed to toll a solemn knell to the departed souls. That dismal sound, together with the wailing of a bereaved mother, were the only sounds that broke the stillness of the night. The castaways upon the reef brooded in silence over the awful solemnity of their situation.

At morning's dawn, low islands were discovered, about ten miles distant. Again all was activity. The holes in the boat were plugged with canvas; spars and driftwood were collected to form a raft on which to float the women and children to a safer place. A little after sunrise, the captain started for the islands, though his boat would scarcely float.

The first island on which he landed presented a somewhat barren appearance. It was covered with pandanus trees, and birds seemed plentiful and very tame;

but a cereful search failed to reveal any water, fruit or vegetables. The boat party then went to another island, where again disappointment awaited them. They sought madly for water, but to no purpose, and late in the afternoon returned to the reef. Women and children were now placed in the boat and sent, in charge of the mate, to the land, while the rest of the party remained on the reef for the second night.

On the morning of the second day, the mate returned with the boat, and the captain immediately sent him away again in search of water, for the want of which they were now nearly choking. Meanwhile, the rest went about lashing together more rafts to carry the provisions and clothing that had been washed ashore. In this way several bags of flour, a barrel of bread, and some peas and beans were saved. About ten o'clock an attempt was made to reach the island by wading along the reef with the rafts in tow, the old and helpless men, of whom there were several, being placed upon them. Energy, perseverance, and, above all, necessity can accomplish the almost impossible. The island was reached. Most of the distance the water was deep; one stretch of over a mile was five feet deep, compelling the shorter men to cling to the rafts. Large numbers of sharks followed in their wake; at one time there were over twenty in sight, and the men had to climb aboard the rafts for safety. Several deep inlets had to be crossed, for which purpose the best swimmers were called into requisition. In one of these places two men were nearly lost. Good luck was at hand when the landing was made, for the shore party had found water by digging holes in the coral sand on the beach. The group had been forty-eight hours in the salt water, and for two days exposed to the rays of the tropical sun, without food or drink.

The history of the two months spent by the *Julia Ann* castaways on this desolate island in the South Pacific is replete with interest. Three days after the first landing, the captain took an exploring party in the boat, and on an island eight miles away, discovered a grove of coconuts. Without something of that kind, their situation would have been desperate, indeed. The food now consisted of shell-fish, turtles, sharks, and coconuts. An attempt was made to cultivate a garden by planting pumpkins, peas, and beans, which came up finely to flourish for a few weeks, then to wither and die.

Repairs on the boat were started. It was small and badly stove, but there seemed no other hope for a final deliverance from captivity. A forge and blacksmith's bellows were contrived to make the necessary nails and iron-work. Several trips made to the wreck resulted in a greater supply of canvas, boards, and many other necessary articles. A lookout was established at the coco island on the chance of signaling a passing ship, and each night turtle hunters were sent out. The party divided itself into families and built huts, which they thatched with the leaves of the pandanus tree. All the provisions found were thrown into one common stock, and equally divided among each mess in the morning. Now the first shock of the disaster was over, and they were becoming more accustomed to their life of hardship.

Five weeks after the wreck, the boat was ready. The attempt to launch forth upon the treacherous sea in so small a craft was desperate; it was the choice between possible death and life-long captivity upon that desolate reef. To satisfy the passengers, Captain Pond proposed to remain with them and to send one of his officers, with a number of the crew, for assistance. The mate, a former whaling captain, objected to going in the boat, saying that he was an old man, and that he preferred to die where he was. The crew, likewise, refused to go without the captain, but volunteered to a man to follow his lead.

The nearest inhabited islands were the Society group, one hundred and eighty miles to windward. There was no hope of reaching them, and the Navigator Islands became the only alternative. Although the distance, some nine hundred miles, was appalling, Pond determined to steer for them. He selected four of his best men for a boat's crew and set the day for his departure.

The gateway from the island offered an unexpected obstacle. Before realizing it, they were imprisoned in an atoll lagoon without an opening to the ocean, an unbroken circle of coral. There was gloomy despair. The ship's crew and officers were scattered in every direction on the reef, to make a systematic search for any break in the rocks that might offer a chance for the launching of the boat. Three days were spent upon the reef in this manner, and a spot finally selected, which, if the boat were carried a hundred yards, and the weather were favorable, offered a hope of success. The captain determined to make the trial on the following day. But his own spirits now seemed crushed; a foreboding of evil came over him. The weather was unsettled and threatening, and he retired to his tent, as he thought, for the last time—unhappy and without hope. The clouds gathered in gloomy grandeur, and a tornado broke over the island. At three o'clock in the morning, he turned out for a walk down the beach, to find, to his consternation, that the boat was gone!

On this alarm the entire colony turned out, and in the gray dawn of morning gathered upon the beach to gaze upon the spot where the night previous they had seen that priceless boat so snugly moored. So great a misfortune could hardly be realized. The compass, nautical instruments, and everything of value, were in the boat, and all of their material had been exhausted in its construction. This loss banished hope; it seemed to seal the doom of the entire party. Some threw themselves in despair upon the beach. Tears trickled down the cheeks of speechless women. Others moaned aloud their sad fate, for the coconuts were nearly exhausted, and starvation stared them in the face. The captain endeavored to cheer them with the hope that the boat had dragged her anchor into deep water, and that, after drifting across the bay, she would anchor herself again off one of the leeward islands.

This eventually proved to be the case, and the boat was recovered, nearly full of water, but uninjured. The weather now seemed to be breaking up; the trade winds blew less steadily, and all appearances indicated a change.

Secretly influenced by a gloomy undefined premonition of evil and disaster, as the result of the proposed attempt to reach the Navigator Islands without charts, the captain now determined on the apparently more desperate course of double-banking the boat with a crew of ten men, and, watching a favorable opportunity, endeavoring to pull to the nearest windward island. This course the mate opposed with all his influence and experience, declaring that he would rather venture alone than with ten mouths to feed; that it would be impossible to pull the boat so deeply loaded, against a head wind and sea, and that there was no place under their lee where they could make a harbor, in the event of encountering what might be expected— easterly weather. In fact, it was a life or death undertaking—success or certain destruction. The crew, with but a single exception, all volunteered, as before, to follow the captain.

At daybreak there came a change of wind; it was now blowing directly towards the Society Islands. The night had been stormy, heavy clouds hung in the western horizon, and the whole firmament was overcast with a drizzly rain. It was their first westerly wind, and the captain gave the order for immediate departure.

Let us remember the situation. The castaways were on a chain of small low islands, entirely surrounded by a coral reef, buffeted with angry breakers and enclosing a beautiful lagoon, ten miles across; at low water one could wade from one island to another. Every man, woman, and boy capable of service started on foot, while the crew pulled the boat, loaded with water and provisions, across the lagoon to the place selected to try the reef, distant about eight miles. The boat was carried over the land some two hundred yards and placed in the breakers, where it was held securely by the united strength of fifteen or twenty men, while her water and provisions were stored. Her crew of ten took their stations, and at the word they were safely launched once more upon the open sea. From now on, night and day, rain or shine, wind or calm, the oars were pulled, spell and spell, without ceasing. On the fourth day from their departure, they landed safely on Bora Bora. This was the only time during the eight weeks since the wreck that the boat could have succeeded in getting to windward, for, on the very day of their arrival at Bora Bora, the regular trade wind again set in and blew strongly from the east.

At Bora Bora, there were no white inhabitants. The king was on a visit to a neighboring island, and the natives at first regarded them with much suspicion, taking them for pirates. However, the captain engaged passage for himself, the second mate and one man, in a small native schooner, expected to sail on the following day for Tahiti, and dispatched the balance of the crew in the boat to the neighboring island of Riatia, with a letter to the British consul, there being no American consul nearer than Tahiti. That night, the captain of the Tahiti-bound schooner, afraid, probably, to embark the strangers, got under way and sailed over to Mopita, to report their arrival to the king. They were left in a bad fix again—no boat and no means of leaving the island.

On receiving the letter, the British consul sent an express over to Captain Lathum, of the schooner *Emma Backer,* and on the neighboring island of Huainea. Captain Lathum got under way without delay, called at Bora Bora, took Captain Pond on board, and proceeded to Scilly Island, where he rescued the passengers, carrying them all in safety to Tahiti.

Captain Pond's troubles did not cease here. Picked off a rock without a shirt to his back, he found himself detained by the French government, at the instance of the British consul, with the unreasonable demand that he provide the means of forwarding his former passengers to California. A lengthy correspondence ensued.

Finally, he was released from arrest. As an American citizen, he demanded a permit to leave the island, and, after much vexation and delay, succeeded in obtaining one, just in time to get a passage in the French ship *Africaine* to Callao, Peru, which vessel was already under way when he boarded her.

10.

Shackleton's Boat Voyage

IN 1916, Sir Ernest Shackleton, noted British explorer, astonished the seagoing world by a very daring small boat exploit. This adventure was the direct outcome of the loss of the *Endurance,* an auxiliary whaling bark, while under orders from the Admiralty to proceed to the Antarctic Continent by way of the Weddel Sea. The *Endurance* expedition was Shackleton's second attempt to reach the South Pole.

It was while the *Endurance* was working her way through the heavy pack ice in the Weddel Sea that she was crushed by the pressure of the floe, and sunk. There was only time enough to rescue some of the stores and equipment from the sinking ship, and these were removed to a spot on the drifting ice which the castaways called Ocean Camp. Here they lived for six months, warding off starvation by eating their dogs.

During the last days of May, 1916, the section of the floe on which the men were encamped rolled and

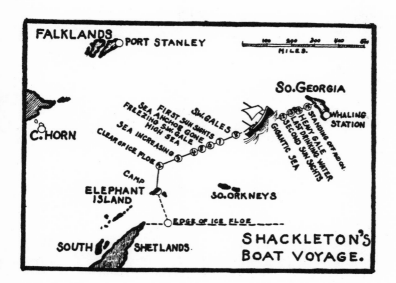

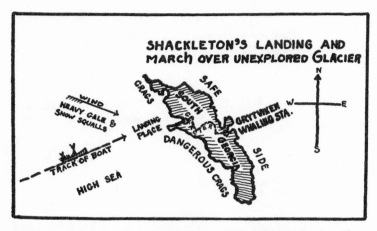

Sketch map to show Sir Ernest Shackleton's landing
on the dangerous side of South Georgia, and the track
of his thirty-six hour march across unexplored glaciers
to whaling station at Grytviken, for assistance.

pitched like a ship on the increasing swell, a sign that the ice pack was breaking up. The high land of Clarence Island, as well as the sharp peaks of Elephant Island, were now unmistakably made out and identified at a distance of about seventy miles.

On the sixth of April the men took to their boats for the last time. They decided to land on Elephant Island, where, according to the Sailing Directions, there was a beach and a cave which might give them shelter. In the imaginations of the distressed mariners the prospect of even such shelter as a cave under the cliffs of a bleak glacier island was pictured as a luxurious haven. But while Elephant Island was only seventy miles distant, ten days of fighting with unknown currents, false leads in the ice, freezing gales, and other incredible hardships were required to reach its shelter.

On a sand spit near the glacier, they hauled out their boats, turned them over and made their camp. There were twenty-eight men, all told, and their stock of emergency rations would normally last about ten weeks. It was the beginning of winter and the action of the ice was already forcing animal and bird life out in the direction of open water, and beyond their island, so any augmentation of their scanty stock by fresh food could not be relied upon. Also, it was too late to hope for rescue by a chance whaler. They were thus faced by starvation.

In this predicament Shackleton resolved on a boat voyage in search of relief. The nearest point from which assistance could be obtained was Port Stanley, in the Falkland Islands. But that was to windward, and though only 540 miles away, was clearly an impossible objective at that time of year in a ship's boat, with its light draft and small sail. Eight hundred miles to leeward was South Georgia Island, the point decided upon. There they might find a whaler and be back with relief within a month, if the sea was clear of ice.

One of the ship's boats, a double-ender named the *James Caird,* was selected for the dash to South Georgia. Shackleton merely mentions her as "an ordinary ship's whaler," which is a loose term applied to any double-ended boat not fitted with tanks and air compartments; if so fitted, it becomes a "life boat." He also remarks that this particular boat never looked large to him, and she looked particularly small in the light of a rough sea voyage. She had been racked as badly as the other two boats by rough handling on the ice, while on the escape from the ice she had been loaded with the bulk of the stores and equipment. The *James Caird* was twenty-two feet long, seven feet beam, and, after being raised up by an additional strake, was a little over three feet deep. Carpenter McNeish, who had a thorough knowledge of boats, was in charge of getting her ready for sea.

To prevent the already weakened boat from buckling in the heavy sea, it was necessary to fasten in a spare mast to the bottom of the boat, by way of a keelson. This did not make for extra room for crew and stowage, under the thwarts. A shelter deck was made of sledge runners boarded over with box covers, and this was fastened down with old nails backed out

of the cases. As it later proved, these nails were altogether too short for their new purpose.

To cover the deck a bolt of new canvas was broken
open. Though frozen stiff, it was thawed out, foot by
foot, over the blubber stove, before it could be cut,
sewed together and fastened in place. The pounding
of heavy seas soon found the weakness in this improvised deck, which leaked at every seam and became but
a sorry shelter for the men beneath. But it enabled
them the better to sustain life by keeping the Primus
stove lighted for the preparation of hot food, one of
the wisest provisions of this hazardous undertaking.

The Primus stove was provided with an aluminum
pot, and six and a half gallons of oil. The stove had
to be protected from the sea and spray which drove
through the deck when it was rough—and that was
most of the time. There was always great difficulty in
keeping the stove alight and preventing the "hoosh"
from splashing out of the pot. It took three men to
do this, one to hold the stove, and the other two to
stand by the pot which had to be lifted clear of the
stove at every heavy roll of the boat. The precious
pannikin of hot "hoosh" was made from the sledge
ration, and the hot milk, their second standby, was
made from milk powder.

The navigating equipment was complete enough for
practical purposes, and comprised a sextant, compass,
chronometer, and, as Shackleton says, "a very inac-
curate German chart of South Georgia Island." The
compass was without binnacle or light; in the night
they had to strike a match to check the course, but this

practice had to be stopped when the matches ran low. A triangular sea anchor, made of heavy canvas, was rigged and got ready for immediate use. In addition to stores and equipment, one thousand pounds of sand ballast in bags, and 250 pounds of ice to supplement the drinking water were put aboard.

While the fitting of the *James Caird* had been drawing to a close, an extra check was kept on the ice and weather conditions. The direction of the wind was all-important in the success of the voyage. Offshore winds opened the leads through the pack, while continued onshore winds closed the pack and locked them in.

On April 23rd, the wind was offshore, blowing storm force, and the island was swept by driving snow and heavy squalls. Shackleton climbed to the summit of the seaward rocks to examine the pack. He found the speed of the ice movement to be great, and observed that the icebergs were passing out to sea at the rate of four or five knots. The sea outside was clear, and he decided to make a start the following morning.

The crew of the *James Caird* consisted of five men besides Shackleton. This made two watches of three men each, the watches to be four hours on and four hours off. As it turned out, this was not too many men for the job on hand, even in a 22-foot boat. The first name on the crew list was Worsley, sailing master of the *Endurance*. He was a wizard at making snapshot observations in high latitudes, where the sun is almost always obscured. Second on the list was Crean, second officer of the *Endurance*. Both Crean and Worsley had been with Shackleton on former Antarctic expeditions.

McNeish, Vincent, and McCarthy completed the roster.

First Officer Wild had been selected to remain behind to keep the camp alive and maintain the morale of the twenty-two left on the sand spit of Elephant Island. Shackleton left the destiny of the survivors in his hands, in case the boat and the relief party never reached South Georgia. Taking all the hazards into consideration, Shackleton did not think that the proposed dash for relief added to the risk of anyone concerned, and prepared to shove off with that conviction, which he also impressed on his crew.

At midday on April 24th, 1916, Shackleton cut loose from the spit of Elephant Island and headed for the open sea. The leads appeared to be clear and the weather was fair and moderate. Everything looked promising. Standing in front of their camp, those who stayed behind appeared a pathetic little group in the eyes of the crew of the boat, so firm was their assurance of success. The men on the beach cheered their shipmates lustily as they set all sail and quickly vanished from sight.

Before nightfall, they were entirely clear of the pack and had open water before them, but they still steered due north to make sure of being clear. The swell was very heavy, making the first night aboard one of extreme discomfort. By running north for the first two days they hoped to get into warmer weather, and also to avoid the lines of pack ice which might be extending beyond the main body. They needed all the advantage they could get from the higher latitude for sailing on the great circle, but they also had to be cautious about possible ice streams. On the third day out they stood away to the east and headed on their course for South Georgia. The wind increased to gale force, while the heavy sea started trouble with the deck, soaking the crew below with icy trickles which were worse than driving spray. Now came the bailing, which gave the watch work enough to keep them warm.

The crew had now settled down to the routine of the voyage. Of comfort there was none. Water leaked in everywhere, thoroughly drenching them. When on deck a sailor will face any kind of weather cheerfully, in expectation of cheer below, but give him the merest trickle near his bunk and he is filled with utter misery and disgust.

The watch below got into their wet sleeping bags (made of reindeer skin), and sought rest under the thwarts on a layer of boulders which formed part of the ballast. They got to know every one of these boulders, and all of their individual characteristics, as they shoved them about in an effort to make room for their aching bones. There was no sleep—only a lapse into drowsy forgetfulness until called to shiver in the cockpit again. The man who then had to bail was considered lucky.

Cramped in their narrow quarters, they suffered severely from cold and sometimes frostbite. Another of their troubles was the chafing of their legs by wet clothes, which had not been changed for seven months. The insides of their thighs were rubbed raw and the pain was made none the less by the cruel bite of salt water. To complete their misery, crawling under the thwarts skinned their knees. But, for all this, there was among them a spirit of good cheer which needed only the merest opportunity to show itself, and in jokes at their own miserable plight their laughter always rang true.

The next day found them hove to under a double-reefed mainsail and the little jigger. Up to this time they had been making from sixty to seventy miles a day, which was good going in that kind of weather. The gale was from the southwest and in the Antarctic that is the cold semicircle. As the gale increased, the double-reefed mainsail had to be taken in, and the sea anchor streamed to keep the boat head to the sea. This gave them more comfort than lying to, but the sea anchor held them so hard that the sea often broke over the boat from end to end. Though shaky and weather worn, their little ship withstood this punishment; but much worse was yet to come to try their endurance.

A new enemy was upon them, the most dreaded of all, King Ice, in a new form. The freezing breath of the southwester had lowered the temperature toward zero, and the spray which froze upon the boat became an added peril. The accumulation of ice began perceptibly to reduce the buoyancy. In turns, the crew crawled out upon the deck, and with tools chipped and picked at it. They all saw and felt that the boat was no longer rising to the seas. Increased effort was demanded if they were to keep afloat.

The next day they began to lighten ship by heaving surplus gear over the side. Some spare oars frozen to the deck were chipped up, and discarded, two being kept for use inshore. Two of the thoroughly wet sleeping bags also went. They weighed about forty pounds each and had become frozen during the night. One of the men was laid up, and the two watches could use the same three bags, which would, also, save them from having to thaw out the frozen bags when they turned in. This reduction of weight relieved the boat somewhat and vigorous chipping did more. She again lifted to the seas. The sea anchor warp then parted and they fell off into the trough of the sea. Only the adequate ballasting kept them from rolling over, as they attacked the frozen mainsail with clubs and beat it until the ice cracked off. When it was finally set with the double reef still in, they came up into the wind again and all breathed more freely. As the boat was drifting off to leeward, there was no chance of recovering the lost sea anchor. They ate their scanty meal, treated their frostbite, and hoped for more moderate weather. There was a threatening sky and the sea still ran high, but at nightfall there came a blessed relief. Both wind and sea dropped and the violent snow squalls became less frequent.

The run, so far, had been made under an obscured sun, by dead reckoning, and it must be remembered that the leaden sky gave the helmsman no marks for steering by night. With no light in the binnacle, the course was kept by wind and sea. What a splendid job they were doing was shown by Worsley's sun sights on the seventh day out. They were exactly on their track and nearly halfway to South Georgia.

The sun came out bright and clear. They actually began to forget their troubles and to take an active interest in their surroundings. The wet sleeping bags were triced up in the rigging and given a chance to dry. Socks and other gear were all over the deck, which began to get dry in spots. The ice melted entirely off the hull. Friendly cape pigeons wheeled and swooped within a few feet of the boat. There was joy of life in the sun, and the hot meal was prepared and eaten in comfort for the first time.

During the next three days the good nor'westerly wind blew hard, and the *James Caird* sailed faster. No bergs were sighted and the men were freed of the fear of ice fields. Although the temperature was rising, they still suffered from the cold, for vitality was declining. An additional hot ration during the night was now required to sustain them. This also meant an additional lighting of the Primus stove with its increasing drain on the solitary tin box of matches.

On the eleventh day, they met high cross seas, the worst they had yet encountered, and passing snow squalls added to their hardships. The gale was from the nor'west, but shifted to the southwest quarter, and it began to freeze again. At midnight, Shackleton himself was at the tiller when he suddenly noticed a line of clear sky directly to windward. He called to the other men that the sky was clearing, but a moment later realized that what he had seen was not a rift in the clouds, but the white crest of an enormous wave. During his twenty-six years of experience at sea he says that he had not yet encountered a sea so gigantic.

It was a mighty upheaval of the ocean, a thing quite apart from the big white-capped seas that had been their tireless enemies for days. In a moment they were in a seething mass of water, but somehow the boat survived, half water-logged, sagging to the dead weight and shuddering at the blow. Then they bailed, fighting for life, and after ten minutes the boat again came up beneath them.

All of the gear was thoroughly wet again. The Primus stove and the aluminum pot were adrift in the bottom of the boat, and portions of the last "hoosh" permeated everything. Not until three hours later, chilled to the point of exhaustion, did they manage to get the Primus alight, make some hot drink, and revive their dejected spirits.

The sky was better on the twelfth day, and Worsley got a second set of sights. This time his observations put them but one hundred miles from the northwest corner of South Georgia. Two more days with favorable wind would put them within sight of land, and none too soon, for their drinking water was running low. The hot drink at night was necessary to sustain life, but the daily allowance of water was reduced to half a pint per man. This was bad enough, but thirst was increased because they were forced to drink brackish water out of a cask that had been stove against the rocks while loading the stores at Elephant Island. Now they discovered that the contents had been spoiled.

On the fourteenth day, at noon, through a rift in the clouds, McCarthy caught a glimpse of the black cliffs of South Georgia. The day had broken thick and stormy, with squalls from the northwest, and they had searched the waters for signs of land. These soon came. First was a bit of kelp, a sure signal of the proximity of land. An hour later they passed a larger piece of kelp, bearing two shags, and by these the mariners knew that they were not more than fifteen miles from shore, for these birds never venture far out to sea. A shag thus posted is as good as a light-house.

Though thirsty, chilled and weak, cheerfulness radiated from the voyagers as they stood inshore to look for a landing place. They soon made out the green tussock grass above the surge-beaten rocks. Ahead, and to the south, hungry rocks showed their teeth close to the surface, and over these the sea broke thirty or forty feet in the air. Thirst had now become a torment, and the condition of the company was desperate, but to have landed at that time would have been suicide. Night was falling, and the weather indications were unfavorable; there was nothing to do but to haul off until the following morning. They stood away on the starboard tack and then hove to in a high westerly sea to wait for daybreak.

The wind then shifted to the northwest and quickly increased to the most violent storm they had yet encountered. The wind and the sea were both driving the boat toward the rocks, but they could do nothing. At 1.00 P.M., through a rift in the flying spray, they caught a glimpse of the huge crags of the island. They were on a dead lee shore and the double-reefed mainsail was set in an effort to claw off. The danger and the increased strain on the boat made them forget their thirst. The afternoon wore away as they edged down the coast with the roar of breakers in their ears, and with a snow-capped mountain towering high above. The chances of escape from the lee shore during the night seemed small, when the wind suddenly shifted, and they were free once more to make a safe offing. With the shift of the wind, the gale moderated, and at this point they met with the first accident to the rigging. The pin that locked the mast to the thwart came adrift. Had this happened when they were clawing off the rocks, the venture would have ended in disaster. As they stood offshore again, they were, as their leader said, "tired to the point of apathy." Their drinking water had long since been finished, the last about a pint of hairy liquid which had been strained through a bit of gauze. At dawn, on the sixteenth day, there was practically no wind, and a high cross sea was running. Progress toward the shore was slow, but it was decided to make a landing at any hazard. Thirst was driving them to it.

About 8.00 A.M. the wind backed to the northwest and threatened another blow. A big indentation in the mountains, which they thought must be King Haakon Bay, had been sighted. They decided to land there and ran before a now freshening gale of wind. Great glaciers they saw, which offered no landing place, and the sea thundered against the naked rocks.

At the approach of dusk, a boulder-strewn beach which made a break in the cliffs on the south side of the

They decided to land there and ran before a now
freshening gale of wind.

bay, was made out, and they turned in that direction. This was to be their landing place, and in the gathering darkness the *James Caird* ended her voyage by racing in on the surf and touching the beach. The sound of a glacier stream, almost directly under their feet, was their welcome greeting, and never was water pure and sweet more needed by sea-worn and storm-beaten mariners.

The whaling station they had to reach was on the eastern side of the island, and between lay a mountain and glacier, which up to now no man had explored. For this, new strength was needed, so a camp was made and much feasting done. It was "hoosh" indeed, but this time made of succulent young albatross, plentiful among the crags. There were great sea elephants enough, strewn about the rocks, to provide food and fuel for months, had they chosen to stay there, but the twenty-two men on Elephant Island were their chief concern.

How the men made an unbroken 36-hour march over the glacier, how they descended to the Grytviken whaling station, secured relief ships, and finally, after almost superhuman effort, rescued their castaway ship-mates before the ice locked them in, is another epic. As for the brave little *James Caird,* she was towed around the island by the Norwegian whalemen, who regarded her with "professional interest," as Shackleton says, and at last, I believe, she found a safe heaven in Liverpool.

11

The Voyage of the Wager's Longboat

IN recounting the adventures of castaway crews in far seas, there is none more varied in tragic or stirring incidents than the boat voyage which grew out of the loss of one of Commodore Anson's squadron on the lower coast of Chile in 1741. It was at the time of the so-called "War of Jenkins' Ear," a naval conflict between Spain and England during the reign of George II, caused by British violation of trading regulations in the West Indies.

Spain attempted to put an end to their illicit trade by cruelty to English smugglers. Captain Jenkins, commander of the *Rebecca of Glasgow,* was the victim of the culminating outrage when the *comandante* of the *Guarda Costa* cut off his ear. Jenkins appeared in London with his starboard cathead in a handkerchief and this fresh tale of open and defiant insult to the flag proved the match to the gunpowder. The storm highly gratified the Bristol merchant class and they demanded

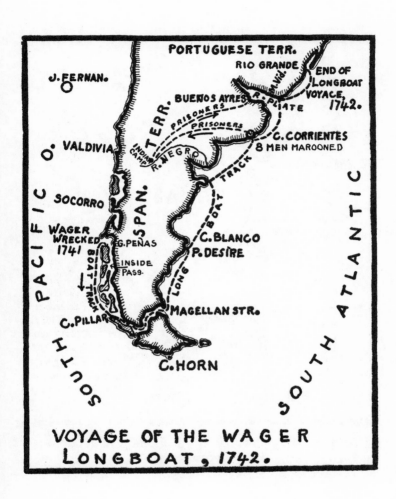

VOYAGE OF THE WAGER
LONGBOAT, 1742.

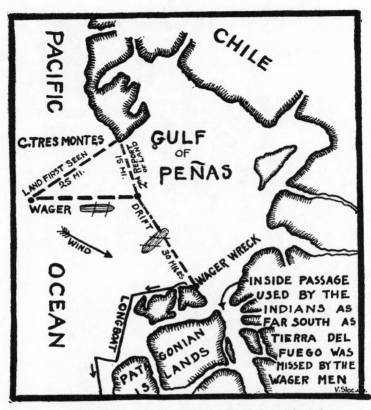

Map of *Wager* wreck and beginning of longboat
voyage

a war, which Prime Minister Walpole declared to be both unjust and uncalled for. During the previous twenty years Walpole had kept England out of war but he was unable to prevent this one which was acclaimed by the people with clanging of bells by day, and huge bonfires by night.

Admiral Vernon's quick and brilliant success at Porto Bello decided the war party to sweep the Don off the Pacific. Popular demand forced the unwilling Admiralty to recall Captain Anson, then cruising on the west coast of Africa, to take charge of this second expedition. Under Anson's flag sailed a force of six frigates and three auxiliaries, all mounting 236 guns and manned by 2000 seamen and marines.

The store ship of the squadron, with which this story has the most to do, was an old converted Indiaman, renamed the *Wager* in honor of the commissioner who was responsible for her purchase and rehabilitation. She was an unwieldy, tubby craft with capacious holds and had spent a long and honorable existence drifting before favorable winds and taking in sail every night on easy trade routes between England and the East Indies. Though greatly out of date in sailing qualities, and long since condemned by the surveyors of Blackwall, Commissioner Wager thought she was quite good enough for Anson. Thus the *Wager,* storeship, high of poop and broad of beam, as well as slow of sail, with some 400 tons of staple provisions and trade merchandise under hatches, waddled astern of the proud array.

Commodore Anson's departure from England was

observed by a display of official pomp and circumstance, his Instructions bearing the signature of the King himself; his broad pennant of command, hoisted to the main on the Centurion, was recognized by a salute of thirteen guns from each of his other ships as they passed in line, sheeting home, for sea. There was great jubilation in the fleet, for every man and boy there expected to come back with pockets filled with Spanish pieces of eight, for prize money and loot paid the bills.

Anson, on reaching the southern coast of Brazil, which was then a colony of neutral Portugal, put into Santa Catherina for a month for the recuperation of his men and for necessary repairs to his ships before starting on the passage around Cape Horn. On the way down the Patagonian coast they put into St. Julian's and there Lieutenant David Cheap was transferred from one of the frigates to take charge of the *Wager*, replacing Captain Kidd, her former commander, who had worried himself to death on the passage out over the unseaworthy state of his ship, and whose last utterance was a prediction of disaster to the *Wager*.

The new captain was the military type of naval officer, who, in that period, acquired commissions more through Court influence than adequate sea experience; he probably was a good gunnery officer on a large combatant ship but he proved to be entirely out of place on a ship which required the direction of a practical sailor, as did the dilapidated *Wager*. He had dash and courage, as well as arrogance and conceit which led him to try to cover his deficiencies by avoiding consultation with more experienced officers.

The *Wager,* being a non-combatant ship, rated only two line officers, the other of which was Beans, the first lieutenant, who was no more at home on board of her than was Cheap; as for personal qualifications he had all of his chief's arrogance and conceit without his dash and courage. In a harmless situation these two would have been a joke, but in the present case they were a tragedy.

They got on very well as long as they were within signal distance of the Commodore, but the fleet scattered in a two-months' battle with foul gales off Cape Horn which sent two of the frigates back to England. Then things began to happen.

Some of the *Wager's* rusty chain-plates came adrift and her mizzenmast went by the board, which loss made her less weatherly than ever. The carpenter made a cap to fit on the stump to ship a jury mast out of a lower stunsail boom, which was not much of a help in holding her to the wind. From the time of reaching the latitude of Magellan Straits the *Wager* was badly handled. Crippled, and sagging to leeward, she staggered along until she suddenly came into view of the snow-capped Cordilleras, which told her navigators that they were altogether too near the coast for safety. A lucky change in the wind gave them a chance to haul off and put the land out of sight. Cheap then seemed to forget the danger he had escaped and resumed his former course which carried him again toward the land, thus mystifying his officers who should have been consulted. When Lieutenant Beans remarked that their rendezvous with the rest of the squadron had been changed from Juan Fernandez (Robinson Crusoe's island), 300 miles off the coast, to Socorro Island which was inshore, Gunner Bulkeley responded in the 18th century sea vernacular:

"This is a very great misfortune for us. We can do nothing with the ship in the condition she is in upon a lee shore, and I am surprised that we should be obliged to go there."

The lieutenant said he found the captain determined to take the course nearest to the rocks, when he should be holding his weather gauge until reaching the latitude of his objective and then fall in with the land.

The gunner was a practical sailor and a navigator who had served many years in the Navy, and he never exchanged watches with the lieutenant without referring to the danger which was uppermost in his mind. The thought of destruction upon a lee shore worried both of the watch officers all the more when they began to see large patches of rock-weed floating by. Of this fresh indication of the proximity of land both the lieutenant and the master's mate were taking note when the gunner again asked, "Gentlemen, what can we do with the ship in the miserable condition she is in on a lee shore?"

"Whenever I have been with the captain," the lieutenant said, "I have always endeavored to persuade him to go to Juan Fernandez, therefore I would have you go to him, he may be persuaded by you though he will not by me."

"If that is the case," responded the gunner, "my going to him is needless."

But as soon as the noon sights were taken the captain sent for the gunner. This was something new, for the master's mate worked all the positions for Cheap, who never took a sight himself. The gunner had been navigator for Captain Kidd on the way out to St. Julian's, where he was replaced by the master's mate, and navigation became no longer a part of his duties.

The gunner knew that something was up as he went down the ladder to the captain's cabin. "Gunner, what longitude have you made?" the captain demanded.

"Sir, 82-30."

"What distance do you reckon yourself from land?"

"Sir, about 60 leagues, but if the two islands we saw are those which are laid down in your chart to lay off Brewer's Straits, and the same current continues with the western swell, we can't be above a third part of the distance off the land."

"As for currents," responded Captain Cheap, indifferently, "there is no accounting for them; sometimes they set one way, and sometimes another."

"Sir, very true; but as the ship has always been under reefed courses, with the mizzenmast gone, she must wholly drive to leeward, and nigher the land than expected."

"I suppose you are not unacquainted of my rendezvous for the Island of Nostra Signora di Socorro, in the latitude of 44°."

"Sir, the ship is in a very bad condition to come in

with the lee shore; and if it is possible to bring the ship to an anchor, we shall never purchase him again."

"I purpose to stand off and on for twenty-four hours; I don't design to come to an anchor; and if I don't see the Commodore, we will go for Juan Fernandez."

"Sir, the ship is a perfect wreck; our mizzenmast gone, with our standing rigging afore and abaft, and all our people down with scurvy; therefore I can't see what we can do with the land."

"It does not signify," concluded the captain, taking no notice of his gunner's suggestions, "I am obliged and determined to go for the first rendezvous." And those were the last navigational orders he was ever to give on the *Wager*.

In the morning, the ship fell in with Cape Tres Montes, the northern promontory of the Gulf of Peñas, and became trapped for the very reasons which the gunner had tried to make the captain understand. They drove on to the south shore of the indentation which was at that time not yet charted.

It is worth while to go back to the details. At eight in the morning, the straps of the fore jeer blocks carrying away, the ship was swung off before the wind and the yard lowered across the rails, to ease up on the repair work. The ship was thus steering directly toward the land, which was sighted by the carpenter who called it to the attention of a boatswain's mate, who agreed that it was plainly land. They reported it to the lieutenant, who, after taking a bearing on the compass, said it was only a cloud. It was impossible that land should bear north-north-west and be on the larboard bow as well. Dismissing the report from his mind, Beans walked across the deck and employed himself in other matters, while the men working on the jeer blocks became absorbed in their own job.

When the gunner came on deck at noon he saw the land broad off the larboard beam and found the ship still running in with the land. He was not long in getting the captain on deck. As soon as the fore yard could be swayed up again to its place, all possible sail was made and the ship wore around on the starboard tack in an attempt to claw off shore.

There was yet no land in sight when they found themselves among submerged rocks and great tumbling seas. It was a fearful night, inky dark and a howling gale of wind with biting, driving rain. The first impact with a sunken rock smashed the rudder, but the mere handful of men that could be mustered on deck skillfully dodged among the breakers by handling sheets, tacks and braces in a manner which displayed consummate seamanship. The ship was finally driven into a snug berth between two small islets, to settle down, a musket shot from the shore, into a convenient position for saving the crew. Their reaction to the disaster was astonishing, for the shock of the grinding hull upon the rocks and the snapping of falling spars aroused many of the men from the lethargy of disease to a fresh interest in life. It took a shipwreck to get them out.

The order in which the abandonment was effected was a violation of the laws of the sea. The captain and the principal officers left the ship first, and, taking refuge from the rain in Indian huts on the beach, gave an exhibition of official unconcern and hoggishness which added to the general confusion. A number of men refused to go ashore when ordered but instead fell to pillaging the ship. Arming themselves with the first weapons that came to their hands, they threatened to murder all who opposed them. Their leader was the boatswain, who, though below for a month, now became very lively. Breaking open the spirit room and broaching a cask of brandy, they all got drunk. Then, to give pandemonium a comic opera aspect, they, mad with liquor, paraded the ship in full dress uniforms which they had found in the officers' quarters. This wild license was but the result of the conditions they had endured and their hilarity was not surprising under the circumstances. Some of them tumbled down into the lower hold to lie in a stupor until drowned by a rising tide, which flowed freely through the broken hull.

When "the tumult and the shouting died," the boatswain hailed the beach for a boat to take him off, as though nothing at all had happened. Finding that no notice was taken of him, he chafed, viewed the captain's wigwam headquarters with rising indignation, and, bringing a four-pounder to bear upon it, fired a shot. The captain appeared, more enraged at the mutinous insult to his authority than at the cannon ball. When the boatswain finally landed, he knocked him down, called him a malingering son of a bitch, and,

When the boatswain landed, the captain felled him
with his cane.

standing over him with a cocked pistol, ordered him to go to work.

From these happenings it is not difficult to surmise the disorder and anarchy which took place when all the people got ashore. The men, knowing that their pay stopped when the ship was lost, decided that they were no longer subject to the orders of their officers. Acting on this one-sided theory, a group talked it over and concluded that they would leave the hard labor of scuttling the wreck for provisions to the ones who knew no better than to do it. The rebels, on refusing duty, and with a show of independence, made a habitation of their own at some distance from the main camp, living on mussels, until they decided that something must be done. Stealing a keg of gunpowder from the store tent, they laid a mine at the captain's wigwam and very nearly blew him up. Having thus enlisted public sympathy, they were at once supplied with the regular camp rations, including the daily whack of half a pint of brandy per man, which should have been enough to ward off melancholy.

During debarkation, the rain descended in torrents, and to make things as livable as possible, the men built a fire under a great tree which gave them a feeling of protection until temporary shelters could be erected, the first of which was an overturned boat. During the five months they were there, the camp grew to a village of eighteen canvas houses with a store tent in the center.

At the end of the first two months, the original one hundred and sixty who landed were reduced by scurvy and accident to a fairly permanent muster of one hundred souls. Food now became the main problem, for the ship's staples had dwindled to a point which obliged them to depend largely on mussels and seaweed like any aquatic animal. The mussels were easy to eat, but it took ingenuity to make the different kinds of seaweed palatable. One kind was found to go down best when dipped in a thin flour batter and fried in tallow candle grease. It was eaten like bread and helped to make the meagre whack of flour go the longest way. Another kind of weed, which the sailors called "dulse" was made into a cream soup by boiling, for in two hours it thickened the water like flour. An effective part of their unwonted diet was the wild celery which grew in profusion on the island, to say nothing of the currant bushes which yielded fruit in due season.

The men lost their best chance of learning how to adapt themselves to life in their new and wild environment when they drove off some Canoe Indians who tried to settle on the island with them. These Indians had quickly nosed out the wreck and at first came in a shy way to trade live sheep and dogs for clothing. After a few such visits in single canoes, five canoes paddled out of the "south lagoon" and landed fifty men, women and children, who pitched their wigwams.

These Indians were reported to be a simple and inoffensive people of low stature, well shaped, of a copper color, with tangled black hair, deeply set eyes and flat noses. The children went naked in spite of the weather which was as cold as an English winter. The older ones wore otter skins and blankets and never seemed to be sensible of stormy weather. If caught without a wigwam they were often seen sleeping in the rain without covering. Never without a fire either on land or in their canoes, they lived continually in smoke which took toll of their eyes.

Like other savages, the males were exempt from hardship and labor, for the females provided the daily food from the bottom of the sea. The women, accordingly, dove into deep water for sea-eggs while their lords squatted by the fire. Holding a small basket in her teeth, a woman would jump out of her canoe into six fathoms of water, to remain under for a length of time which made her appear as amphibious as a seal.

As the Canoe Indians are now known to frequent the reaches immediately to the southward of the Gulf, it is certain that the "south lagoon" out of which the canoes came could have been none other than Tarn Bay, leading into Messier Channel which is the head of the passage to Fuegian waters. Had the confidence of the Indians been intelligently cultivated, valuable knowledge of the channels back of the islands might have been gained which would have been of great use later. Some of the white men attempted liberties with the wives of the Indians. Although the women were slaves and drudges, the tribe had great regard for the unwritten law. In a single night the Indians vanished. Later in the season other natives visited the island, but they were distant and hostile, with no disposition to trade.

Captain Cheap, undaunted by catastrophe, and

mindful of his orders to join the Commodore "wherever he might be found" determined to fit up the boats and to make his way to Valdivia. With a hundred men "in health" he was confident that he could board and master any Spanish vessel he should meet in those seas. If he gained an enemy coaster loaded with flour, so much the better; then, with supplies replenished and with a vessel again under his feet, he could go on to Juan Fernandez. Should he meet with no prize on the way, his boats could still carry him there.

Reasoning in this way, he cheerfully ordered the carpenter to saw the longboat in two and to stretch her out to carry sixty men under the hatches. This new boat would be the flagship of his flotilla. Carpenter Cummins considered that twelve feet added to the length of the boat would make it large enough, and the work of reconstruction was started at once, with a sail hung over the job to keep the rain off. There was no unusual problem in regard to materials, tools or hardware, for the wreck supplied everything but the additional timbers in the center of the boat. These were hewn out of beech which grew on the island.

When the new schooner was completed after four months of work, she measured up to 23 tons. Her length was 40 feet; breadth of beam 10 feet; depth of hold 4 feet; draught 5 feet.

The captain's Valdivia project was due to fail largely through his shooting, in a fit of anger, of Midshipman Cozens, who died fourteen days later. This act so embittered the crew against the Captain that they were no longer inclined to listen to his orders.

Gunner Bulkeley became the new leader. He had come upon Narborough's "Voyages," a book written seventy years before, describing the Straits of Magellan. It became clear to him that a boat voyage by that route to Brazil could be the means of escape from the island. Bulkeley had the ability to carry out the project as well as the confidence of the men, but he was to encounter great difficulties.

Under pressure, Bulkeley drew up a formal paper setting forth that: "We whose names are undermentioned, do, upon mature Consideration, think it the best, surest and most safe way, for the Preservation of the Body of the People on the Spot, to proceed through the Streights of Magellan to England. Dated at a desolate Island, on the coast of Patagonia, in the Latitude of 47 Deg. and 40 Min. in the South Seas, this 2nd day of August 1741."

This document, duly signed by all the officers except Lieutenant Beans, the purser, and the surgeon, and by twenty-five seamen, was publicly read to Captain Cheap at the usual noon gathering before the store tent. The captain rightfully regarded the paper as a mutinous instrument, and although angered, declared that he was agreeable to anything "for the Preservation of the People." He secretly resolved to get the better of the gunner and his adherents. In order to accomplish that purpose he hoped to take advantage of his opponent's contemplative tendencies, for the latter was often seen reading his Thomas à Kempis.

One night the wily Lieutenant Beans called upon the warrant officers in their quarters with a new proposal, namely, that since a place for divine service on each Sabbath Day was wanting, it would be proper to use their commodious tent for that purpose. The officers remembered that the duty of public prayer had been entirely neglected on board, and they took it that religion had little to do with this proposal. What if they were surprised during their devotions and their arms taken from them in order to frustrate their plans and to prevent their return to England by the Straits of Magellan or any other way?

On discovering that the captain was trying to undermine them, the "Magellans" were now obliged to act with resolution to defeat his official influence, and the time had come for a showdown. The men were now forced either to face charges by the Admiralty for deserting their lawful commander or to boldly arrest him on some technical charge and carry him with them as a prisoner to England. This problem was neatly solved by the officer in charge of the marines, who ordered the captain's arrest for murdering the Midshipman Cozens. That worked, and Cheap, who took his change of fortune with admirable courage and dignity, was led as a prisoner to the tent where he was to be confined until the sailing of the longboat.

On his way he met Beans who had replaced him in command. Ironically calling him "captain," he apologized for not pulling off his hat, "because," he said, "my hands are confined," adding, "you shall be called to an account for this in England."

Issuing a formal statement that he never intended to go to the southward, Cheap further said: "Gentlemen, I do not want to go off in any of your craft and I have more honor than to turn my back upon my enemies. I never designed to go for England, and would rather chuse to be shot by you; There is not a man on the beach who dare to engage me; but this is what I feared." He then parleyed for release to go his own way after the departure of the Magellans, a request that was put to vote and granted. "Let him stay and be damned," chorused the crew, who again swore that they did not want to go to a Spanish prison.

At daylight on October 12th, the longboat, now named the *Speedwell,* was launched and provisioned. Reasonable requests by the captain in regard to a share in the stores and equipment were readily agreed to. He also sent word to the rebels to learn if they would go with him in the yawl and the barge which had been assigned to him by the mutineers. They agreed. Cheap then wished the Magellans safe and well to England.

The longboat put into a snug fiord at the offshore end of Wager Island, before heading for sea, to make the final preparations and to cook, on shore, the twelve days' rations for their run down the coast. There was no galley on board and that was the estimated length of time they expected it would take to reach the Straits. They were accompanied for a short distance by the barge in charge of Midshipman Byron, who was supposed to be a part of the Cheap outfit. John Byron, at that time but 17 years old, was to become a noted explorer of the Pacific, a fighting admiral, and an ancestor of a great poet who became proud of referring to a book on the wreck of the *Wager* as his "Grand dad's Tale."

It is not clear whether the future admiral intended to desert Cheap at the last moment or whether he was just looking Beans and his "mutineers" over before their final departure.

Wager Island is the northernmost part of a great archipelago which reaches from the Gulf of Peñas to Fuegian waters. It is mountainous and bold like the mainland and intersected by deep and tortuous channels which bewilder the imagination. The entire Patagonian coast from Valdivia to Cape Horn presents a maze of salt water sounds and fiords almost as secret today as when the buccaneers chose them for their hiding places.

Between the archipelago and the mainland is a smooth water route all the way south; that is, it may be said to be smooth, for the space between the shores is so confined that even a wind of great fury cannot kick up a sea sufficiently high to swamp a well-appointed ship's boat. In many respects the Patagonian channels resemble the inland waterways of our own Alaska, which are quite comfortable for the navigation of moderate sized motor boats.

The Patagonian coast, outside, is wild and rough, battered almost constantly by the westerly gales which raise mountainous seas. Of the inland route to the south, the longboat knew nothing. They were obliged to sail and explore for places of refuge at the same time, an interesting experience in the exercise of self-reliance which the modern yachtsman, with his closely checked coasting chart, is denied. There is a strange thrill in not quite knowing. A large part of the longboat's track down the coast was from 5 to 10 miles off, and inside of the 50-fathom line, making her fall in with thick settlements of rocks, both visible and submerged. The submerged rocks blind-break in heavy seas.

The Magellan party, in charge of Lieutenant Beans and Bulkeley, with the carpenter and master's mate as assistants, was now ready to sail in two boats; the longboat with sixty people on board and the cutter with twelve. At the first good slant they put to sea and before night made the shelter of Breaksea Island where they found a fine landlocked and sandy bay. In two days they weighed and passed between Cape Dyer and Dundee Rock which stood out of the sea like a great ship. A strong northwest gale with a high following sea now drove the boats southward at a good speed. To prevent separation during the night the cutter passed her painter to the longboat which was of greater length and weight and therefore sailed faster through the heavy seas. At daybreak they were off Cape Primero, having covered 129 miles in twenty-four hours since leaving Breaksea. During the fearful night they drove past many blind breakers but managed to escape.

At 6 A.M. they opened the Gulf of Trinidad, hauled in and made the harbor of Port Henry. Here the small vessels lay secure in a cove which nature had formed like a dock. There was no occasion to let go an anchor, but just to run alongside the land and make fast, bow

and stern, under a perpendicular cliff. Here they found
the land very high and steep on each side with great
waterfalls all along the coast. They liked this haven
of rest but they thought that the outlying dangers were
too great for "any ship to fall in with the land." They
took advantage of the bad weather by baking more
cakes upon the rocks, and left on the third day to
round Cape Rugged. At the pitch of this cape they
obtained their first meridian altitude of the sun in
latitude 50, which checks exactly. This accuracy was
due to the use of the new "pig yoke" quadrant invented
for sailors by astronomer Hadley, which measured
celestial angles by reflection instead of by guess as did
the old cross-staff that Columbus used to discover
America.

Twenty-five miles south of Cape Rugged, after sailing in smooth water under the lee of some small
islands, they found a bay with a fine sandy beach and
anchored there until morning. At 7 A.M. they weighed
to fall in with a rough tumbling sea and by night they
had doubled Cape West Cliff on Duke of York Island
and anchored in Port Morales. With a strong wind
blowing directly in the bay they found it "an indifferent
place of shelter."

While in Port Morales the cutter broke adrift on
a dark, stormy night and was lost together with Seaman Stewart, who was alone on board. It was their
first stroke of bad luck. Besides the loss of a life, it
also meant the loss of future means of going ashore
in shoal water, for the longboat was not beachable.
There should have been four men in the cutter at all

times to handle the oars in case of accident, and for this sheer disobedience of her crew Bulkeley gave all hands hell.

"We have seventy-one men in this vessel and not above six of you that give yourselves the least concern for your lives, being ripe for mutiny and destruction; this is a great affliction to the lieutenant, the carpenter and myself, and we know not what to do to bring you under command. We are weary of our lives. Therefore, unless you alter your conduct and subject yourselves to command, we will leave you to yourselves and take our own chances in this desolate part of the globe rather than give ourselves any more concern about so many thoughtless wretches."

Strong language, this, to arouse victims of apathy, for life on board was beginning to be unbearable; it was heard said that the boat was worse than any jail in England. Stench from the wet clothes on so many bodies in the crowded hold made the air unfit to breathe. The *Speedwell* was already crowded beyond capacity and the cutter crew could see that the loss of the boat was their own fault, so they offered to go ashore for the preservation of them all. They entered a formal request to that effect and signed the logbook to attest that they were not being put off "contrary to their inclinations." The longboat was hauled close to the rocks to allow them to land with whatever supplies could be spared. The men assured Lieutenant Beans that they expected to do well; to find the cutter and to return to Wager Island. In case the cutter should not be found, they could make a canoe. That was the last ever seen of that brave, self-sacrificing crew.

By morning the wind dropped to a light breeze and, shipping her oars, the *Speedwell* pulled out of Morales. Outside they caught a strong fair wind which boomed them southward again so well that on the next day some high land came into sight which was visible for twenty miles. A point bearing southeast and with no land to the southward of it was rightly taken for Cape Victory. Four islands they next sighted proved to be the "Islands of Direction" (*Evangelistas*) mentioned in Narborough, which they had on board as their only guide to the Straits. By a sight for latitude, made two days before, and by dead reckoning since, the gunner knew that they were in the entrance to the Strait.

A hard northwest gale set in, driving them before it under bare poles. Never in their lives, said they, in any part of the world, had they seen such a sea as ran here. Every wave seemed likely to swallow them. When the weather cleared, they sighted the north shore and put in among the rocks for shelter. Twenty-seven days from the start, the longboat anchored in a spot as smooth as a mill pond on the south side of Condor Island. Their twelve-day ration prepared before leaving, which was supposed to carry them well into the Straits, was now long gone.

The next day, with the wind much abated, they weighed and ran further in and came to under a steep rock which hung over the vessel. Looking up, they saw two Indians peering over the edge. These made signs for the men to come ashore and two of the crew did so, going unarmed to allay suspicion, for the Indians had no weapons but their clubs for killing seal. The Indians fled as the men came toward them, but the next day they brought a mangy dog which the sailors killed at once and ate, for they had had no food but raw flour for nearly a week.

In three days, the men, somewhat refreshed, left Condor Island in light weather and steered to the southward until they came in sight of the south shore, which appeared like an island stretching to the east. On the western extremity of the island they made out two hummocks like sugar loaves, and to the south of these, a large point of rocks, forming all of the landmarks identifying Cape Pillar. Narborough had plainly stated that Cape Pillar was on the right hand of the entrance of the Straits on going in, but Lieutenant Beans contended that, granting it was Cape Pillar which they saw, they were still wrong, for according to his way of thinking they would be in a blind sound to the northward of the Strait. Master's mate Jones agreed with Beans, Narborough to the contrary notwithstanding. As it was coming on night and the weather was by this time too boisterous to beat out around the cape in search of the supposed "right passage," they anchored in Port Churraca, on the south side of the Strait, to settle the argument. The gunner had been right in the first place, and now he was more assured than ever that they were at the entrance of the Straits of Magellan.

It is difficult to account for the strange controversy raised by Lieutenant Beans, for he must have been as hungry and as eager to reach the end of the terrible voyage as anyone else in the boat. At least a dozen men in the boat were lying in a coma, waiting for the end. As for information about the Straits, neither he nor the master's mate could possibly know more about them than was given in Narborough's account. It was the same kind of official conduct that the lieutenant had exhibited when he refused to believe that Cape Tres Montes was anything more than a cloud on the horizon when everyone else on the deck declared it to be land. The same manner of thinking was now to be the cause of 150 miles of extra sailing, the loss of seventeen days with the crew starving, and the loss of at least five more lives.

On the gunner's insistence that they give the "north sound" a try, the lieutenant agreed to set sail, and, running before a light fair wind for five hours, they came abreast of the flat summit of Cape Lunes at the entrance of Long Reach. It was an unmistakable landmark rising a sheer thousand feet from the sea and it was well identified. The very name, which is the Spanish word for "Monday," indicated that it was plotted by Sarmiento, who had made a survey eighty-six years earlier than Narborough. But that meant nothing to the lieutenant.

The gunner warmed up and offered to stake his life on the issue that they were in the straits. The lieutenant and the master's mate then agreed to run a few more miles down the reaches, bordered on each hand by rocky mountains covered with snow. They passed through Crooked Reach, only a mile and a half wide, at the point where it is guarded by Cape Quad, but they passed the Cape in the rain without sighting it. The longboat was then doing well and was only fifty miles from Cape Froward, the turning point in the Straits toward the north. Both Beans and the master's mate gave it to the gunner that he was wrong and they were for running toward the Atlantic no longer, though it was blowing a hard fair wind and another league would have convinced everybody. The lieutenant and the master's mate had their way. After eighteen days of fearful beating back to the Pacific, over ground already covered, the longboat came for the second time within sight of Cape Pillar. It took all this cruel hardship to make the lieutenant recognize his error and to interpose no more objections to the navigation. The master's mate was only his jackal. The crew, who got the worst of it, took on new hope as a brisk wind bowled them back toward home. On the morning of the second day they were abreast of Cape Froward.

At Friend Bay, across Froward Reach, they raised some smoke, and, putting in, managed to get ashore to trade with the Indians for seal and dogs which they cooked and ate on the rocks. On leaving they seized a bark canoe for a tender but that was soon towed under and lost. Not stopping for anything, they made Fresh Water Bay on the third day, coming to anchor for an hour in seven fathoms. Why they did not water here is unexplainable for it is a natural watering place, the River Aquafresca emptying there after tumbling down the mountains. On the following day they anchored off the northern end of Elizabeth Island, thirty-eight miles further along, still looking for wood and water.

They weighed again next day and stood for the Narrows to make the Foreland. In the afternoon they hauled in for Fish Cove, expecting to land and to shoot some guanacoes, but the wind blew them out into the Narrows again where they met the flood which here runs very strong. At midnight they anchored in five fathoms about a mile from the shore. Weighing early in the morning, they soon got out of the Narrows to haul in for a shallow bay on the north shore to again seek for water.

As there was no tender, some one strong enough to stand the cold water had to swim ashore, and this the boatswain was able and willing to do. After half an hour's search he came back down to the beach and sang out for the boat to send a cask ashore. That done, they took their anchor aboard and removed two miles farther out where they thought there would be no danger of stranding. They discovered, however, that it ebbed dry for three miles out and that the boat settled on foul ground which would have stove her to pieces had there been any sea on. While the boat was high and dry, they got out all of the casks to be filled and managed to put most of them on board at next high water. Then it came on to blow.

On December 11th, at noon, with a strong fair wind, they stood out of the bay for Cape Virgins and entered the Atlantic just a month from the time they first sighted Cape Pillar, on the Pacific side. Had it not been for Beans' ill-advised order, they would have been in Rio Grande rather than just rounding the pitch of the Virgins. On the 275-mile run to Port Desire they passed St. Julian's without putting in for their salt, a second inexplicable tragedy. Captain Cheap had referred to St. Julian's while he was glibly discussing the proposed boat voyage in council, remarking, "When we come to St. Julian's we shall be sure of salt in plenty for our provisions, without which our fowls (penguin) will not keep above two or three days." All concerned were well acquainted with the salinas at that port which supplied the squadron on the way out, and the failure of the longboat to go in there for her salt before reaching Port Desire cost them dearly and added the last fatal touch to their misery.

They lay for ten days in Port Desire recuperating from the Magellan punishment, and on the first day there they killed more seal and penguin in half an hour than they could take on board. But there was no way of keeping it to the end of the voyage and there were yet 1,500 miles to go to reach Rio Grande. Some of the men, gorging themselves on the tough meat, became very sick. A water party found "Peckett's Well" in the very place described by Narborough. Although the flow of water was very limited, producing but thirty gallons per day, they took full advantage of it in filling up.

Life for the men in the *Speedwell* was now intolerable, and their numbers were slowly reduced by accident and starvation. Between the time of passing the

Virgins and arriving at Rio Grande, thirteen human beings, reduced to skeletons, were cast into the sea. From Cape Pillar to the Virgins the toll had been seventeen.

On leaving Port Desire, an argument about the flour allowance was settled by serving out the whole remaining lot at once, which amounted to three and a half pounds per man. Aside from this there was nothing but the high seal, which only a third of the men could choke down. That was to be their subsistence for the month or more it would take to arrive at Brazil, or to put them beyond the reach of enemy Spaniards.

Fourteen days after leaving Port Desire, land was sighted to the southwest of Cape Corrientes and, after cruising along a league from the shore, they came to anchor in a sandy bight which they called Shoalwater Bay. Roaming over the grassy shore they could discern horses more numerous than the sheep in their own Dorset and Wiltshire. The prospect animated the boat's crew who were now at the bitter end. Enemy or no enemy, they were obliged to land, for to sail farther without meat or water meant certain death. Having no small boat on board for a tender, fourteen of the ablest leaped into the sea to swim watercasks and muskets through the surf. On the rocks was an abundance of seal which were shot and cut up into quarters to be sent on board. Meanwhile, the wind came on to blow so hard that it was impossible to load the meat, so that the men left on board were in a worse plight than ever, for now they were actually starving in the sight of plenty. Unable to endure longer the torture of watching the beach party roast and eat their meat, they stripped off and fell to chewing a sealskin hatch cover.

At dawn it was fine and calm, which made it possible to veer in close to the shore. A line was sent on shore to pull in the seal. In addition to the seal, a horse had been shot that very morning bearing the brand "AR", which indicated that Spaniards were not far off. As no sudden change in the weather was expected, several of the men, always keeping a lookout for enemies, scattered to try a shot at the wild dogs which were running with the horses. The meat and water safe on deck, seven of the shore party returned on board, among them the boatswain, the carpenter, and a lieutenant of marines.

No sooner were they on board than a breeze came in and kicked up a sea which obliged the boat to weigh and then to come to anchor again in deeper water, a league off shore. The dog hunters, numbering eight, returning to the shore, found the vessel out of reach and a high surf already tumbling in. During the night the gale increased in force, carrying the line of breakers out to the anchorage of the longboat, which was now forced to make sail to avoid foundering. Had her cable parted, all on board would have perished. Before weighing, a scuttled puncheon was sent ashore containing clothing, four muskets with ball, powder, flints, a kettle and some candles; also a letter informing them of the boat's danger and of the impossibility of her riding it out till they could get off. The Eight thus

abandoned on the beach, after examining the message
of the puncheon, sank on their knees and made signals
of despair as they watched their only link with home
disappear from sight. Before night the longboat, finding that she could not clear the land, came to anchor
two leagues from the shore to ride out a hard gale
and a great sea.

Three days later the *Speedwell* anchored at the
north shore of the La Plata estuary, and the boatswain
again swam ashore to look for water. He was met
at the beach by two men on horseback who took him
away to their caravan. Several others, seeing that the
boatswain had gotten through, also swam ashore to
fill water, of which by this time there was not a drop
on board. One of the men drank so much that, in
attempting to swim back, he sank before reaching the
vessel and was drowned. That day they were able to
get one cask of water on board.

On the day following, both the gunner and the carpenter swam ashore where four of the inhabitants
came down on horseback to meet them, and although
Spaniards, they could speak Portuguese, a language the
gunner understood. The four horsemen explained that
they were fishermen from Monte Video, which was
two days' journey away, and that they sold their fish
salted and dried in Buenos Aires. Yes, they were on
land belonging to the King of Portugal, but there were
many settlements of Spanish fishermen over the border
and no one cared. The fishermen were very communicative. England was still at war with Spain and there
were many Spanish men-of-war in the La Plata waters,

belonging to the squadron of Pizzaro which had been
sent out to intercept Anson at Cape Horn. The ships
were now stationed all about; only a few weeks before,
a 74-gun ship had parted from her anchors in a great
storm to drive on the shoals of English Bank; the ship
was lost and every man perished. That must have been
a storm similar to the one that came upon Cape Corrientes but a few days before, when the eight men were
left on the beach at the mercy of Providence. The
account of the loss of the seventy-four was interesting
to the Englishmen but they became alarmed when told
of another one of Pizzaro's war ships which was pa-
trolling the coast all the way to Rio Grande. Here, at
the very end of the voyage, capture looked them in
the face.

The fishermen were hospitable and invited the two
strangers to get up behind them to ride to the caravan,
where they were entertained with jerked beef and
white bread. Of the beef there was none to be bought,
but at the sight of gold the fishermen consented to
part with twenty-six tu'penny loaves for four guineas,
which, after all, was not a worse deal than when members of the longboat party sold their distressed shipmates their ration of flour at a guinea a pound, and
ate mussels themselves. In principle, that was next to
cannibalism. The *patrone,* on selling the sailors the
bread, said that if this trading became known to the
Governor of Buenos Ayres, they would all be hanged.
He then offered to get them, in two hours, ducks sufficient to serve all on board if they would but lend him
a musket, which they did. But after the Englishmen

got back to the caravan they noticed that one fisherman and one horse were missing. Suspecting that the man had gone to betray them to the military, they did not wait for the ducks but shoved off with the water and made ready to sail on the morrow for Rio Grande. With nothing now to sustain life but water, and with all hands starving, there were yet 300 miles to go. For the next week there was drifting with little winds and calms until after rounding Cape Santa Maria, which greeted them with thunder, lightning and rain. That opened the last stretch up the coast.

On January 27th, the gunner got a meridian altitude of the sun and by the latitude so obtained reckoned that the *Speedwell* would be in port the following morning. On the 28th of January, 1742, they anchored on the east shore of the Rio Grande, 116 days from Wager Island, having covered a sailing distance of 3000 miles. When the Portuguese governor heard the story of the *Speedwell,* he was first incredulous and then, amazed. He took them for Spanish spies making a reconnaissance survey of his coast. Beans, passing the buck as usual, pointed to the gunner as the "pilot," and the latter was thoroughly questioned. The Governor wanted to know if there were a chart on board, and if not, how they could hit the bar and venture into such a hazardous place.

The gunner responded that "as for a chart he had none of any kind but that he had a good observation the day before and their vessel drew so little water, that they kept their lead going and in the necessity they were in, they were obliged to venture, and had they not seen the opening they must have been compelled to run the vessel ashore." Bulkeley was then examined concerning all the places the boat had stopped, from the Virgins to the Rio Grande, and particularly on what had happened when they were sailing by Cape Santa Maria, where the Spanish man-of-war was reported. The Governor, after thoroughly satisfying himself that he had before him some genuine English seamen in distress, embraced the officers and extended them hospitality as well as the freedom of the port, entertaining them well and ordering the sick to be properly cared for in hospitals. Beans and Pemberton were taken by the Governor to his villa in the country where they remained three weeks.

People flocked to view the longboat and marveled that thirty men could be stowed in so small a vessel; that she had once contained twice that number was beyond their comprehension.

From Rio Grande, the survivors were sent on various ships to England by way of Portugal. Lieutenant Beans reached England first and told a story derogatory to both Gunner Bulkeley and Carpenter Cummins, to whom he probably owed his life. His was such a tale of piracy and mutiny that the two warrant officers responsible for the success of the voyage, and for saving one-third of the crew, were not permitted to land on first reaching Spithead, within sight of their homes; instead they were detained two weeks on the ship as felons, awaiting transfer to the prison ship at Portsmouth. Special instructions were issued from the Admiralty to prevent their escape.

In a fortnight their status was changed to that of prisoners at large, and they were allowed to go home, only to be reminded by every neighbor they met: "You are going to be hanged." "For God's sake, what for?" asked Bulkeley, "for not being drowned?"

To quote Bulkeley: "On the following Sunday we were had up to Prayers, where there was a great Congregation, the Text was taken out of the Psalms. 'Them that go down to the Deep, and occupy their Business in Waters, see the works of the Lord.' In the Latter Part of the Sermon, these Words were applied: 'Men should not feed themselves up in vain Notions or Expectations of a reprieve of Pardon, for how often are Men deceived even at their last Moments. And men that have seen so many Providences of the Divine Being, it's not to be doubted but they are prepared',' etc.

When, three years later, Captain Cheap returned to England on a French ship, as an exchanged prisoner, after a long imprisonment in Valdivia, the specifications of the court martial were altered into a mild inquiry "to know how the *Wager* was wrecked." The blame was placed upon Lieutenant Beans "for failure to put the wheel over soon enough after the ship struck, and so remained fast between the rocks," although it may be recalled that the rudder was already unshipped. Nothing was said about Cape Tres Montes, and coming in with the land in sight for an entire watch on deck. Beans got off with a perfunctory reprimand, everyone else concerned was honorably acquitted, and all survivors received pay up to the time the ship was lost.

Commodore Anson, who by that time had returned from a round-the-world trip full of glory and political power, insisted that two important changes be made in the Navy regulations. Thereafter, a seaman's pay was continued after a wreck; and secondly, a corps of marines was established on a permanent basis, thus making them entirely distinct from the army. In his wisdom, he made it impossible for a gang of castaways to refuse to salvage provisions thrown up on the beach, on the ground that they were not being paid for such work; impossible, also, for a mere captain of marines to arrest the commanding officer of his ship even for shooting one of his midshipmen.

For a time, John Bulkeley was placed in command of a coast guard cutter chasing smugglers in the English Channel, and later he had a privateer of forty guns in the same waters. However, after giving up the sea he came to America and settled in Philadelphia, a natural thing to do, for it was Peter Bulkeley, a forebear of his, who had founded Concord and assisted in the settlement of New Plymouth Colony.

The experiences of Midshipman Morris and his seven shipmates after they had been abandoned by the longboat at Cape Corrientes comprised the strangest adventures of the *Wager* castaways. They were marooned on a grassy plain bordering the La Plata, about 250 miles due south of the Spanish town of Buenos Ayres. The Pampas, extending for 600 miles to the Andes, were the home of countless herds of wild horses, the descendants of the few turned loose by Mendoza 200 years before when he had tried to found Buenos Ayres. The Pampas were also the stamping grounds of several tribes of Patagonian Indians who roamed from Buenos Ayres to the Straits of Magellan.

As soon as Morris and his men were able to get their bearings, they resolved to make themselves comfortable until strong enough to reach civilization. As it was yet the dry season, their first step was to bivouac in a ravine between the cliffs of the coast with the sky for a roof, and where a nearby spring supplied them with water. They lived on seal and armadillos which they boiled with seaweed to give a savor of salt; later they were obliged to revert to the very primitive method of eating meat raw like carnivorous animals.

After a month of good living, they felt able to commence the long march ahead. Weighted down by muskets, knapsacks stuffed with dried meat and the seal bladders filled with water, they managed to travel sixty miles in two days, only to find the country burned up with the drought and themselves dependent upon the water in their own small canteens. Fearing that they would perish when the water was gone, they wisely retraced their steps to their first base and decided to wait for the rainy season. In camp they could live indefinitely, for they had flints to strike fire and they could obtain animal food by hitting a seal on the nose with a club.

In holes in the ground they found four litters of wild dogs consisting of thirteen newly whelped pups. This "Thirteen" was a lucky find which the men carried home. The pups, raised on seal broth, forgot their wild relatives and became self-respecting hunters of armadillos and partridges for the camp.

Each man hunted with a brace of these dogs, one luckily bringing down a deer and another taking two wild pigs, a boar and a sow, which were mated. Their progeny put seal meat at a discount for the time being.

Rain clouds appearing, they made a second attempt to reach Buenos Ayres. Followed by their dogs and pigs, and equipped as formerly, they set out along the seashore, but this time they were driven back by storms which theatened to undo and destroy them in their unprotected condition for travel. They made their way back and built, under a cliff, a hut of giant thistle stalks lashed together with sealskin thongs. Before the weather became worse they thatched the roof and sides with reeds, and here humans, dogs and pigs resumed their community life.

The party divided into two watches, ship fashion, since their hunting had become systematized. One watch performed the duties of the day, such as catching a seal on the beach, hunting on the plains with the dogs, or gathering firewood from a copse of trees about two miles away. While they were in the woods one day, Clinch came running out, crying, "The Lord have mercy on us, here is a great tyger." With only one hatchet for defense, they took to their heels with the "tyger" gleefully after them. When they realized that the cat was gaining and that there was no escape by flight, they suddenly halted, faced about, and clapping their hands, yelled at their pursuer. The astonished "tyger" just sat back on his tail and gazed in blank wonder, while the men, one by one, quietly turned and slowly walked off. Puma and jaguar both occur in the Pampas, but in this case the animal was very likely a jaguar for they saw a number of such afterwards, while foraging, and shot one with a flintlock musket.

Before long human beasts of prey were to descend upon them. The watch, returning at evening after a seal hunt, noticed the unusual behavior of their dogs who sniffed suspiciously as they approached camp, when suddenly Morris cried, "Our hut is pulled down and everything taken away."

"Ay," cried the others, "and something else has happened, for yonder lie poor Guy Broadwater and Ben Smith murder'd."

Their bodies were not yet cold. One had had his throat cut and the other had been stabbed with a knife. Rushing toward the ruined hut they found that everything had been taken away; their muskets, powder and ball were gone, as well as the flints used to make fire. Nothing was left.

Such a hideous act in their solitude, by an unseen and unknown enemy, filled them with unconquerable fear. They were thoroughly terrified. What became of Allen and Clinch was never learned. Expecting the return of the murderers at any moment, they moved away during the first part of the night to return to camp before dawn, and at daylight, with their bare hands they hollowed out two trenches and laid their shipmates away. The braces of dogs which had belonged to the dead stood off on a knoll and howled, refusing to answer to their names or to come down for food until darkness came on again. The loss of the flints made the men doubly helpless for there was now no means of making a fire to cook meat.

Deeply depressed, the remaining four filled their knapsacks again with dried seal, put on their sealskin jackets and boots, and started out a third time for Buenos Ayres. With their dogs and pigs they followed the trend of the coast so that they would come into the La Plata where they hoped to find some inhabited place. Traveling was hard for they were brought to a low state of health by eating raw meat. At the end of ten days they came upon the cape of the river, finding creeks and swamps which they could not cross. Once more they returned to their old habitation. Now, eleven months after their first attempt to reach Buenos Ayres, they saw a dozen mounted Indians gallop up to their hut and dismount. After looking about and satisfying their curiosity, they motioned Morris and his three companions to get up behind them to be carried off. The Indians rode with their captives to a camp in a range of low hills inside of Cape Corrientes. Many of these hills have remarkable crater-like formations lined with interior cliffs, usually with an opening at one side; such an odd hollow hill was used by the Indians as a natural corral into which they drove their wild horses. On their arrival, they saw a dozen other Indians with four hundred horses taken by them in hunting. The Indians treated their captives kindly, killed a horse for them, kindled a fire, and for the first time in three months, the sailors ate cooked flesh. Their stomachs lined with suitable food, and blankets instead of rags covering their backs, fears slipped away and the men began to enjoy life and the country spread out about them; they were to see many wonders of the life in Patagonia.

The following day they broke camp and rode for nineteen days to the south and west, coming finally into a valley between two mountains where there was excellent pasture for the horses, and where stood a dozen huts made of poles covered with horse hides, which were inhabited by another party of Indians with their families. In this village, the captives were regarded with great wonder by the women and children, while the men gathered in small clusters and gambled for them. Morris observed that nothing of any great value was exchanged. One Indian acquired the four for a pair of Spanish spurs. At another time an ostrich plume head dress was the purchase price, while at the third sale they went for a small brass pan. The last exchange was made by dice throwing.

During the month's stay at this village, other parties brought in horses until fifteen hundred were counted. With these they set out for their home settlement of Huichin, on the Rio Negro, at its junction with the Limé, close by the modern village of Neuquen. Here lived the great Cacique Cangapol who was the head of all minor chiefs of a district stretching for hundreds of miles. Traveling slowly by day, camping comfortably at night, and living on the horses which they drove before them, at the end of forty days they reached Huichin.

On their arrival, the Cacique promptly claimed the four prisoners as his own personal property, and when he was ready he received them in the council house to hear their story. He was sitting on the floor surrounded by his headmen, complacently smoking a long reed pipe. His kindly bearing immediately set the prisoners at their ease. Mustering enough Spanish to get along, they soon reached a mutual understanding. The Cacique inquired from what country they came and in what manner they had reached this place. Morris was the spokesman:

"We are Englismen, lost in the South Seas, our ship, an English man-of-war, was wrecked as we were about to fight our enemies the Spaniards. We were eight in number left on a desolate part of the coast towards the rising sun; two of our number were murdered and two more were carried away; our hut was pulled down and robbed; all these evils came upon us by Indians, maybe your own tribesmen, we do not know."

On hearing all of this, the chief looked very grave and held a council in his own language with his headmen. The Indians insisted that they knew nothing about it, but that the white men might have been mistaken for Spaniards by a group of San Antonio Indians, for the *campo maestro* from Buenos Ayres had but a few months before made a raid on this band and killed a great number of San Antonio people,

arousing their deepest enmity. Such was the explana-
tion made by the headmen.

When Cangapol found that his prisoners were at
war with his own enemies, he was greatly pleased and
he offered them as wives four Spanish women prisoners
he had recently captured in a skirmish near Buenos
Ayres. He then asked the prisoners if they were great
men in their own country and was assured by them that
they were warrior chiefs with many followers and
many horses.

When spring came, the horse hunting started again.
The Cacique allowed three of the men to go with the
hunting party, but kept John Duck, who was as dark
as any of the Indians, for which reason the chief would
not believe that he was an Englishman like the others.
The truth was that Duck was an English mulatto.

A parley for ransom was conducted at a distance of
100 miles from Buenos Ayres, and at its conclusion
the three Englishmen were sold to the Spanish governor for thirty pesos—about eight dollars—each, to
be held as prisoners of war. With sixteen other prisoners, Midshipman Morris, together with Seamen
Andrew and Cooper, of the *Wager,* were thrown into
the guardship, and a year later were sent in the *Asia*
to Spain, to be exchanged. They arrived in London,
rejoicing, on April 28th, 1746, just three years after
their longboat shipmates.

12.

The Voyage of the Jeannette's Boats

THE story of the *Jeannette's* boats properly begins with the sinking of that vessel through the ice, when about five hundred miles to the north of the Siberian coast. The *Jeannette* was an Arctic steamer, formerly the British gunboat *Pandora,* owned by James Gordon Bennett, New York newspaper man, and commanded by G. W. De Long, a lieutenant in the United States Navy.

The attempt of the *Jeannette* to reach the North Pole was based on two mistaken theories. The first was that the warm Japan Current, which was known to flow north through Bering Strait, could be expected to melt navigable leads through the ice. The second was that Wrangel Island was the terminating promontory of a great expanse of land which stretched over the top of the world, to join Greenland on the Atlantic side. The shores of this supposed land were thought to afford a convenient base for a dash to the Pole, which would need but one summer to accomplish.

On the 8th of July, 1879, the *Jeannette,* with a complement of thirty-three men, left San Francisco. Soon after leaving St. Michael's and passing through the Straits, De Long boldly jammed his vessel into the drifting ice, expecting to make winter quarters at Wrangel Island. As he was helplessly swept past Herald Island and came in sight of Wrangel, he gradually became convinced that it was not part of a friendly continent. Clutched by the ice floe, the *Jeannette* was carried over the very spot marked "mountains" on the chart. The ship passed fifty miles to the north of Wrangel Island, as she drifted west.

After twenty months of crooked and sometimes retrogressive drifting from this point, the *Jeannette,* on June 12th, 1881, was crushed by the ice and went to the bottom. Not a life was lost at that time and the crew was in good health and spirits. As the need for abandoning the vessel and escaping to the Siberian coast had been imminent for some months before the *Jeannette* sank, the men took their new home on the ice largely as a matter of routine. The entire organization of the ship had been transferred to the ice in such a masterly manner that, once in their snug camp, and after they had been piped down for the night, one of the men treated his mates to a harmonica serenade. This was not a devil-may-care attitude in the face of a desperate situation, but an open expression of relief over the final disappearance of the ship under

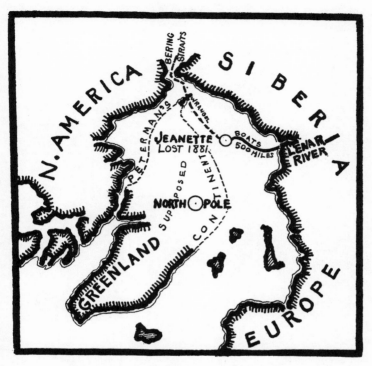

Jeannette expedition to North Pole

the ice. They had no longer to worry about her, and they were now homeward bound.

They were in Latitude 77° 18′ and it was about a hundred and fifty miles, in a southwesterly direction, to New Siberia Island. Once to the south of that island, De Long expected to find open water, but that hundred and fifty miles of sledging between was of the worst possible nature, for at no time of the year is traveling over the rotting ice worse than it is in summer. In winter, the ice, though cold, is dry. Just at this time the snow was soft enough for men to sink into. At the very best, it was wet and slushy going; at the worst, progress was sometimes impossible.

The three boats selected for the journey were mounted on sledges, while four dog sledges were loaded with full rations for sixty days. There were thirty-three men and forty dogs.

The three boats used by the expedition were all of English build, being part of the equipment of the ship before coming under American ownership. De Long's boat, officially the "first cutter," was an open boat, twenty feet long, six feet beam, and thirty inches deep. She was clinker built, copper fastened, fitted with mast and dipping lug, and pulled six oars. She had the greatest capacity of the three, and was an excellent sea boat. With Captain De Long were Dr. Ambler (surgeon), Mr. Collins (meteorologist), Nindemann, Ericson, Gortz, Noros, Dressler, Iverson, Kaack, Boyd, Lee, Ah Sam, Alexey (Eskimo hunter)—fourteen persons.

Lieutenant Chipp's boat, the "second cutter," was

the smallest and least efficient of the three, being only sixteen feet long, five feet beam, and thirty inches deep. She was clinker built, copper fastened, pulled four oars, and was fitted with mast and dipping lug. With Lieutenant Chipp were Mr. Dunbar (whaling captain), Sweetman (carpenter), Starr, Warren, Kuehne, Johnson, and Sharvell—eight persons.

Chief Engineer Melville's was the whaleboat; twenty-five feet long, five feet six inches beam, and twenty-six inches deep; copper fastened, and clinker built. She pulled six oars and was rigged with mast and dipping lug. With Chief Engineer Melville were Lieutenant Danenhower (on sick list due to partial blindness), Mr. Newcomb, (naturalist), Cole (bosun), Leach, Mansen, Wilson, Bartlett, Lauderback, Charles Tong Sing, Anequin (Eskimo hunter)—eleven persons. The whaleboat was the best sailer of the three, and she was pronounced by the master boatbuilder at Mare Island to be the best fastened boat he ever saw, which accounts for her survival after the awful punishment she got by being dragged over and through the ice. The second cutter, by being so short, was racked the least of the three boats. Before leaving Semenovski, they were all fitted with weather cloths.

The general procedure of the march was for Dunbar, the ice pilot, to go in advance with a party of four. Melville followed Dunbar by a quarter of a mile, with nearly all hands and the dogs, dragging the heavy provisions. All hands then marched back and dragged one boat at a time, until the quarter-mile stage was made and then they were ready for the next one. The best

speed they could make thus was from one to two miles
a day. No labor could have been harder, and no greater
endurance could have been shown by human beings,
fighting for life in this open and moving Arctic wilderness. The unnatural expedient of turning "night" into
"day" was adopted to relieve them from the glare of
the ice and the heat of the sun. This enabled them to
sleep sounder and warmer while, at the same time,
their clothes could be drying on the boats and tent
tops. It always froze at night.

Immediately after they had broken their first camp,
the floe, upon which they had lived for two days while
organizing the march, suddenly split under their feet,
just as it had done under the *Jeannette*. With their
boats and gear, they jumped from one piece of ice to
another, finally getting on one which was large enough
to camp on for the night. Next to the labor of dragging boats and sledges, the greatest hardship was the
constant wetting from wading through knee deep
slush. At the end of three weeks of toiling over the
sharp ice, not one man had a tight pair of moccasins.
Many a time, at the end of a march, their bare feet
were on the ice, in spite of all that leather from the
oar-looms, or canvas, could do.

After marching a week on a supposedly southward
course toward New Siberia Island, De Long found, by
the first meridian altitude of the sun he was able to get
during that time, that they had been carried northward
three miles for every mile made in the opposite direction. The ice was slipping under them. They were now
in Latitude 77° 42′, the record latitude attained in the

Polar Seas northward of Siberia. Shifting their course across the current stream, they made twenty-one miles to the good in the following week. The men, who had grown morose and despondent on suspecting the fearful truth of their position, burst into cheers upon the public announcement of their new progress.

After many more days of painful marching and camping on the floes, Dunbar thought that he sighted a dark line of open water to the westward. This dark line proved to be an undiscovered island, towards which the course was changed. In another day the sun broke through upon some blue mountain peaks, the sight of which filled them with new life and hope. Approaching the land, they found the ice looser, the leads more frequent, and game more plentiful. Soon they had seal in the pot; then a bear supplied a feast for men and dogs. The bear was cooked by using its own blubber for fuel, saving the rapidly diminishing supply of alcohol.

Forty-six days after the sinking of the *Jeannette,* they landed and pitched camp on Bennett Island, as De Long called it. There they repaired the battered boats. On the beach and under the great mountains, ten days were spent working on their gear, preparatory to the next stage of the journey. The men were sunburned, lean, ragged and hungry. Prospects began to look hopeless, for by this time they should have been beyond New Siberia Island, on the open sea and sailing toward the Lena River.

On leaving Bennett Island, they found a mile of water between the beach and the nearest floe. It required two trips by the deeply laden boats to transport all their provisions, sledges, camp equipment and the four remaining dogs. The journey now became a combination of open water and floe work of the most strenuous kind. When a floe was to be crossed, the boats were run alongside the ice, emptied of their freight, hauled over the floe on their sledges, launched and reladen. Then they were off again to work with sail, oar and tow rope until the next obstacle was encountered.

So long as the wind, which put the ice in motion, made open water for them, their progress to the south was rapid, but when it crowded the pack together it seemed that they would never get out. At length, after a good day's run with a freshening breeze, they were finally forced by the gale and the crowding of the ice, with approaching darkness, to haul out on the floe. Pitching their tents near the edge, they ate their supper of pemmican and then crawled, wretchedly wet and cold, into their sleeping bags. As bad as it was, they were not to be undisturbed, for at midnight they were turned out by the watch into a howling snow storm and told that the floe was breaking up. Shifting boats and tents to more solid ice, they were piped down again to their watch below.

At dawn they launched the boats and, after a fairly good day's work, brought up against an old rotten pack full of holes and water spaces, on which they hauled out to pitch tents and remain two days. Then, taking every lead that opened southward, they worked their way in the general direction of the New Siberian

Islands, the leads becoming larger and more frequent as they progressed. The ice was all in motion and the lanes widened into great bays covered with the first whitecaps they had seen for months. They now dodged in and out of the floe openings, working with tiller and sail to avoid striking the sharp edges of the ice.

The ice shut in and kept them prisoners for ten days. Then it seemed looser than usual and they sailed south rapidly between Faddejew and New Siberia Islands. At first it looked as if they would be swept through the channel without getting a chance to land on Faddejew, but, by great effort, they did so. They pitched their camp on the high mossy tundra, and enjoyed a night's rest on solid ground.

Between Feddejew and Kotelnoi they got into shoal water and all one night they beat among heavy breakers. They then landed under the lee of a detached sand spit off the east end of Kotelnoi, where they pitched their tents as night came on, worn out, and thankful for a rest.

The next day they were held up by a hard snow storm, but the second morning released them. Soon they were under way, scudding through the lanes of broken ice until they came under the land to see the mountains raising their snowy peaks above them. Rounding a point of land together, they hauled out on the lee side of another sand spit and camped. Here driftwood was abundant and, gathering great heaps of it, they soon built a fire of gratifying warmth.

Breaking camp the next morning, the boats rounded the spit and all stood to the westward, some of the men preferring to run alongside the boat on the beach as long as they could. Driftwood on the beach bore axe marks, the first tangible evidence that other human beings were not far off. They hauled out and camped for the night on the southwestern coast of Kotelnoi, under a long line of almost vertical cliffs.

Next morning they started across the open ocean for the Lena Delta by the way of Stoblovski. As the boats were heeled over before a stiff breeze, they suddenly came upon the weather side of a great floe, over which the sea was breaking heavily. To collide with it meant destruction. "Down sail! Out oars!" They pulled for their lives. The sea roared against the cold bleak mass of ice, the men, blinded by wind and freezing spray, strained at the oars, their bare hands frozen and bleeding. At last they weathered the danger. As they faced the death-dealing sea and the murderous ice edge, they found new life and strength. As night closed down, the wind became fitful, blowing in heavy gusts, and the sea ran high. Each helmsman steered with his ear tuned to the roar of the breakers, while a man held the turn of the sheet with a frozen hand. At midnight, upon tacking to avoid another danger, the boats were swept by seas which filled them to the thwarts, almost swamping them. Finally they ran into a field of stream ice which calmed the sea and afforded some shelter.

When day broke, it found the crews of the boats shivering together in heaps, their wits either drowned or frozen. The sea soon calmed and a warm sun broke through the clouds to thaw them out, and before long the men came alive again and bright with hope. Stoblovski was just then coming in sight. At dusk, having been well warmed by the sun, they hauled out on a floe, cleaned the boats, wrung out their clothing, and, after a meal of pemmican and hot tea, crept, still soaked, into their sleeping bags, under the cover of their tents.

The next day was one of sunshine, and, after toiling all day at oar, tow rope and sail, they camped again on the floe. The water had just begun to shoal and they could hear the roar of the surf on Semenovski. When morning dawned it revealed to them the muddy cliffs of the island, not more then five hundred yards distant.

Upon landing, a hunting party soon killed a deer, which dressed to a hundred twenty pounds of good sweet venison. This they broiled over a driftwood fire and, as the bread had long since given out, it was washed down straight with plenty of hot tea. After this feast they enjoyed the almost forgotten sensation of having a stomachful of palatable food, and the prospect of a night's sound sleep on solid ground, with a good soup on the morrow. Though the weather looked ominous, it was decided that it was dangerous, on account of the lack of food, to delay sailing any longer than absolutely necessary.

With no thought in their minds except that of reaching the Lena Delta, ninety miles across a sea quite clear of floating ice, they launched their boats about eight in the morning. Getting under way at once, they sailed with a good breeze under the lee of the island and ran briskly to the southward towards

Wassilewski. Passing through the channel between the islands, Wassilewski was soon sighted in the distance, and, just before noon, they hauled alongside of a floe for the last dinner they were ever to eat together. De Long, Chipp and Melville discussed their chances and the comparative sailing qualities of their respective boats. Chipp, although he always liked his boat, was better satisfied when De Long relieved him of one of his men. De Long reiterated his orders to keep within hail if possible, and also as to what to do in case of separation.

Soon after casting off from the floe, the wind and sea increased, making it impracticable for the boats to sail in formation or even to keep together. The second cutter, Lieutenant Chipp's, performing badly, fell far astern, while the whaleboat was nearly capsized several times by being obliged to jibe to keep from passing the first cutter. To avoid being boarded by the following sea, the whale boat made sail enough to range ahead, De Long at the time standing up in his boat and apparently waving his assent to Melville. The whaleboat then shot ahead with the wind four points on the port quarter and made good weather of it until dark. Her crew had seen the little second cutter broach to and disappear in the high sea; in their opinion, that was the last of Chipp and his crew. No trace of her was ever found. De Long, as his diary reveals, thought that both the second cutter and the whaleboat had certainly foundered that night.

Soon after De Long lost sight of the other two boats, his mast step was carried away. This accident obliged him to ride to his sea anchor and drift off to leeward. The weather, for him, increased to a heavy gale with a tremendous sea. His boat shipped a good deal of water because the sea anchor watched abeam. In attempting to set a riding sail, the sheet parted and both sail and yard were lost. Then, rigging a larger and heavier sea anchor of two oars and the mast, he managed to ride out the gale to it. When wind and sea moderated, he set a jury sail made of a sled cover and thereafter could do no more than keep off before the wind.

In this crippled condition, De Long projected a landfall at Cape Sagastuir, on the north side of the Lena Delta, where he expected to find a native settlement. The cape could be identified by one of the mouths of the Lena, and it was here that the first cutter grounded a week after leaving Semenovski. The crew were starved and frostbitten. With feet disabled, walking was nearly impossible. Determined not to die in their tracks, they first made a search for the settlement which they hoped to find. (It was determined long afterwards that it had been shifted twenty-five miles to the westward of the cape.) Then began their march to the southward.

The beginning of the peak of eventual disaster was when they ate Snoozer, the remaining dog. Blocked on their way south by an arm of the great river, they halted, to perish of exposure and starvation—all except two. Those were Nindemann and Noros, whom De Long had dispatched on a forced march up the Lena in a vain quest for timely succor.

The crew of the whaleboat, on the night of the oncoming gale, made a sea anchor of some of her gear and laid to for fear of running into pieces of young ice, which would have been a menace in the darkness. For twenty hours they held on to the drag before it became possible to get under way without being boarded by a sea. The upper gudgeon on the stern-post had carried away, so an oar was rigged to take the place of the disabled rudder. The last of the drinking water was ruined by salt. Without sighting land, the boat grounded in two feet of water on the shoals of Cape Barkin and cruised for two days more seeking some trace of the two other boats which were to reach the Delta if possible. Coming upon a deserted and dilapidated hut by one of the mouths of the Lena River, they found shelter and water that was wholesome to drink. They built a fire to warm their chilled and benumbed bodies, ate the last of their pemmican, and then searched again for more signs of native life. Afterwards they learned that no native had been living near Cape Barkin for two years. On sailing into the Delta, which they thought looked like the Mississippi River of their homeland, they met a canoe with three natives who piloted them to Jamaveloch, a settlement of Yakuts large enough to give aid.

The Lena Yakuts could not understand the strangers' language, but signs and pantomime served. They were well disposed, but had nothing except their own diet of putrid goose and a limited supply of fish to feed the lame and half famished men.

While the party were healing their frostbitten sores

in a *yuort* which had been assigned to them by the head man of the village, a native brought to them a Russian trader who was also a criminal exile. His name was Kusma and to the Americanski he was a good man. They found that they could understand each other. A bargain was made at once between Melville and Kusma by which Kusma was to receive the whale-boat and five hundred rubles to make a sledge trip to Belun, the nearest point of communication with St. Petersburg and the United States.

At the end of eighteen days, the faithful Kusma returned after a hard journey over mountain passes and broken river ice. He was the bearer of startling news, for, in addition to an official letter from the Cossack commandant at Belun, he also brought a message from the two seamen whom De Long had dispatched from his last camp. At first Melville was not sure but that De Long or even Chipp had reached Belun. Now, armed with military authority from Belun, he at once ordered a fresh dog team to be ready on the morrow. In due course, he arrived at Belun.

When Melville first appeared before him, Noros failed to recognize his former shipmate. He gave the newcomer a casual glance and resumed cutting a loaf of black bread with which he was busy. Quite undramatically, Melville then introduced himself, saying, "Hullo, Noros, how do you do?"

There was a cry from Noros. "My God, Mr. Melville! Are *you* alive?"

Then Nindemann cried out: "We thought you were

all dead, and that we two were the only ones left alive. We were sure the 'whaleboats' were all dead, and the 'second cutters' too."

Melville then heard the story of the disaster which had befallen De Long's party. Twenty-five days had elapsed since Noros and Nindemann had parted from their companions, to take up the forced march which was to save their lives. To search for De Long and his crew was in vain.

Note: Though too late for rescue, Melville, after a march which is remarkable in the annals of Arctic exploration, and months of searching, at last found the frozen bodies of De Long and his crew buried in the snow.

13

The Tofua Castaways

THE story of the mutiny on the *H. M. S. Bounty* is written upon the face of the South Pacific Ocean, and it has enthralled humanity ever since the beginning of English maritime history. The mutiny itself was an event of outstanding importance in the early days of exploration and discovery. The *Bounty,* while on the King's business, had cruised among the Society Islands until the sailors had become intimate with the natives, especially those of Tahiti. The charm of the islands and the attractions of the native women caused them to forget both their country and their ship. They had become demoralized by the voluptuous life, and the discipline of the ship had become intolerable. After setting sail for a return voyage to the old poverty and the paving stones of England, they longed for the comforts and indulgences of Tahiti.

While there, three of the crew had tried desertion from the ship, but had been recaptured. Desertion in the Society Islands always turned out that way, for a ship with an armed force could bring sufficient pressure upon the native chiefs to compel the return of the sailors. Desertion being impossible, the obvious alternative was to seize the ship and to heave the captain himself over the side as a short cut to a continued life in this land of plenty. With unbelievable secrecy a plot was hatched on the ship with that end in view. The malcontents decided that the *Bounty,* with a complement of only forty-four persons, would be an easy ship to surprise, since fifty-seven per cent of the crew were in favor of the beach. Accordingly, the majority organized a mutiny and carried the plan into effect, sailing the ship back to Tahiti.

Upon their arrival there, sixteen of the mutineers voted to stay, while the ringleader and eight of his men, together with a number of native men and women, headed the vessel to the remote and uninhabited island of Pitcairn, a thousand miles to the south and west of Tahiti. Arriving at Pitcairn, her contingent of mutineers destroyed the *Bounty,* thereby successfully hiding themselves from justice.

My story, however, deals with Captain Bligh's escape in the launch after having been driven from the ship into the sea, and not with the subsequent fate of the mutineers, which is in itself another story. I have always regarded the act of the mutineers to be one of potential wholesale murder, for the turning of fellow beings adrift among islands infested with cannibals, without so much as one musket to defend themselves, is nothing less. Such an example of sordid cruelty excites interest but never admiration.

My earliest impressions of life were received in Australian waters and naturally I became familiar with the South Seas. In our family, the names of explorers and discoverers were household words. Cannibals, loathed and feared, were right next door and not sufficiently distant to be a joke, while gruesome tragedies like the murder of Commodore Goodenough were events of our own current history.

During my early voyages in a sailing ship, I had begun to think of Pitcairn as one of the half mythical islands which we read and dream of, but never expect to see, for, previous to the opening of the Panama Canal it was far removed from the path of the merchant ship. Now it has been brought on the steamer track and is frequently sighted by ships bound to and fro between the Canal and Australian waters. A good part of the fun of voyaging is to rediscover the places we have read of and have seen pictured in the atlas, and so to verify romance and geography.

The only time that I ever sighted Pitcairn was while I was second mate of the steamer *Donald McKay,* on a passage from Noumea to the Canal. Our last landfall from it was the volcanic island of Rapa Iti, at a distance of ten miles. It was an interesting view. I had carefully spaced off the chart and determined that we were to pass historic Pitcairn during the hours of daylight, which was better luck than we had had on any previous voyage.

At noon, September 28th, while relieving the bridge,

I made out the Island, and by two P.M. had completed and entered the four-point bearing in the logbook. When abeam it was twenty-two miles off. There was not much to see of it at such a distance, merely the bare outline, which was but slightly more positive in value than the dark rain clouds which hung low over the 2000-foot peak, as clouds have a way of doing over high tropical mountains. I made a quick sketch of it in my notebook and then, for the remaining two hours of the watch, my glasses were glued to the vanishing island until it had faded into the purple atmosphere. I had seen Pitcairn, and it was a great moment in a lifetime. I then began a fresh study of Bligh's boat exploit by overhauling all the matter relating to it that I could find in the chart house, and checking his course on our general sailing chart.

On the next voyage to Sydney I was lucky enough to find Bligh's *Narrative* of the mutiny which had been printed in London in 1790. The book as an antique cost me three guineas, which I gladly paid, though my unimaginative shipmates considered that sum far too much to pay for a book yellow with age. To me it was a gold mine, containing as it did a very fine copperplate print of the builder's draught of the famous launch, which was built for the *Bounty* under Bligh's own supervision.

As a means of vivifying history I set to work building a scale model of the launch. As the form of the model developed, I was astonished and delighted at the little ship which the photographs show. The original launch was twenty-three feet in length, six feet, nine inches beam, two feet, nine inches deep, seven inches freeboard, and every inch a boat. The design seems to have been the usual one for a ship's boat at that time, judging from drawings in the Atlas of Captain Cook's *Voyages*. From the description in the *Narrative,* and from marginal sketches in Bligh's log, kept in the launch and preserved in the Mitchell Library in Sydney, she was rigged with a double dipping lug, the usual boat rig of the period.

The first intention of the "committee of arrangements" was to turn Bligh adrift in the sixteen-foot cutter which was nested inside of the launch and which could carry only six men on the thwarts and in the stern sheets. Besides being much smaller than the launch, it was stove in the bilge by pounding on the beach, and leaked badly. The intention of murder was evident right here, for the only difference between being turned adrift in the cutter and being forced to walk the plank was that the former death would be the more prolonged.

While the ringleader was guarding the commander abaft the mizzenmast, with a drawn bayonet at his throat, the rest of the mutineers were holding a violent altercation over the selection of the boat. With a grim sense of decency, they finally hoisted out the better of the two. To this decision, Captain Bligh and his party owed their lives; it also explained the reason why some of the gang did not swing to the yard-arm of the *Brunswick* in Portsmouth, when they were afterwards captured by the *Pandora* in Tahiti.

The seizure of the *Bounty* was made at daylight on

the 28th of April, 1789, while she was on the homeward bound passage about thirty miles from the Island
of Tofua, of the Tonga group. The launch being
ready, the ringleader said; "Come Captain Bligh, your
officers are in the boat and you must go with them;
if you make the least resistance you will instantly be
put to death." Bligh's statement at this point is: ". . .
Without any further ceremony, holding me by the cord
which tied my hands, with a tribe of armed ruffians
about me, I was forced over the side where they un-
tied my hands. Being in the boat, we were veered
astern by a rope. A few pieces of pork were then
thrown to us, as well as a quadrant and four cutlasses,
and then we were at length cast adrift in the open
ocean."

The ship's carpenter, who had been ordered into the
launch, was allowed to take his tools notwithstanding
much opposition, "Damn his eyes, he'll have a vessel
built in a month and find his way home."

Bligh's clerk had managed to secure for him his
commission and his journal, but he was not allowed to
have a chart, a nautical almanac or a chronometer. On
asking for firearms as a protection against cannibals,
Bligh had been derided and was ironically told that, as
he was well acquainted with the people where he was
going, he did not need them. As a matter of fact, he
was too well acquainted with the people of his destination, and, furthermore, he was the only man on the
ship who knew anything at all about the islands. Com-
pared with what Bligh had previously done in the
Pacific, the *Bounty* voyage had been like a pleasure

excursion. Everything had been mapped out in advance from the time of their leaving England, and they had run no unusual risk from natives.

The Tongas, near which the launch was cast adrift, are fourteen hundred miles to the eastward of Tahiti, just to windward of the Fijis, and they form a group of islands and reefs extending 180 miles north and south and 50 miles east and west. Tongatabu is at the south end and Vavau is at the extreme north end of the group, with Namuka and Tofua near the center. On the outward voyages of both the *Resolution* and the *Bounty,* Bligh had visited the Tongas and had formed an agreeable acquaintance with the wily King Poulaho at Tongatabu. In the presence of white men in great ships with a plentiful show of armed force, Poulaho was on his good behavior and had lavished favors and entertainment upon his visitors.

The island of Tofua lies by itself, to the westward of a line of reefs. It is a conspicuous mark of dreary aspect, standing nearly two thousand feet out of the sea, which makes it visible at a great distance to passing vessels. From the time of its discovery by Tasman until two centuries afterwards, Tofua had acquired notoriety for treacherous attacks by natives on the crews of visiting ships. They had even been known to board small vessels and to murder all hands. Bligh could not say from his former knowledge of the island whether or not it was inhabited, but he knew that it was inferior to the other islands of the group and that large numbers of natives were seen there only at particular times.

The Tongans cruised in large outrigger canoes capable of sailing and holding their own under the lee of the entire extent of the group. If ever they were blown off to the Fijis, they themselves, in turn, might furnish the chief dish for a cannibal feast.

Tofua was barely visible when the launch hoisted sail and shipped oars on a calm sea. On pulling away from the ship, Bligh decided to land on Tofua, and later to reach Tongatabu and seek the aid of Poulaho. Long after dark, they reached the island and laid on their oars all night under the lee. All that was visible through the gloom was the rocky coast. In the morning, the launch came to a grapnel within twenty yards of a stony beach in a cove. Some of the men went ashore and climbed the cliffs, returning with only twenty coconuts, which supplied one apiece for their first dinner. An attempt was made to put to sea but, bad weather preventing, the launch was moored in the cove, one grapnel out ahead and a second grapnel astern on the beach. Four men were left on board for an anchor watch while the rest landed to explore and to forage.

The cove was lined with cliffs and the men hauled themselves up the precipice by long vines which were the only means of reaching the interior plateau, and which had been fixed to the rocks by the natives for that purpose. On the top of the level elevation they found a few deserted huts and a small plantain walk. Separating, they explored the plateau to within two miles of a volcanic peak and then all descended the precipice, to eat a ration of pork and plantain at the cove.

At the head of the cove, about 150 yards from the water, they found a cave, and here, after setting an anchor watch, all hands turned in to sleep. Bligh felt disposed to stay here and prepare for his long voyage, rather than to risk going to Tongatabu.

At dawn a party ascended to the plateau where they met two men, a woman and a child, and, on their return, they reported several plantations where supplies might be obtained. This information was encouraging and made it probable that the launch could get away as soon as weather permitted.

Soon afterwards, thirty natives lowered themselves down the cliffs and showed a disposition to trade a few coconuts and plantains. Both of these were scarce, while water was only to be obtained a gallon at a time on this lava island. At sunset the natives left the white men in possession of the cove, which fact might signify their return in the morning with a good supply of fruit and water.

In the morning, the natives came down the precipice in greater numbers than before, and at the same time two well-filled canoes came sailing around the north side of the island. In one of the canoes was Makavow, an old chief of the windward islands, and with him, Negete, a younger man of importance. To each of these were presented a shirt and a knife. Bligh and Negete had met before, on very amicable terms, at Namuka while on the *Bounty*. The latter professed to be very glad to see Bligh. It was now that the muskets denied by the mutineers were to be badly needed, for Bligh was aware of the sinister meaning of so many warriors on the beach. It was soon discovered that the white men had no firearms, and a marked change was noted in the conduct of the natives. When the chiefs appeared on the beach it was a signal for open hostilities. Bligh, who already had been in two massacres, saw the intention of a general massacre right here, when the natives, numbering more than two hundred, commenced knocking stones together. Towards noon, some of the natives attempted to haul out the launch, as they always did before murdering a landing crew, but Bligh brandished his cutlass in such a manner that Negete chased them away from the line and they became quiet for a while. The crew felt the horror of their position but put on a front of unconcern as they began to load the launch to shove off. With the savages milling about them, they ate their dinner of coconut and breadfruit standing, well aware that if they were caught off guard they would certainly be seized. Bligh told his people to keep steady until sunset when something might happen for the better. But the clatter of the stones grew louder as the natives lined the beach and lighted fires, before stoning their intended victims to death. They were ten to one.

At sunset, on the command being given to shove off, each man shouldered his load and resolutely marched down the beach and through the line of savages, without so much as looking around. It was a tense moment. The chiefs then inquired of Bligh if he were not going to remain on shore during the night, when, upon being given the negative, Makavow, the old cannibal chief, declared: Matte," the equivalent of which was "We will kill you."

As the crew were dragging Bligh and the carpenter into the boat, Norton unwisely jumped back into the surf to pick up the stern grapnel. At once, he was knocked down by the natives who took hold of the grapnel themselves and started to drag the boat back on shore, at the same time beating Norton on the head with stones until he was killed. Bligh cut the sternfast with his pocket knife and the released launch was hauled out to the head grapnel. As soon as Norton was knocked down and killed, the boat was bombarded with a shower of stones directed with great accuracy and force. No one in the boat was seriously hurt, as they got out the oars and started to pull for the sea. Twelve savages, thinking to get the better of the boat, loaded some canoes with stones and paddled around, keeping up the bombardment until dark, when, defeated, they hauled off shore. During the attack they were careful not to come within close range of the launch. With their advantage, they could easily have overpowered and murdered the whole crew. Why they did not was a mystery. Providentially, the lives of the Englishmen were saved by the delayed attack of the natives, due really to the friendliness of Negete.

Such a sample of hospitality handed out to defenceless visitors to the Tongas convinced everyone in the launch that it would be useless to see King Poulaho. If not actually massacred at Tongatabu, there would be a long chance of losing their boat and gear. In the morning, Bligh told his men that the only chance for life would be to make the Dutch island of Timor, fully 3600 miles to the westward and directly to leeward. It would take at least eight weeks for the voyage, even if favored with the strong southeast trades; this port, however, would be an advantageous one, because Timor, with its European settlement, was the nearest point of communication with England. Bligh settled down to the conviction that it would be too hazardous to attempt another landing in the Pacific Islands and that he must so arrange that the provisions in the boat would last them until they reached Timor. There was less in the boat now than when they touched at Tofua, because the breadfruit had been mashed up and the bread greatly damaged during the stone attack from the beach. Here, Bligh's character was shown in his capacity for swift decision in matters of grave importance. On what part of the island the settlement was situated he did not know, but he knew that the center of Timor was in latitude ten degrees south, and near the eastern end of Java. Failing to find relief on Timor, they could still make Batavia, in Java.

On taking account of supplies in the boat, it was estimated that an allowance of an ounce of bread and a quarter of a pint of water a day would carry them through. This would mean, practically, slow starvation, but all hands solemnly pledged themselves to this plan. To be exact the supply in the boat, expected to last eight weeks, consisted of: one hundred and fifty pounds of hard bread, twenty-eight gallons of water, twenty pounds of salt pork, three bottles of wine, five quarts of rum and a few coconuts. The breadfruit had been trampled upon and spoiled. Some of the bread was also damaged and to preserve this it was stowed in the carpenter's chest, after his kit had been removed to the bottom of the boat. Later on the voyage, the allowance of bread was standardized by rigging up a pair of scales made of two cocoanut shells, and using a pistol bullet for a weight. The meager allowance of water was even more of a hardship; a quarter of a pint, less than half a glassful, just enough to wet the throat.

The navigating equipment consisted of a compass, a quadrant, a book of "latitudes and longitudes," together with Bligh's own recollections of places obtained during his voyage with Captain Cook. How Bligh ever managed to get his latitudes by observation has always been somewhat of a mystery to me. A possible solution is that he may have had a secret notation of the sun's declination and the daily rates of change and made up a table in the boat. In the time of Cook and Bligh, the navigator, dependent upon himself, was much more resourceful than those of the present time. Bligh's longitudes were by dead reckoning, using Tofua as the prime meridian.

After cleaning out the boat and putting it in order, Bligh decided upon a start. It was eight o'clock at night when they bore away before the wind under a reefed lug foresail, and, having divided the crew into two watches, they had prayers, thanking God for their "miraculous preservation" . . . as Bligh said, "Fully confident of His gracious support, I found myself more at ease than I had been for some time past."

During the night, the wind increased in force and at daybreak the sun rose fiery and red, which was taken as an indication of heavy weather to come. By eight in the morning, the wind increased to a gale and the sea ran high enough to becalm the sail while in the troughs. All possible sail had to be carried to prevent the boat from being boarded and swamped by the following seas. Bailing had to be smart with no let-up. This work was for their lives. They could do no more than keep dead before the sea but the boat displayed such wonderful sea-going qualities that they soon recovered their fear of foundering.

On the second day, although the sea increased, Bligh hauled the course to the northward as much as the boat would stand, for he intended that the voyage should be used for something more than simply sailing to Timor. By so doing, not only was better weather to be expected, but there would be a chance to do some exploring. Misfortune, privation and danger did not destroy the discoverer's instinct in Bligh, for he knew that he was headed for a large group of important and undiscovered islands which the natives of the Friendly Islands called "Feejee." The direction of these islands had been pointed out to both Cook and Bligh. The natives had an idea of their distance and extent, as well, and Cook considered them to bear west-northwest from Tongatabu. The people in these islands, they said, were mighty in battle and voyaged to other islands in great war canoes. Tasman had reported some of the smaller of these islands that are in the northeast section of the group, and, in 1773, Cook had discovered Turtle Island, which is at the extreme southeast, and the most outlying island of them all.

With keen expectancy, Bligh held his west-northwest course with the firm assurance that beyond all these he would see the real "Feejees." It was this quality of optimism and imagination which made him superior to the troubles in the launch, and which infused in his people a spirit of confidence which eventually carried them through. He could foresee not only the outcome of his plans to reach Timor but an opportunity to make discoveries as well.

After a second day of gales and high seas they began, one by one, to sight the outlying islands of the group. Though drenched and chilled from constant wetting, as were all the crew, Bligh was careful to keep a close account of his runs and navigation. A log was improvised, and, by counting the seconds, they could get the speed "with some degree of exactness." He made a running survey, with sketches, of the islands which, for the purpose of identification, were indicated by letters, as, "K" Island, "L" Island, etc. This survey was accurate enough to enable him later to check up and to verify his own discoveries on his succeeding voyage to these islands in the *Providence*. The launch's track through the Fiji group resembled a steamer's direct track, and shows an avoidance of the cannibal islands. To this boatload of castaways the islands looked fair and delectable, for there was food and water for the mere taking, but they had learned their lesson at Tofua and dared not land without firearms.

Bligh entered the group between the islands of Mothe and Namuka, then, steering northwest, passed Vanua Vatu and Mola; he proceeded northward between the islands of Koro and Makongai, and, after making the Makongai passage, suddenly and without a warning ripple, the launch ran over a coral shoal carrying but four feet of water. This identifies the point where, at sunset, Bligh came between the two great islands of Vanua Levu and Viti Levu.

Entering the Vitu-ira Channel, he set the course for the night at west by north, according to his own account. We are here able to check up on his steering, for the actual magnetic course on this run was west by north and a quarter north. It was as direct a course for Yasawa and the Round Island passage to sea as though he had really known that it was there—a magnificent piece of seamanship. In the morning, the launch sighted some large sailing canoes heading out from Yasawa Island, but, taking no chances with more hostilities, she held her weather gauge with the wind on the starboard beam, and managed to outsail them to the open.

This passage of Bligh in the *Bounty's* launch among the Fiji Islands made him the first white man to record the discovery of the larger and western islands of the group. In the light of modern research, Bligh was the actual discoverer of the Fiji Islands (first known as "Bligh's Islands"), although credit was long given to

Dumont d'Urville, who arrived there thirty-eight years later.

Once back on the open ocean, the launch ran into a heavy rain squall, and, for the first time since leaving Tofua, they were able to completely quench thirst and to collect water. They filled twenty gallons. This was the fifth day from Tofua and 420 miles had been covered, a daily average of 84 miles. They had yet 600 miles to look forward to in the run to the New Hebrides, and Bligh took care to instruct his people in the route to Timor. This he did in the way of general conversation, in which he reiterated distances and courses as well as descriptions of New Guinea (which was to be avoided) and New Holland, as the Dutch called Australia, with her inland sea behind the great reefs. The crew knew nothing about Timor, some not even the name. These talks were good psychology and cannot be taken as an indication of despair, for, as nature became exhausted and they grew weaker in body, the spirit of the whole crew rose, from their captain's example, and nobody thought of giving up. Timor was their only thought. A week later, after sailing before storms and with heavy rains, they made the New Hebrides.

During this time Bligh carried on a regular routine of improvement in the boat, which helped to keep the men's minds occupied and less self-centered. He contrived a weather cloth to keep the heaviest sprays off. The quarters of the boat were raised nine inches by having the seats of the stern sheets nailed on, which prevented some of the sea from breaking over the stern, though two men had to bale constantly to keep the boat from swamping. A pair of shrouds was fitted to each mast, and a grommet was seized to each quarter so that it would be possible to steer with an oar if the rudder should be carried away.

From Vanua Levu to the Great Reef of Australia (now called the Barrier Reef) was the longest pull of the voyage, 1380 miles, and this they made in fourteen days, an average of nearly 100 miles per day, with the weather conditions similar to those experienced on the run from the Fijis. Had the weather been calm and hot, they would have perished from thirst, but the sixteen days of continual rain which accompanied the driving gale soaked their skins and relieved them from the most maddening of all torments. Chilled from the constant soaking in fresh water, they dipped their clothes over the side, wringing them out of the salt water and putting them on again, for greater warmth. This gave more of the effect of a change of dry clothing than can readily be imagined, and, in fact, it was so pleasurable that they wrung their clothes until they were in rags.

Extreme hunger now began to show itself but this was eased up on several occasions by the catching of sea birds by hand. Once caught, the bird was killed and divided among all hands, on the "who shall have this" method. One man divided the bird into nineteen parts, among them the bill, offal, webbed feet and contents of the maw. He would then call out to another man who had been blindfolded, "Who shall have this?" pointing to one of the portions. The blindfolded

one, in turn, called out the name of the man who was
to get the indicated morsel, and who dared not growl
at his luck. The blood was carefully saved and given
to one or perhaps two of them, who were drooping
the most. The boatswain paid Bligh the compliment of
telling him that he looked worse than the rest of the
men, though Bligh himself says that after the first
pangs, he felt no hunger.

On part of this run, Bligh feared that the scend of
the sea would drive them too far to the north and onto
the coast of New Guinea, which had a most evil reputation for cannibalism, and which, one may add, has
not yet been lost.

Before daylight, on May 28th, just a month after
having been cast off from the *Bounty,* the helmsman
reported the sound of breakers booming against a reef,
and the launch was hauled into the wind. By nine in
the morning a break in the reef was found through
which they passed into smooth water. Hardship was
for a time forgotten, as anyone who ever ran into
shelter will realize. This gap in the Great Barrier Reef
has ever since been called Bligh Boat Entrance, and is
in latitude 12-51 S. It was here that Bligh found that
he had outrun his dead reckoning longitude by only
one degree and nine minutes—a feat in navigation.

On the 29th, they found a fine sandy point and a
bay at an island which was a little removed from the
mainland. Here they landed and named the island
"Restoration," not altogether on account of their own
salvation, but because of the anniversary of the restoration of King Charles II, which came on that date.

Near the shore, they discovered fireplaces and shell heaps which had been left by the natives, but there was nothing to alarm them for the night. They took the precaution, however, to set a watch, half of the party sleeping in the boat to guard against surprise. In the morning, everyone was keen for something to eat and quickly searched for food, which they found in plenty in the form of rock oysters, and best of all, there was water in abundance. A copper kettle was produced from the boat, a fire was kindled with a magnifying glass, and they all sat down to a pint of oyster stew each, which was reported as not too bad. All the men had pains in their joints from the wet clothes and exposure, and from knocking about in the boat. In addition, most of them suffered from dizziness, headache, and loss of sight, as from a violent tenesmus. Except for baling, there had been no exercise since leaving Tofua.

On entering the passage through the reef, the lower rudder gudgeon, which was a strap on the rudder itself, carried away and was lost. Again, luck was with them, for, in the heavy following sea in crossing the Pacific, it is doubtful if they could have held her before it with a steering oar, had not a staple that answered the purpose been found in the carpenter's kit, which saved the use of the rudder for the rest of the voyage.

There were 175 miles of sailing inside of the Barrier Reef to Torres Strait, the entrance to the Arafura Sea, from which it would be another 1100 miles to Timor. Accordingly, renewed preparations were made for this last long stretch, and a good "tuck out," as they say in Australia, was laid in. After the oyster feed, they went berrying, tasting a bit gingerly at first, trying the effect of the fruit, but, after observing the birds eagerly eating the berries, every man went ahead and had his fill. Then, after a second oyster stew, they separated for the night, one-half sleeping on shore and the other half on the boat.

On Sunday, May the 30th, the boat was prepared for sea and watered to her capacity, which was only sixty gallons. The third oyster stew, to which the remaining two pounds of salt pork were added, comprised their last dinner. After a final oyster hunt, everything was put into the boat. This being the Sabbath Day, Bligh had prayers as usual. He believed in God, but at the same time he inculcated the doctrine of self-reliance by telling his men to "keep the powder dry."

As the crew was preparing to launch the boat, after these three days of rest and recuperation, twenty natives came running down on the opposite shore, waving their arms, shouting and gesturing for them to come nearer. This proved that the white men had been discovered. As the blacks had no canoes, Bligh passed them as closely as could be done with safety, and observed that they were entirely naked, of evil facial expression, and that their hair was bushy and short. Each was armed with a spear and a boomerang.

The next day, while sailing close to shore, they saw another party of blacks running towards them, making signals for them to land. Since there were no signs of canoes, Bligh laid his boat close to the rocks and beckoned them to approach, but none would do so. These blacks were armed in the same manner as those seen from Restoration Island.

Bearing off to an island four miles from the coast, the launch was beached in smooth water. This was named Sunday Island. Oysters and clams were procured and rain water was dipped from the hollows of the rocks. Bligh walked to the highest part of the island to view the main coast and to plan his route for the night. There, on the north side, in a sandy bay he came upon an old canoe, half buried in the beach. It was the kind built by the natives of Papua, just across Torres Strait, the very people that he wanted to have the least to do with, for they were the worst of man-eaters. The construction of the canoe was unmistakably Melanesian. It was thirty feet long, made of three pieces, the bottom entire, to which the sides were sewn in the usual way with rattan. It had a sharp projecting prow, rudely carved, in resemblance of the head of a fish; the extreme breadth was about three feet and it was capable of carrying twenty men. The discovery of so large a canoe of this type was startling and confirmed him in his purpose of seeking a more retired place for the night.

After dining again on the usual fare of stewed oysters and clams, they launched the boat and made for a key where they arrived at dark and came to a grapnel for the night. At dawn of day they landed and, though they found a wigwam and other signs of Australian natives, they decided to rest here for a while. The majority of them passed the afternoon in sleep. Nelson, before mentioned, was becoming very weak and could take only a small piece of bread soaked in wine. Others, though distressed with intestinal pains, continued to fill up on oysters and a kind of tropical bean which Nelson identified as a "Dolicho." During the night, some of the men went on a bird and turtle hunt. They found no turtles but returned with twelve noddies. Lamb, a boy of sixteen, confessed to having eaten nine noddies, raw, on the spot, for which breach of duty he was disciplined by a licking.

In the morning, the invalids being much better after their night's sleep, the launch shoved off to head into the Arafura Sea, bound for Timor, a run of 1100 miles. This the launch accomplished in ten days, averaging 110 miles a day, before half a gale and a rough sea. Two men were kept constantly baling to prevent the boat from foundering. This speed in a heavy sea was magnificent work for a boat of the launch's size, and all the more remarkable considering that the crew was in a state of starvation.

They had spent just six days on the coast of Australia. The good food and water, the relief from inactivity in cramped quarters in the boat, and rest at night were a godsend which certainly preserved their lives. At best, they were deplorable objects, but hope of relief within eight or ten days buoyed their spirits.

The sea, high and breaking over the boat, made the men miserably wet and cold. Nelson was low; Ledward, the surgeon, and Lebogue, a hardy old seaman, appeared to be rapidly sinking.

Timor was just coming into sight. The launch was reeling off more than a hundred miles a day when there came a visible change for the worse in several of the men. Extreme weakness, swollen legs, hollow and ghastly faces, and undue inclination to sleep, together with a loss of understanding, were the alarming symptoms which indicated the end.

Birds and rock-weed began to appear, showing that they were not far from land. At three the next morning they saw the high loom of Timor and hauled on the wind until daylight. It is a mountainous island, 250 miles long, and later they found that they had made the landfall at about the center, on the south and west side. The actual sight of the island at daylight was scarcely credible to the exhausted crew. It seemed hardly possible that, in an open boat, poorly provided, they should have been able to reach the coast of Timor in forty-one days after leaving Tofua, a distance of more than 3600 miles according to their log, and that, notwithstanding their extreme distress, no one had perished on the voyage.

Bligh had a faint idea that the Dutch settlement was situated on the southwest part of the island, so at daylight he bore away along the shore. A great surf which broke against the shore made landing out of the question. The gale moderated to a fresh breeze on the port beam. After running all day, and fearful of passing the cape in the dark, they hove to for the night under a double-reefed foresail. At two in the morning they stood inshore until daylight, when they could see the southernmost land bearing west. Coming to the

Strait, with Rotti on the port hand, they came to a grapnel in a sandy bay to examine the coast. There was yet no sign of the Dutch settlement. Getting under weigh, the launch continued along shore until, coming to a small bay, they saw signs of habitation and natives running about. Here a pilot was taken on board who told them that their port could be reached on the next day, and with a light breeze they cruised along the coast until dark when they again came to a grapnel for the night.

On entering the harbor at dawn, the report of two cannon fired from the shipping in the roads filled the launch with new life. On beginning to lose ground on each tack while beating in against a very light air, the men took to their oars and found to their surprise and delight that they could still pull to some effect. At sunrise they came to anchor off a small fort and town which the pilot said was Kupang.

The launch took on the character of a foreign ship in distress by formally setting a jack in the main shrouds and waiting for official recognition from the port authorities. In a short time she was hailed from the fort and directed to land in front of the guns. There was no need of all that warlike precaution against an invading enemy, for, had the specter crew of the *Flying Dutchman* landed at Kupang, the European garrison could have been no more horrified than it was at the spectacle presented to it, as the launch drew closer. If the cause of their ghastly appearance had not been at once known, it would have excited terror rather than pity. Clothed in rags, with bodies which were nothing but skin and bone, and running with sores, they were lifted out of the boat to dry land.

Governor Van Este, himself too sick to attend personally to their relief, directed from his bed that the men be hospitably cared for. His son-in-law, Lieutenant Governor Wanjon, did everything in the way of providing food and medicine to alleviate their distress. Most of them were not long in manifesting signs of returning health, but three of the men remained in a critical condition. Nelson, the scientist to the *Bounty* expedition who had been very low ever since leaving Australia, was the first to die. He was a man of sterling character, and Captain Bligh's best friend both on the ship and in the launch.

The time of the sailing of the Dutch fleet from Batavia was regulated by the occurrence of cyclonic storms in the Indian Ocean, the worst season being from January to March inclusive. Thus, in two months the October fleet was to sail for Holland via the Cape of Good Hope, and Bligh set about to secure his arrival at Batavia in time for his people to go. Should he miss that fleet, they would all have to wait four months for the next sailing.

At Kupang he secured a thirty-four foot schooner modeled like a home galliot, very commodious for the length, and suitable for carrying the crew on the remaining 1200-mile voyage to Batavia. This new acquisition was placed in commission under the name of the *H.M.S. Resource*. At the time of making the purchase for the British Government, there was doubt of obtaining money from official sources to buy the vessel.

This breach was filled by the friendly Wanjon, who went down into his own pocket to get Bligh and his men to Batavia on time. Besides provisions, Wanjon saw to it that the *Resource* was equipped with swivels and small arms against Malay pirates who swarmed the coasts. To help Bligh find his way through the maze, he was provided with a Dutch map of the islands, which was to be returned from Batavia with the loaned armament. This was the extreme mark of state confidence, for the Dutch were reticent about telling commercial rivals much about their East Indian possessions. Until their final return home, the Englishmen were the guests of the Dutch Government.

During the stay of the launch crew at Kupang, Bligh and some of his men paid their respects to the native king, whose residence was four miles back in the country. The king, an elderly man, received his visitors with a show of great respect, ordering tea, rice cakes, roasted corn, tapa (dried buffalo meat), and a pint of arrak, which appeared to be all that he had on hand. The day was saved, however, for, on a hint from Wanjon, the Englishmen had tactfully brought along a full demijohn. The king explained that his shortage was due to a civil war fomented among his people by the Portuguese, who occupied Dilli, a settlement on the north end of the island. The rebellious tribesmen had ravaged his plantations, he explained, and had made produce very scarce. "There still remains my wild honey," he said, "for the rebels do not care to do with the bees." In Kupang, a native was seen to come to market with two potatoes to barter for his day's chewing of narcotic betel nut.

The Dutch settlement of Kupang on Timor was made in 1630, about a century after the Portuguese had founded their settlement of Dilli on the opposite end of the island two hundred miles away. The opposing interests contrived to avoid open conflict in the sandalwood and beeswax trade during the years that they had been in the same field. "Getting the natives a-fighting is an indirect move on the part of the Portuguese," Wanjon explained, "to embarrass the production of the sandalwood and beeswax on our end of the island." Thus, on an island with an area of 12,450 square miles, about the size of Maryland, were found all the elements of an economic war. The Malays had small vessels on the coast, but they were indolent and allowed the more industrious Chinese to carry on their inter-island traffic.

On August 22nd, the *Resource,* being ready for sea, sailed, with the launch in tow, from Kupang. Passing out, she exchanged salutes with the fort and with the shipping at anchor. Drifting along the south side of high Flores Island, she stood through the Straits of Mangaryn before a stiff breeze. Then, sailing leisurely to the north of Sumbawa, Lombok and Bali Islands, she reached Surabaya in twenty-eight days.

Governor Opperhooft was very hospitable and helped the Englishmen to enjoy his fine little town which was a short distance up a small river. The beautiful mountain scenery was an attraction to some, but they did not dare venture far into the country on account of many fierce tigers which made travel dangerous. The *Resource* remained in Surabaya four days in order to sail in company with some other small vessels. It was customary for small fleets to keep together in mutual protection against the Malay pirate. They worked their way through the intricate strait of Madura, keeping a good lookout for Malays until reaching Samarang, a Dutch fortified town, next in importance to Batavia. Here, the *Resource* replaced her mainmast, which had been sprung on the way from Surabaya, and then departed for Batavia under convoy of a six swivel galley.

On October 1st, the *Resource,* with the survivors of the *Bounty's* launch on board and with the famous launch herself in tow, anchored in Batavia road. Riding there also were a Dutch man-of-war and twenty sail of Dutch East India ships, some of which were to comprise the October fleet.

In Batavia, the *Resource* was sold at public auction to the account of the British Government, as was also the little *Bounty* launch. They wanted to save her, but it was found to their great regret that there was no way to convey her to England. The Governor-General, who arranged everything, had three hundred invalids on his hands to be sent home. He was no less hospitable than the others had been in Java, but he was obliged to tell Bligh that the homeward bound ships were so crowded that all of his men could not go together on one ship, but that they would have to be separated as occasion made fit. Bligh, with his clerk and one seaman, were the first to leave Batavia, which they did on the packet *Vlydte,* bound for Middleburgh. The other victims of the mutiny followed promptly, until all the twelve survivors of those who were forced over the side and into the launch off Tofua, reached their native country.

When Captain Bligh reported back to the Admiralty to account for the *Bounty,* he was immediately given another and a larger ship, together with a tender, to sail again for the South Seas to fulfill his previous orders. On the completion of that commission, he was elected Fellow of the Royal Society, for eminence in navigation and science.

He fought at Dogger Bank, at Gibraltar and at Camperdown. In 1801, he "led the 54-gun Glatton" at the battle of Copenhagen, under Lord Nelson, who, having sent for him after the action, said, in the presence of several officers: "Bligh, I have sent for you to thank you. You have supported me nobly."

After twenty-one years a Post Captain, he was, in 1811, promoted to the rank of Rear-Admiral, and to that of Vice-Admiral in 1814. He died in 1817, at the age of sixty-four. His was a great career, and his name distinguishes many places in the southern hemisphere.

The subsequent history of the mutineers may be related in a few words. The sixteen left at Tahiti were captured by the *H.M.S. Pandora,* and those who lived to reach England were court-martialled on board the *H.M.S. Brunswick* in Portsmouth. Three were executed.

Nothing very certain is known of the lives of the nine who sailed with ringleader Fletcher Christian on the *Bounty*, to Pitcairn, except that they followed very closely in the footsteps of other lawless adventurers in the South Pacific. It was not long before they began to quarrel about their women; some drank themselves to death on liquor which they themselves distilled; others were ushered out of this life by mutual destruction. A Tahitian man killed Christian for stealing his wife. Only one of the mutineers lived more than four years after setting the launch adrift off Tofua. Such were the ancestors of the present Pitcairn Islanders.

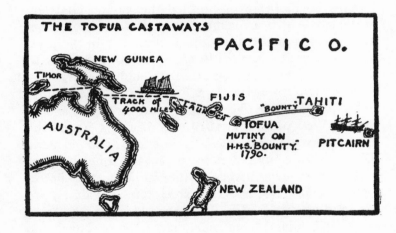

14

The Tawiti Castaway

HENRY, as the Maoris of New Zealand called him, outdid the fictional Robinson Crusoe in his remarkable experience when living with them. He was an English missionary of the rugged and adventurous type most likely to survive the dangers and rigors of life among the heathen of the Pacific Islands, and so was chosen to labor with the Ngaphuis who owned the Bay of Islands.

The evil reputation of this particular group of Maoris seems to have been entirely justified by the reports of navigators from the days of the earliest discoverers. Accounts of native treachery, bloodthirsty butchery, and cannibalism constitute a dark page in their history. It is a page of single and wholesale murders accompanied by the capture, burning, and pillaging of ships which touched their shores.

The peak of this native terrorism was reached when the notorious chief Hongi led the Ngaphuis, and, strangely enough, an over-zealous missionary, deceived by Hongi's cunning, became the innocent cause of many of the uprisings. Hongi, a professed convert to the faith, was taken triumphantly to England, as an exhibit of what missionary skill could accomplish in improving the savage. Decorated with elaborate tattooing, he was a picturesque figure who commanded much attention by his native dignity and haughty bearing, but while assuming the ways of civilization Hongi was chiefly absorbed in his discoveries about muskets, and eagerly learned all that he could about their use. On his return to the Bay of Islands he had secured 300 of these lethal weapons, which none of his political opponents possessed, and started a war for their extermination.

The New South Wales Government had apparently winked at this shipment of arms to Hongi, for their statesmen may have considered that there were too many Maoris or that this up-to-date method of man destruction would prove a stimulus to Australian trade. Whatever the motive, British guns eventually solved the Maori problem by colonization, so that by the time Henry reached the islands the tomahawk had long since been buried in their inter-tribal strifes.

Henry, by diplomacy and tact, gradually won the friendship of the Maoris and frequently went with them on their fishing expeditions. Many a time he was invited to go with Chief Monganui and his five wives in their old whale boat to Black Rock, two miles beyond Cape Brett, and a trip of sixteen miles from the settlement, which consumed an entire day if the wind was right.

One Friday Henry took a fancy to go to Black Rock, but for reasons of convenience none of the natives would go with him, so he made ready his own little sail boat and started off by himself. The boat, sixteen feet long, was beamy and able, and rigged with a single sail on a gaff. Anticipating a night in the boat, he took blankets but no supplies except a bit of food, some water in bottles and his pipe. Hooks and lines were part of his equipment as a matter of course. Confidently, he sailed out by the great promontory which the discoverer, Captain Cook, had named for one of his navigators. Henry had never sailed alone outside of Cape Brett before and the long heave of the Pacific imbued him with a wild desire to push out into deeper water where he could see the high surge dashing over Black Rock in the far distance.

Reaching the fishing ground, he anchored and in three hours had caught a fairly large mess of rock cod. Suddenly he noticed that the wind had changed and was now blowing freshly from off shore, directly from the point to which he wished to return. Boats were often blown away by these changes in the direction of the wind and Henry became panic-stricken. A more experienced sailor would probably have shifted his anchorage to the new lee of the rocks and waited for the wind to change again in his favor, but Henry, hoisting sail, attempted to beat against the rising wind and sea. The boat was not weatherly and made too much leeway. After a few futile tacks he fetched altogether too far to leeward of the rocks to anchor again, and in desperation he took in sail and started to pull on his oars against wind and sea. After two hours of this strenuous pulling, he became exhausted, and, as he was losing ground as well, he unshipped the oars and allowed the boat to drift helplessly as it would. Terror threw him into a state of coma and when he finally aroused himself he found that the sun was setting and that the land was fading from sight. To lend him courage, the moon rose clear and full to light the sea for the night.

Before morning the wind and sea moderated and the rising sun revealed the peaks of some small but high islands upon which, he had heard, the Maoris sometimes landed when blown off shore in just such a wind as had carried him away. These islands were south and east from Cape Brett, and on clear days could be seen from the main shore. Henry bore for these in a light breeze and towards sundown made a landing on a steep shingle beach in a little bay. No doubt he was faint for want of food and tired to the point of apathy, for, instead of hauling his boat safely upon the beach, he anchored it off by means of a long rope in addition to the warp, and then, rolling himself up in his blankets, went to sleep upon the ground near the water.

He was awakened during the night by the sound of a great wind among the trees and by the roar of breakers against the point of land where he was resting. The tide had fallen considerably since the boat was anchored out, and it was now pounding upon the

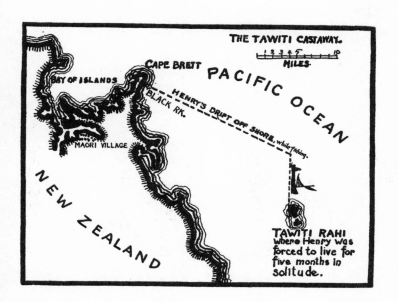

THE TAWITI CASTAWAY.

MILES.

PACIFIC OCEAN

CAPE BRETT

BAY OF ISLANDS

HENRY'S DRIFT OFF SHORE, while fishing.

BLACK RK.

MAORI VILLAGE

NEW ZEALAND

TAWITI RAHI
where Henry was
forced to live for
five months in
solitude.

shingle at the risk of going to pieces. While trying to move the boat to a more sheltered part of the bay, Henry was caught by a tumbling breaker, larger than any of the others, which hurled both him and the boat high upon the rocks. He was blinded by the salt water and shocked into insensibility. In the morning he found himself much worse off than when he first landed. His boat was smashed up and completely ruined; his hooks and line were gone; his catch of cod was washed out of the boat; his water bottles were broken, and his pipe and tobacco had disappeared. On making an inventory of his possessions, after having been so strangely thrown into this place, he found that he had nothing left but a jack-knife, a pair of blankets, a few pieces of broken glass, a torn boat sail and a stove boat. Even the long rope had been lost through his carelessness in leaving it too near the water. He was totally unarmed and had no wrecked ship from which to draw supplies, tools, or domestic animals for companions.

The bay was enclosed by a high rocky rampart and above this was a forest of high trees. At the base of the rampart was a rock covered with oysters and Henry fed upon these by the use of a stone, as a prehistoric cave man might have done. On the flat section of ground about the bay was a pool into which flowed a stream of clear water, and, after drinking his fill, he plunged into the pool and gratefully washed off all traces of the soaking he had had in the salt water. This bath both refreshed him and helped to clear his mind, but for the first day or so he could do nothing but wander aimlessly about within his small enclosure, unable to make any plan in particular for the continuance of his existence. He naturally gravitated to the stove boat and tried, in an impractical way with his jack-knife, to mend the gap in her bottom. It took him two days to conclude that all efforts in that direction were a waste of time.

For a few nights he slept in a cave, but it was not tight at the top and the floor became wet when it rained, so with his jack-knife he set about building a small hut in the manner of the Maoris. Bulrushes were found in a swamp and on these he worked for a few days, cutting and tying them in bundles. He was glad of the work, for it left him so tired by night that he had no inclination to brood over his troubles.

Henry decided on keeping the second Sunday on the island as a day of rest from manual labor. It was rather a change of occupation, for he made his first climb up the rocky pathway and into the forest where he found, growing among the trees, an abundance of an edible wild palm, which he at once recognized as the Nikau of the Maoris. The nutritious heart of this palm is about two inches thick and a foot long, and this, with the oysters, made a fine supper for him that evening. The day was warm and sunny, which, after a week of wet weather, was very cheering. During the afternoon walk he had selected a location for his hut and had spent the rest of the evening in designing it. He had no books to read, as the more favored Robinson Crusoe had, and to keep articulate he resolved on reciting psalms and singing songs. These performances served a double purpose, for they also comforted and soothed his troubled mind.

Early the next morning, after the usual visit to the oyster rocks, he went, with a feeling of renewed energy, to his boat and tore off a plank to fashion into a spade, for building operations were to begin immediately. Then, digging a small trench around the spot selected for the hut, he made a perfectly level space fourteen feet long by ten feet wide, which he cleared of all grass and plants. Far up in the forest, he cut down four straight branches forked at the end, for the corners of the hut. That was but the beginning of his task, for two entire days were spent in cutting and carrying the wood down to the building site, and three days more in erecting the framework, after which it was covered with the bulrushes, and the details completed.

Henry had frequently seen Maoris strike fire by the friction of two sticks, and once or twice he had tried it himself, but without success. Now, however, the obtaining of fire was of vital consequence, so he searched for a flint-like stone, thinking to strike a fire with the aid of his knife, but found no stone suitable for the purpose. The only alternative was an effort to obtain fire in the Maori way.

Two fire-sticks of dry wood were made: a lower stick, which was a foot and a half long and somewhat flat, and the rubbing stick, about a foot long and an inch square, with one end brought to a rounded point. Kneeling down, the fire maker placed the lower stick on the ground, with the near end raised a few inches;

then he grasped the rubbing stick with both hands, thumbs underneath and fingers placed flat on its upper surface, one hand overriding the other. By rubbing the pointed end on the under stick, and by exerting considerable pressure, a groove about four inches long was soon formed, in which a quantity of fine dust soon collected. This dust was carefully brushed into the farther end of the groove. Heavy pressure was now applied on the rubbing stick and the movement, at first slow, was gradually increased in speed as the groove became heated. His sense of smell gave Henry, now despondent and perspiring at every pore from his efforts, his first inkling that fire was at hand. The groove darkened in color, a very faint wisp of smoke appeared, the dust turned black, and a small red spot was seen in the center of it. This small red spot was live fire, which he emptied on some dried ferns and *manuka* twigs, very resinous and inflammable, to be tenderly fanned into a blaze.

This fire, so laboriously acquired, was never allowed to go out. Henry kept a good stock of firewood at hand and a hole dug in the floor of his hut was always kept well filled with hot embers; besides, there was a pile of dry purin sticks ready for light at night.

Provided with a shelter and fire, there still remained the ever present problem of getting food. The labor of breaking open oysters occupied much of his time and very considerably shortened the length of the day, but at his best he was never able to collect sufficient quantities to completely satisfy his hunger, and he was continually tortured by the memory of his former substantial meals. With a gun he could have done better in the way of food, as he saw plenty of wild ducks on the small pond and parrots and pigeons in the forest. He endeavored to hit the ducks with stones but never succeeded in getting one. He tried making a bow and arrows, but his attempts proved futile. However, he was able to add another dish to his meagre fare, namely the fern root, of which there was an abundance growing in and about the forest.

He even lacked the comfort of a drop of water at hand, when he awoke at night with a nagging thirst, for there was no vessel in which to keep it. Later on he made a pot from soft clay, but, in spite of being baked in a fire to harden it, the pot was so very porous that the water seeped through during the night and by morning the vessel would be empty.

Henry had now spent about three weeks on the island, and the hope of getting away daily grew less and less, until, at times, when thinking over his situation, he was well-nigh driven to despair. Then he would courageously gather himself together and search for new tasks.

One morning he found a large shark, which had been washed up by the tide. It was past eating, but it occurred to him that he had seen the Maoris make fish hooks out of sharks' teeth. He had already experimented in the making of hooks out of the copper nails of his boat, but had found that the metal was too soft and bent too easily to hold a fish.

In six evenings, with his knife, some stones, the broken glass, and some bent wood, he made two Maori

fish hooks sufficiently sharp and strong to catch any
fish he might find off the rocks. Another week was spent
in twisting raw flax into fishing lines. The following
morning he was up with the early dawn to try out his
fishing gear, and soon caught a large rock cod. Roasted
at the fire, that rock cod made several sumptuous
meals, seasoned with salt found, deposited by evapora-
tion, in the crevices of the rocks.

Life on the island now settled down to more or less
of a routine for Henry. Awakening early, he went to
the spring for a bath, then to the rocks, obtaining either
oysters or fish for breakfast, after which he searched
the forest for a supply of dry firewood. Once in his
wanderings he found, growing among the shrubs, a
large orange colored pod producing a very fragrant
pepper, with which he frequently flavored his fish.

Then came the preparation for the midday meal,
usually consisting of fish and wild cabbage, which grew
at the foot of the rocks. His diet was made less monotonous by changing the method of cooking: on one day
he would broil the fish and another day would cook
it in a native *kapura,* with hot ashes, in a hole.

Afternoons were usually spent walking in the forest, but he did not dare to penetrate very far lest he
lose his way. At dusk he went down to the pond and
caught a few eels, ready for bait the following morning. As soon as it was dark, he went into his hut, threw
a few sticks on the fire to make a light, and busied
himself in making hooks or lines. Then, replenishing
his fire with enough fuel to last until morning, he rolled
himself in his blanket and slept soundly until daylight.

Thus the time passed slowly away. Each day found him with less hope and despair slowly settling over him. He moved about mechanically, wondering if relief would ever come.

He kept the reckoning of time by daily repeating to himself the name and date of that particular day. Seven weeks and two days had passed, when, as he was coming from the forest with a load of wood, he looked towards the sea and sighted a vessel. He had always expected to see a sail, but the appearance of one startled him. Greatly excited, he threw down the wood and rushed over the rocks to his hut to get his blankets to hang in a tree as a signal. Then, thinking that the smoke of a fire would be seen more plainly, he hurried to obtain some fire, light the pile of wood he had thrown down, and then climbed into the tree to hang out the blankets. But the fire was made of dry wood and burned too brightly to make much smoke. It was now too late to place green branches upon it, for the vessel faded slowly out of sight and no one aboard had noticed his attempts at signaling her! Despair closed in.

That evening he caught, as usual, several small eels, and placed them upon the roof of his hut to be ready for the morning's fishing. In the middle of the night he was aroused by a strange scratching, scrambling noise upon the roof, and went out at once to see what it could be. In the darkness, he saw two fiery balls of light glaring at him from the top of the hut, and the next moment a dark object flew at him with a loud hiss, and disappeared. It was a large cat, which he had never seen before, and which he never saw afterwards, although it could be heard yowling in the forest. Was this animal also a castaway from some lost ship?

The next two or three days he walked about in a daze, and it was during this time that he later found he had lost three days' reckoning.

Walking into the forest one day farther than he had ever ventured before, Henry came upon a gully, where he stumbled over a tree root and rolled down the side, landing upon some tobacco plants. He eagerly gathered all he could find and then returned to the hut, where he hung the tobacco leaves on a string of flax and set to work making a pipe from clay, which proved to be a great success. At last he could smoke!

His feeling of utter solitude was increased by the absence of animal life and the stillness. With the exception of birds, bees, and an occasional lizard, the only living thing he had seen was the cat, which had probably swum ashore from some passing ship.

Wild pigeons abounded, and he learned to make snares which, from time to time, caught a number of birds. He watched the courses of the bees in the hope of finding honey, and finally traced an immense swarm to a tree which he felled by burning, and was finally rewarded by finding the largest stock of honey he had ever seen taken from a tree. A part of the mass was three seasons old and of a deep yellow color with brown wax; the rest was of a pale straw color, in white combs. Afterwards, he discovered two more bee trees and took out the contents, storing the honey in the clay vessels which he had made. The honey and pigeons were delicious additions to his menus.

Henry had frequently noticed what appeared to be the footprints of an animal on the pathway leading up the rocks into the forest, and one day, as he was returning with a load of firewood, he thought that he heard the bleating of animals. Quietly laying down the load, he looked below and saw a herd of wild goats licking the salt on the rocks. Stealing quietly down to make a sudden rush, he approached within fifty yards of them. One goat, suddenly observing him, gave a loud bleat of warning to the others and they all rushed up the rocks where he could not follow. When well out of reach, they turned around to stare at him. Nothing could be done, so he returned for his wood and tried to devise some method of catching one later on. However, all the devices which passed through his mind were equally futile.

Some days later he came upon six goats, separated from the herd, browsing on some bushes near the spring. He had their wind, and crept upon them as stealthily as he could. As the distance between them grew less, the space between the pool and the steep rocks also narrowed, giving the goats less room to rush past him. At length they saw him and for a moment stood as though paralyzed. Five goats then passed him as he rushed upon them; but one leaped upon a large stone in the water and stood there, bleating. Henry made one bound toward her, seized her by the neck, and held on tightly. He decided that she was the very goat he would have chosen. The question was how to get her home. His quandary was very soon solved. The stone upon which they both stood was covered with a green slimy moss, and he felt his feet slipping from under him. The goat made a sudden break and down came both man and goat into the water, thus forcing Henry to loosen his hold. The goat beat him in swimming to the edge of the pond and, with a loud bleat, rushed up the rocks after her mates. Many a time afterwards, he sat planning on how to secure a goat; for even one goat as a companion would have been most welcome. All his plans were to no purpose, for he never caught a goat.

One bright moonlight night Henry fell short of wood; so he had to turn out and go up into the forest. He was startled by a shrill whistle close behind him and, glancing cautiously around, he saw a kiwi moving. It was good eating, so, looking around for a suitable stick, he started forward to strike a blow at the bird. It ran off quickly, but he managed to overtake it, whereupon the bird threw itself on its back and struck out at him with its legs, ripping up his trousers with a sharp hind claw, and tearing the skin of his leg. The kiwi escaped, but in a day or two he found kiwi eggs, which made another welcome addition to the monotonous fish and oyster diet.

Four and a half long weary months passed. Regularly, three or four times a day, he went up to the rocks, trying to sight a sail. A long time had elapsed since he had seen the last one, and the hope of ever seeing another became fainter every day. At length, one day, he detected a small speck far out to sea.

Upon his return from a walk in the forest, he found that the speck had grown larger and plainer. The white sails of a vessel were now glistening in the sun! Would she ever come near enough to be signaled? Soon the smoke of his fire curled up among the trees. She was coming closer and Henry now saw that it was a large schooner, probably bound to Auckland. As the schooner drew nearer, his heart palpitated so that he could distinctly hear its anxious beats.

"They see the smoke. They see it!" he cried, as she suddenly hauled up to the wind and he could hear her sails flap sharply against the masts. In his excitement, he screamed and shouted in a vain hope that the people on board would hear his cries.

"Do they really see the smoke? Will they lower a boat for me?"

The few minutes of suspense during which she lay aback seemed like hours, or even years.

"I know they see the smoke—I know it!" he cried. "Why do they not lower a boat and pull off?"

"They are going!" he shrieked, as he saw the head of the vessel slowly turn, and the sails again belly out to the wind. "They are going! Oh, my God, they are going, and leaving me here. Have mercy, have mercy, and do not utterly forsake me!"

He threw himself down, face to the ground, for he dared not look again. He felt as if he were going mad. Finally, he arose and took one last look at the receding ship, which for the second time became a small speck in the distance.

He sat for hours, silently looking down into the deep

blue water where all things looked so peaceful that the thought crept into his mind: "Would it not be better to roll off this rock, and seek that resting place? It would be but one plunge, a very brief pang, and then to sleep." Overwhelmed by the wickedness of his thoughts, he rushed down to his hut, fell on his knees and prayed for patience and submission.

Four more weary weeks passed without special incident. Each day he fished, gathered wood, roamed through the forest, and formed futile plans for catching goats. Henry had now lived on the island for five and a half months.

One night he was startled by hearing a bumping sound on the beach. He jumped up and listened, wondering if the high tide had lifted his old boat from the rocks. On second thought, he knew this was impossible, for the boat had been almost completely dismantled for one purpose or another.

He heard footsteps, and then a loud gruff voice saying, *"Kumea, kumea."* He knew that voice well, but thought he must be dreaming.

Rushing out, he saw by the light of the moon, five or six dusky figures trying to haul up a large boat out of reach of the breakers. With a loud shout of joy he ran forward, and then stood amazed and appalled at the sudden yell which escaped from the new arrivals. They stopped dragging the boat and hastily tumbled aboard her again.

"Kowai koe (Who are you) ?" shouted a loud voice.

"Ko Henare ahau (I am Henry)," he replied.

"Stop," answered the voice, "or I throw this," at

the same time brandishing a small tomahawk. Henry stood stock still, while the figure moved toward the boat.

"Stop, Monganui," cried Henry, in an agony of fear lest they should go off and leave him. "I am Henry— do not leave me."

"*Ka teka koe* (You lie)!" Monganui exclaimed. "Henry is dead. You are his spirit."

"No, no," Henry answered, "I swear to you I am Henry. Come and touch me, and see whether I am not flesh and blood."

"No," Monganui replied, "I do not believe you. You are a spirit, and I shall go." Monganui made toward the boat, but suddenly he turned and stood still, calling to Henry, "Do you see that stone?"

"Yes."

"Take it up then." Henry did so.

"Now do you see that tree?" pointing to the very tree to which Henry had tied his boat when he first landed.

"I see it."

"Throw the stone at it." Henry obeyed, hitting the tree with good aim.

"Ah," Monganui said, "no ghost could do that!"

"May I come to you?"

"Yes," said Monganui, still hesitating.

Henry went up to him with the usual Maori salute, "*Tena koutou.*" Monganui caught hold of him, grasping his hand so hard that he flinched.

"Ah," he said, "that is real flesh and blood." Then,

looking Henry full in the face, he said, "And you look something like Henry, only thinner."

"*You* live here five months, Monganui," Henry replied, "and try to keep stout on it!"

As soon as Monganui fully realized that this man was really Henry and not a spirit, he asked innumerable questions, for he wanted to know what had happened and how Henry had managed to live so long alone.

The others, who were the chief's five wives, had been listening all this time in the boat, but now, on Monganui's order, reluctantly came out. The boat was pulled high up on the beach, the women casting frequent side glances of doubt and fear on the supposed ghost. But the "ghost" contrived once or twice to knock against them rather roughly, as only flesh and blood could possibly do, and so set their minds somewhat at rest.

Monganui went to the hut with Henry, while the women made a shelter for the night with the oars of the boat and their blankets. The Maori chief remained in the hut after eating and, when the two men had lighted their pipes, Henry related his adventures of the last few months. He was frequently interrupted by Monganui's exclamations of astonishment.

In turn, Henry inquired of Monganui why he had come to the island. The chief replied that he had been fishing at Black Rock, when it had come on to blow very fresh. So hard did it blow at last that, despite having a whaleboat and crew, they could not pull against the wind, and so ran before it to the islands.

When the men awoke in the morning, the wives were already astir, with a fire lighted, and potatoes and fish cooking in an iron pot. The women looked somewhat doubtfully at the "ghost," but when it took a potato out of the pot and deliberately peeled and ate it, they seemed considerably relieved. No ghost could eat a potato!

Monganui took it for granted that Henry would leave the island with him, as soon as the weather moderated, and, as a change seemed likely within a few hours, he arranged for an early start the next day.

The morning opened clear and fine, with the wind in the right direction for the homeward sailing. All were astir early and in a bustle of preparation. When breakfast was over, the things were put on board and soon all was ready for the take-off.

Looking at the boat, Henry's courage failed him, for, despite his long and lonely stay upon the island, he could not overcome the fear of trusting himself, for so long a trip, to that old whaleboat, deeply laden as she was, and leaking, as was her habit of old. He decided to remain on the island, and, when it came to the point of getting in, drew back, much to Monganui's astonishment. "I will stay," Henry said. "Should you land safely, please go to Kororaika and tell the white people I am here and that I have been living here nearly six months. Seek the magistrate there, and ask him to send a small vessel for me. I will remain patiently here until it arrives."

"But Henry," Monganui answered eagerly, "there

is room. The sea is quiet, and I am sure I can find my way home again. Do come with us."

The Maoris were in the boat and prepared to start, when up jumped the chief again. He ran to Henry and, pressing his nose against the latter's, said, "Now Henry, now for the last time."

"No, Monganui, I feel that I cannot go."

After the departure of Monganui, Henry rushed away to his hut, but soon climbed the rock and looked for the boat. As he watched it sailing away, he felt that he had been a fool and a coward, and shrieked for them to come back.

Alone once more, he prayed that the Maoris might land safely and send some means of rescue. Perhaps he would never get away from that horrible place. He felt that he could not wait long; that in a short time he would become mad!

Six days of waiting followed, before Henry again sighted a small dark speck on the distant sea. A small schooner was surely approaching the island. Again, he lighted a fire, and the smoke soon curled upwards in dense clouds. At sea, a gun was fired. Henry could not hear the report, but he could see the small puff of white smoke fading slowly away.

Henry scarcely knew what passed during the next few hours, but he had a faint memory of dancing, jumping, whooping, crying and laughing. He rushed back and forth again and again from the rocks to his hut.

A small boat containing two men rapidly pulled towards the shore. He rushed down to meet them, and,

He had a faint memory of dancing, jumping,
whooping, crying and laughing.

as they grounded on the pebbles, one of the Maoris leaped out and rushed up to him, threw his arms about his neck, and, rubbing noses, cried like a child. Henry felt his hand grasped by the other one. They were two of his native boys. Taking his blankets and the things that Monganui had left with him, he boarded the boat, which immediately pulled off to the schooner. From two English sailors he heard his own native tongue spoken for the first time in six months, and it sounded strangely in his ears.

In the early morning of the next day, they neared the land. He saw the fateful Black Rocks, and the dreaded Cape Brett loomed up once more. As they rounded the point, the houses on the beach appeared, and on the well known pier stood a number of whites and Maoris, eagerly looking towards the small vessel as she swept up the bay.

Once more Henry was in the boat, being rapidly rowed toward the pier. A deafening cheer saluted him. In landing, as he tried to mount the last step, he fell unconscious on his face. Many hours later, he came to himself in a friend's home, "You would make a good Maori," declared Monganui, who was standing by.